Going Off Alarming

Also by Danny Baker

Going to Sea in a Sieve

Going Off Alarming

A MEMOIR

WEIDENFELD & NICOLSON
LONDON

First published in Great Britain in 2014
by Weidenfeld & Nicolson

1 3 5 7 9 10 8 6 4 2

Extract in chapter 15 from *Classic Football Debates*
by Danny Baker and Danny Kelly reprinted
by permission of The Random House Group Ltd

A CIP catalogue record for this book
is available from the British Library.

ISBN- 978 02978 7011 1

Typeset by Input Data Services Ltd, Bridgwater, Somerset

Printed and bound by CPI Group (UK) Ltd, Croydon, CR0 4YY

Weidenfeld & Nicolson

The Orion Publishing Group Ltd
Orion House
5 Upper Saint Martin's Lane
London, WC2H 9EA
www.orionbooks.co.uk

The Orion Publishing Group's policy is to use papers
that are natural, renewable and recyclable products and made from
wood grown in sustainable forests. The logging and manufacturing
processes are expected to conform to the environmental
regulations of the country of origin.

The true propellers and turbos amid all these words are Bonnie and Sonny. This is from your dad, kids. Mancie, you'll just have to sit up on your cloud and be born in the next one, OK?

Preface

For what it's worth I would like to dedicate this book to my brother Mickey. If there's any detectable chronology at all in these volumes then Mickey died just after the last one finished and this one begins. Following a fellow docker's enormously boozy leaving do, he went home to bed and simply didn't wake up again. I've wrestled with how to place his sudden passing into the cavalcade of events that gather in these pages, but no matter how I approach it the problem always remains the same; I am just no good at morbid reportage. All the stories told here are true and all, I hope, contain something fresh, surprising and entertaining for the reader. To simply write out the tragic impact of Michael's death on the people around him seems to me, in a literary sense, obvious and strangely banal. In my own reading tastes I have never had the slightest interest in poking about in other people's bad news, whether in book, magazine or broadcast, and this is possibly why I have no idea how to serve such stuff up as a cracking good chapter. I grant that some may see the reticence to dwell on the dark months immediately following Mick dying as the psychological key to everything else contained here, but I'm afraid it really isn't. There is no long-subsumed secret sorrow here from which to unburden myself. To put it simply: my brother died. How do you think it fucking felt? There are more than enough misery memoirs out there if people want to bizarrely nose about in the grief of others and, as I say, I am genuinely not armed with whatever heart-wrenching tools are required to guide an audience through the universal details or even how to make them interesting. I'm absolutely certain when it comes to publicizing this volume, interviewers will narrow their eyes and say, 'You seem to skip over your brother's death. Why is that?' as though this would have been the really interesting part of my tale. The media is funny like that. So when that happens I will offer them a phrase that my mum would say whenever somebody started going on about how terrible life is and, for my money, it's something you really don't hear often enough these days. Once anyone began edging toward what we now label 'confessional', Mum would lean forward and touch their arm. 'Ooh love,' she'd coo, not a little alarmed at being trapped by all the drawn-out gloom, 'We've all got our problems, mate, and besides . . . it's none of our business, is it?'

So here's to you, Mickey, his wife Jane and daughter Alex. Family.

Introduction

They say you never hear the shot that kills you, so at least I knew I wasn't going to die.

I had definitely heard the slug as it left the pistol, a ballistic snap identical to the spit of a log fire, and besides, the sharp pain and fast-blossoming bloodstain were located on the outside of my right knee so unless my assailant had tipped his bullets with cyanide, my life was probably not hanging in the balance. However, shot I most certainly had been and I now doubled over to grasp my punctured leg, turning about in small alarmed hops while emitting shocked choking sounds like a dog trying to sick up a feather. None of my friends appeared to have noticed the gunfire and continued to amble along Jamaica Road in their shared drunken buzz. We had been having a 'late one' in any of the various Bermondsey pubs that took a relaxed attitude to the legal drinking hours and were now meandering back through the borough, here and there losing a few from our original strength of fourteen as we passed the streets and estates where most of us still lived with our parents. There was little traffic this Sunday night and so I had got a pretty good look at the passing bottle-green Rover from which someone had just held a pistol out of the rear window and fired.

'I been shot! Someone just fucking shot me!' I bleated after my group while actually trying to put most of the alarm I felt into my facial expression rather than the pitch of the message – after all, it was nearly 1 a.m. and we were passing some flats where dozens of people we knew were fast asleep. Even in such a crisis I was aware that if any of them saw my dad the next day and said, 'Here, your Danny was pissed and causing a row outside our block last night,' it would really put the tin hat on affairs. So it was more in the style of a strangulated stage whisper that I drew attention to having just become a victim of what we now call a drive-by.

John Hannon reacted first. 'Shot? What y'talking about, shot?' he asked almost wearily, as if I'd asked him to help me find a shirt button.

'Shot!' I cried, stage whisper rising toward boiling kettle. 'Some fucker in a car just got me in the leg!'

John turned to the rest of the chaps. With a chuckle in his voice he jerked a thumb toward my buckled pose and chortled, 'Baker's just got shot!' And everyone began laughing.

Crowding around me under the street lighting they saw that the 'bullet', an inch-long chrome slug, had buried itself into the top of my knee right up to the yellow flights that adorned its base. Unconcerned with my pain, they seemed more intrigued as to who might have done it. The car I had identified to them was now well down the road and as it receded in the gloom it gave no clue as to its occupants. After a few moments dwelling on possible local suspects it was agreed – though not by me – that this was merely the work of a little mob from over East London, 'just fucking about, having a laugh.' The Rotherhithe Tunnel under the Thames lies at the end of Jamaica Road towards which the car sped and this would logically take them back to their own part of town. Case closed.

Forming my index, middle finger and thumb into a claw, I set about pulling the slim bullet out. In silence, my friends gathered about me to take in the gore. This was a mistake. For in turning all my attention to the injury I had stupidly dropped my guard and carelessly become the softest of targets. And it was literally the softest of targets that was about to receive a slapstick second blast. Believing the immediate threat to be over, none of us had double-checked that the mystery car had actually driven into the Rotherhithe Tunnel. It hadn't. On arriving at the roundabout at the subway's entrance it had in fact turned around and was coming back up towards us on the other side of the road. I certainly couldn't see this because I was facing away from the road. Bent over. From my pistol packin' tormentor's vantage point, I was now presenting the fullest and most irresistible of targets. I fancy I was waving my rear end around a little, thus making the bullseye even more alluring.

Crack.

The dirty double-dip bastards shot me right up the arse. This time I not only heard the report, I was forced to process their wild whoops of glee as the car sped off once again – in the direction of Tower Bridge. I of course snapped violently upright as though I were spring-loaded, both hands grasping the under-fire cheeks, and turning the phrase, 'Fucking hell, they've just shot me up the arse!' into one long strangulated word. Now, if you thought my colleagues' reaction after the first attack was possibly callous, I'm sure you must concede this occasion deserved nothing short of roars. Shocked as I was, I knew even at the moment of impact that being shot up the arse was, comically, a classic. By morning the sketch would be all over South-East London with pensioners, priests and close family members having to stuff handkerchiefs into their mouths in failed efforts to stifle outright guffaws. The only thing that might temper the hilarity would be a genuine sense of awe at what terrific marksmen these maniacs were. In those days my arse wasn't anything like the size it would grow to be and, while never of a supermodel slimness, to land a dart almost centre-buttock from a moving car was little short of miraculous. If I had reported the incident I dare say the police would have narrowed the immediate search down to any army snipers on leave, but the fact is, I didn't report it. In working-class areas in the late seventies people didn't stride, or in my case hobble, to the local nick to alert the authorities there was a skylarking little mob with an air pistol on the loose, any more than the police expressed an interest in the tremendously common punch-ups in our local pubs. It just seemed to be part of the game. Compensation culture, trauma and counselling may be the options today, but back then if you got shot up the arse in front of your friends you simply had to take the gag on the chin, so to speak.

Those of you who bought the first book in this series may be wondering why, when that one ended with my earliest TV appearances in 1982, we're now back in the late seventies again. Well, since that book was published I have had countless friends and family members get in touch to say how come I hadn't included this story or that tale in the covered time frame – especially those that took place away from the show-business spotlight (a beam that was about to start shining into my life with ever greater force during the eighties). For example the incident of which you have just read. How, various chums have enquired, could I possibly have omitted that saga from any serious history of the times? Was I ashamed of being shot twice, once up the arse, in Jamaica Road? Did I feel I was somehow to blame for it, had brought it on myself, and by burying the memory hoped to shut out the truth? How long should a man live with such a secret? By sharing with the world that I had been shot up the arse in Jamaica Road I hope now to help all those who have been similarly assailed. In that era, a sharp injury to the backside while colleagues looked on was seen as somehow humorous. Thank God, we've moved on since then. I believe it's a tragedy that in the twenty-first century we still have no idea how many other innocent late-night revellers in the seventies took gunfire to the rump and have ever since kept this outrageous fact hidden from even their nearest and dearest. From another angle there might possibly be an argument that that well-aimed pellet to my rear in some way spurred me on to my later successes by forcing me to show there was so much more to me than a simple patsy who presented his buttocks as a challenge for strangers' firearms. Of course, nobody in the public eye would wish to be defined by the inevitable newspaper headline: baker: i was shot up the arse as a young man, accompanied as it doubtless would be by a photograph of myself looking grave but obviously relieved to have become unburdened. Yet how can I possibly hope to offer up a full picture of myself without including that awful night when I bent over in Bermondsey? I owe it to all of us who were shot up the arse back then and then suffered silently in the following years – particularly when sitting down too fast. I still have the small round scar which, if I position a mirror just so, I can gaze at and reflect upon those times in my life when not everything smelled as sweet as it does now. Maybe it is high time I 'got it out there', as they say.

So, diligent chronicler that I am, though I will earnestly attempt to move the biographical arc forward over the next couple of hundred pages, forgive me if the narrative becomes somewhat off-kilter at times. The difference between life and fiction is that life doesn't have to make sense. If by retrospectively dropping my trousers every few pages I can reveal a fuller picture of myself during these years, then so be it.

Besides. Being shot up the arse. In front of your mates.

Fucking hell. What else did I forget?

Teas, Light Refreshments And Minerals

To say that nobody in my family had ever been in show business would be an understatement. I may as well reveal that none of my mother's collection of teapots had ever spoken to her or that our tortoise, Tom, was not the local MP. Although – and less than fifty words in, here comes our first diversion – I can see why I just put those two examples in harness. Our tortoise, Tom, completely destroyed my mother's teapot collection, trashing it into smithereens as thoroughly as Keith Moon hepped up on a five-drug cocktail.

Tortoises, by nature, are not destructive animals and, until the Great Teapot Massacre, the only time Tom had been shouted at was when he had lunched too well on my father's tomato plants. My dad's voice actually woke me that morning. He was up early to go to work in the docks and had gone out in the back garden because, as he later told me, 'I thought I heard someone chuck a wallet over the wall last night.' Anyway, the old man wasn't a bad gardener and as he was out there anyway he decided to quickly do a job that was normally one of my duties. His favourite flowers were chrysanthemums – or as he always called them, 'crizzants'. He had once read in a magazine called *Titbits* that the greatest threat to the healthy chrysanthemum was the earwig and the best way to keep these pests off the plants was to fill a small flowerpot with straw, put this upside down on a stick and then place it beside the vulnerable flora. The idea was that Brer Earwig, journeying with a few friends to have a slap-up meal amidst my old man's cherished crizzants, would see the straw up the stick and immediately alert his company that there had been a change of venue. Apparently earwigs are attracted to compacted straw in the same way some old actresses are drawn to cat-rescue centres. Therefore every few days it would be my job to evict these insects from their new digs and, to quote *Apocalypse Now*, 'terminate with extreme prejudice'. Well, I know it's wicked, and these days I am so respectful of any living thing that even Buddhists might find me a bit wet, but back then I approached this grisly task with out-and-out relish. I became tremendously inventive in coming up with new and shocking ways to dispatch these pincered squatters to the great flowerpot in the sky. Indeed I, as my mum once told me with shaking head, was 'a fucker for it'. Seriously, if earwigs have any kind of oral history then I am surely recalled as their own Vlad the Impaler and invoked by mother earwigs as a final resort when the little ones are playing up. However, on this particular morning my dad had deprived me of my murderous fun by deciding to do it himself. It was as he was shaking the bundles of straw and stepping upon any of the half-asleep occupants that tumbled out that his eye fell on his tomato plants.

'Oh, you little ponce!' I heard him shout (my brother and I shared a bedroom that faced on to the garden). 'You wilful little fucker! Where are you?'

Scrambling up to the window I looked out to see why the old man was creating ructions at barely seven in the morning.

'Where the fucking hell you hiding, you THING!' he bellowed, while making a frantic patrol of our small patch of green laid out below the railway arches. This garden, roughly twelve feet by six, sat at the end of our block of twelve council flats arranged on two storeys. We were the first flat on the ground floor and as such had a six-foot wall enclosing us on two sides at the back to separate our scratchy turf from the municipal builder's yard on the other side. You could drive a car down our turning almost as far as our garden, but not quite, and so when one of my dad's few work mates who had a motor would come to pick him up they would get as close as they could and then 'pump up'. It was one of these short blasts from an idling Granada that I heard next. Dad, by now in something of a righteous fury, sprang over the roadside wall and, placing his fingertips atop it and standing on tiptoe, roared, 'Two seconds, George!

I'm about to aim the poxy tortoise on to the fucking railway – mind I don't hit you!'

I had absolutely no idea at that point what Tom the tortoise could possibly have done. Usually Spud – the name by which my dad, Fred, was universally known – doted on the creature. He fed him by hand most days, and when he found out that Tom was partial to Bourbon biscuits – I don't recall how – he laid in packets of the things so he wouldn't run short. On more than one occasion I heard him say proudly that Tom was 'the best thing I ever got out of the dock' – meaning that his little shelled pal had been smuggled out of the port gates one day when the dockers were unloading them as cargo bound for the pet stores of Britain. When I think about the endless booty that my old man had liberated from his place of work over the years this really was some claim. And now he was threatening to launch the rugged little reptile on to the electrified tracks.

Eventually he located Tom in, of all places, the wooden fruit box that was Tom's actual house, stowed on the back porch. Pulling the sleepy pet from his lair, he carted him up the path and stood above the five or so tomato plants from which each year we harvested an impressive amount of fruit. This year, it seemed, we were going to be below the usual quota.

'I've fucking told you and told you – THAT'S your one there. Leave. These. Alone.' My dad was still holding our bemused tortoise by the shell and up at face level. 'You've taken fucking great lumps off all them! I'm not having it. That one. That's yours.'

Satisfied it was no major crisis, I slid back into bed.

'What's Dad shouting about?' mumbled my brother, Mike, from his single bed two feet away.

'Oh, he's got the hump with Tom,' I answered, not entirely unaware that this line probably wouldn't play outside our immediate family. In our house, actually in the entire world, every living thing was fair play for one of the old man's notoriously explosive 'volleys' if the provocation warranted it. He often spoke to our dog Blackie as though he was a particularly irritating cellmate and they were doing twenty years together. If, for example, the dog broke wind while reposing in front of the fire, Dad would say, 'Are you gonna do that all night, you dirty bastard? One more and I'll stick an air freshener right up your arse.'

Following outbursts like this, my mum wouldn't even look up from her book but just say calmly, 'He don't know what you're saying, Fred. It's all noise to him.'

Should Blackie lazily turn round to see what the outburst was about, Spud would follow up with:

'He knows all right. Don't keep looking at me like that, Black – I'm too old at the game and you're too close to that fire. Drop another one and you're going on it.'

Any time a rogue bluebottle arrived in the living room and buzzed by his bald head he would allow it a few laps and then say, completely normally, 'Go on. Land on my fucking leg. See what you get.' If our budgerigar Joey was in a particularly good mood and was chirping to express just how well the world stood with her at that moment, Dad might say directly to her, 'I'm trying to watch the fucking telly here,' and then turning to the rest of us say, 'Ain't it all right, eh? A poxy bird in charge.' However, it was he who brought all our many and varied pets into the house and he who dutifully took care of each and every one. If anything, he respected them as equals and as such expected them to take some no-nonsense advice when required. This even extended to a lizard he'd chanced across on the quay and brought home in a paper bag. For a few days it lived in my sister's small, wooden, pink-satin-lined sewing box that, because we figured the reptile must have come from a hot climate, we put on the top shelf of the airing cupboard by the immersion heater. The lizard remained disappointingly inert at first, completely ignoring the pieces of lemon we had provided for its dinner. Dad naturally advised my brother and I to tell it to 'liven its fucking ideas up'. My brother duly went to have a look at it – possibly to deliver this caustic piece of pep talk – and as soon as the lid of the sewing box was open half an inch, it bolted out at lightning speed into the furthest reaches of the narrow airing cupboard itself. The whole family gathered around to see if we could spot it, the old man shining a torch about the un-ironed piles of shirts, blouses, pillowcases, football socks and underwear that clogged up the shelves. My mum refused to make the job easier by emptying the space because, as she fairly reasoned, 'I'm not taking all that lot out and have to put it all back in again, because none of you mob'll help me AND its all for a bleedin' tupenny-ha'penny lizard.'

Eventually, though, this is just what she did and we all took an item each, shaking it nervously, with our hearts in our mouths, all too aware one of these pieces was sure to reveal a surprise package. We were actually very close to calling off the search when suddenly from inside one of Michael's V-necked pullovers our fugitive made a break for it. The collective scream that went up almost shattered the lantern-style light fixture hanging from the passage ceiling. The lizard now skedaddled into the bathroom at the other end of the short landing and we hared off in pursuit. Dad spotted it first. Or rather, he spotted a portion of it. Sticking out of a tiny gap under the skirting board was a glimpse of lizard tail. Shushing us all quiet, he gingerly crouched down and with his thumb and finger made a sudden grab. Now I don't know about you but I thought all this stuff about lizards being able to snap off their tails at will and without prior written notice was a bunch of hooey. However, as my father slowly retrieved from the bathroom wall nothing more than three inches of twitching gristle, this wonder of nature was laid bare to us all. My sister Sharon probably best summed up the spectacle when she declared it to be the single most revolting thing anyone had ever seen. Dad, on the other hand, seemed fascinated by the still-jerking sliver of lizard and inspected it closely.

'Fucking hell, look,' he said, 'I got the poor bastard's arse.'

Now the reason I give such weight to this story is that Spud, who on the surface seemed so indifferent to the sensibilities of different life forms, refused to simply chuck that lizard's tail away. He formally buried it, wrapped in a Handy Andies tissue, in the reptile section of our garden previously only occupied by my brother's two terrapins – called, I promise you, Terry and Pin – that had proved such a short-lived failure just a few months before. So yes, verbally he made no allowance for any domestic fish or four-leggers but, by the same token, always did the right thing by them.

It was very rare that we got to see my mum in a fury – which finally brings us to the time Tom smashed her teapots. As anyone who has ever kept a tortoise will tell you, they are, at heart, vagabonds: rugged, rootless creatures within whom the wanderlust runs very deep. Our Tom, possibly because his earliest memories would have been aboard that ship bound for the London docks, was as restless as the ocean itself and recognized no man-made boundaries. Tom knew that, thanks to the four-foot fence that separated us from the Brimbles' garden next door, his dreams of a life on the open road were destined to remain unfulfilled; he would never be able to scale this towering barrier, let alone vault over it. After a few frustrating years, however, it dawned on him that there might be another way. Employing a thoroughness that only someone to whom time is no object can muster, he began to tunnel down. Though they're renowned for being slow, let me tell you a tortoise with a plan can actually shift solid earth like a gravedigger on piecework. The first time Tom performed his subterranean escape he was hailed on both sides of the fence as something of a marvel. His audience grew less appreciative once he started repeating the gag on the hour, every hour. We began to wonder if he was quite right in the head. In the early stages, Mrs Brimble would laugh at the sight of him mooching about her garden and tap on our back window with her wedding ring to alert my mum to the wayward pet's latest bid for freedom. After a while, this lapsed into an exasperated, 'Bleedin' 'ell, Bet – can't you keep this tortoise of yours under control? My ice plant ain't got a leaf left on it.'

We had always gotten along wonderfully with all our neighbours and Tom's adventures underground were the first time any kind of strain had ever been put upon east–west relations in the block. The difficulty, of course, was just how does one corral such a determined beast? Tortoise collars, leads and harnesses were then very much things of the future. Actually, now I think about it, they still are. So what was to be done? My brother suggested that a small hole might be drilled through the back of Tom's shell through which a piece of string could be affixed, but this was soon voted down as both cruel and demeaning. Besides, to what would the other end of the string be attached? When Michael said some sort of metal ring embedded in the wall, Dad pointed out, 'He's a tortoise, not fucking King Kong.'

Within days though the situation had escalated to a point where some sort of action had to be taken. Tom, having fully mapped out the Brimbles' yard, now turned his roving eye to the next fence standing in his way: the one separating him from the undoubtedly lush lawn at number 15. Decision made, his front legs began furiously excavating once more and within hours he was emerging into the hitherto uncharted territory of Mr & Mrs Punt's cherished dahlia beds. Forty-eight hours after that – having been returned to us five times – he was managing to get as far as the Dalligans' geraniums at number 21. Enough was enough and my father was forced to erect a wire mesh stockade that restricted Tom's beat to the small concrete porch area immediately outside our back door. This was not meant to be a permanent enclosure but, as Dad said, 'Just till he gets the idea.' The only idea Tom got was that there might be New Worlds to be discovered beyond the rough mat that lay at the threshold to our front room. And so he became a house-tortoise, entering our home at a moment's notice should anyone leave the back door open more than a few inches. During the summer, this would be the norm. It was very common to hear Mum break off washing up at the kitchen sink to look down over her shoulder and say, 'Oh, hello. What do you bleedin' want?' as Tom appeared, charging around on his latest lap. The apogee of Tom's perambulations came one day when there was a knock at our door and a man we had never seen before was standing on the doorstep holding our tortoise in his left hand.

'Mrs Baker,' began the fellow. 'I've just got off the number one bus up at the top of the turning and I nearly trod on this tortoise. The man from the post office says he's yours.'

Well, Mum couldn't thank the chap enough, although Tom, clearly furious at such busy-bodying, had withdrawn deep into his shell and was refusing to assist in the inquest. I later got the blame for leaving the front door open, 'When you know full well he'd be off like a shot.'

It was a few nights after this, while we were watching *Take Your Pick* with Michael Miles – a wonderful and extremely popular peak-time games show in which members of the public could win tiny caravans, a carpet or £50 in five-pound notes – that Tom's indoor visa was abruptly cancelled.

My mother, like most 1960s mothers, loved a knick-knack. In our front room we had a madly contemporary, if mass-produced, glass-fronted cabinet full of things like chalk poodles, Toby jugs, little highly glazed ladies' boots as well as decorative ash trays and faux Georgian porcelain figurines. What my mum liked best though was a novelty teapot. Since these were too large to fit into the spaces in the cabinet, she displayed her collection on a tall but narrow corner unit that could house about three teapots on each of its five triangular shelves. As we sat watching *Take Your Pick* that night, the fixture, which stood a few feet behind our television set, was full to capacity. Never the sturdiest of structures, it was nevertheless well grounded by the combined weight of Mum's pride and joys and topped by her favourite piece of all, a china cabbage leaf arrangement whose lid featured several caterpillars hurrying away from a radish.

I can't remember which of us first noticed that the entire column had begun to move. Not too much initially, but before long it was swaying back and forth like a Japanese city bank during one of their regular earthquakes. It turned out Tom the Tortoise had strolled into the front room earlier that afternoon and, having patrolled his usual haunts, decided to find somewhere enclosed and shady to take a nap. The base of my mother's teapot unit offered just such a darkened area, a space at floor level where the unit's feet supported the bottom-most shelf. The gap was about four inches high which, happily, if at a pinch, was exactly the same height as Tom himself. Having snuggled into this retreat he had dozed off facing the wall. Now, many hours later, it seemed Tom had awoken and had momentarily forgotten where he was. What's more, this accommodation no longer exactly fit his requirements. Somehow the den appeared to have shrunk. Or possibly he had swelled. Whatever the science involved, Tom the Tortoise suddenly felt constrained and horribly claustrophobic. In an attempt to free up a little shell space he began vigorously shunting himself to and fro, and it was this repeated motion that had manifested itself in the upper decks of the unit. As the giddy rhythm gathered pace, Mum leapt from her chair, one arm outstretched, shrieking 'Fred! Do something!' But it was too late. Like Tom, Fred had only just surfaced, the fatal combination of a hard day's work, an open fire and average TV having sent him off into a beautiful kip. Helpless to prevent disaster, we looked on as with one final lurch Mum's teapot collection toppled forward like a punchy heavyweight who'd taken one too many on the chin. The noise! Dear God, the cacophony of that moment what with the shattering pottery, the impact of shelving on television set, our massed family screams as we rose to our feet and, because one unseen teapot had yanked the aerial out of its socket, a burst of loud white noise cutting across it all. Amid the sobs and recriminations I looked over the wreckage and there was Tom, free at last and casually making his way toward the back door, his thoughts seemingly anchored on that half a strawberry he had earmarked for supper. Mum, absolutely distraught, saw him too. Taking her slipper off, she hurled it at him as hard as she could.

'You fucker! You destructive little fucker!' she screeched. The slipper missed its target and Tom appeared not to notice. Arriving at the back door he saw it to be closed. I swear he then craned his scaly old neck round to peer at our hysterical tableau. He followed this up with a sanguine look that seemed to say, 'I say, could one of you get this for me? Don't know about you lot, but I'm starving.'

Mum cried all the next day and the Great Tortoise Teapot Disaster would be something she measured all other breakages and disappointments against for the rest of her life. Needless to add, our garden door was never, ever, allowed to be left open after that and Tom remained penned in on the porch until some concrete mix was applied to the base of the four-foot fence between us and the Brimbles, bringing to a close that particular avenue of reptile escape.

Anyway, the point is, nobody in my family had ever been in show business. But in the spring of 1982, without actually trying, in show business was exactly where I found myself.

Are You Having Any Fun?

There's a school of thought that many people drive themselves to become famous to either please, or spite, their parents. In my case, I became famous because it was convenient. It was, in a physical sense, literally handy. The TV programme that I'd almost sleepwalked on to, the *Six O'Clock Show*, was made at the London Weekend Television studios, roughly fifteen minutes from my front door.

I cannot emphasize enough how significant a factor that was in the decision to adopt a comparatively sedate career after my wilder years working in a hip record store, getting mixed up in the birth of punk rock and particularly my recent tutti-frutti hurricane ride on the *New Musical Express*. I've often wondered how keen I would have been to pursue a life in front of the lens had the programme been made by the BBC, who were way across town, a thousand miles away in Shepherd's Bush. In London traffic, Shepherd's Bush could be a two-hour trek from my place in Bermondsey, and I don't know if I could have stuck such a tedious commute for long. I fully accept people may curl a lip and feel such world-weary posturing is unforgivably lofty, given what a huge break landing a gig in TV might seem. However, in my defence I would offer that until just a few months previously, I'd been going all over the world getting paid to hook up with exotic, half-crazed drug-fuelled pop stars in fantastically fancy-pants hotels, notorious bars and sold-out stadiums. In that light, I promise you, even the most exciting discussion about a regional news programme's proposed running order starts to look a bit pale around the gills. Throw into that mix the grim subterranean meeting rooms of the BBC's TV

Centre and you may glimpse why the shot simply wasn't on the board.

So the workplace being just up the road became the tipping point in what some of my *NME* colleagues came to gleefully refer to as 'Tin-pot Elvis going in the army'. Something else that soothed the realization that my Vegas days were over was the fact that LWT were willing to pay me an absolute fucking fortune: £500 for my initial appearances, rising to £750 by the summer of '82 – and this show was on every week, forty-two weeks a year. Those of you who read the previous book will know that these huge amounts of money, from the fanfare of receipt to the tinkling of the last tanner as it disappeared down the drain, lasted me about five days. Having been well schooled in the theory of largesse by my father, I now set out to eclipse his reckless reputation rather in the manner George Formby's screen career swallowed up the legend of his old man on the stage. The size of the budget was never the point. To live high on the hog had always been second nature to us as a family and I had viewed every rising sun like the call to some euphoric theme park for as long as I could remember. My true thinking toward this latest splash from the cash stream was that I thought they were absolutely insane to be offering such sums to me at all. Five hundred quid? OK, if you insist. I had no agent. I had no reputation. I had no real ambition to actually do this 'for a living', whatever that meant. Yet here they were, walking up to me not only with a wheelbarrow full of ten-pound notes each Friday but, without prompting or so much as a blackmailer's note, regularly asking if I could possibly carry this other sack of twenties away as though it were stinking up their bins and I was on my way to the furnace. Which, in one sense of course, I was.

I can clearly remember the day I stood by the LWT lift on the tenth floor and Barry Cox, a lovely fellow who acted as some sort of executive on our harlequinade, sidled up to me with an almost embarrassed shuffle and asked if he could have a quick word. I honestly thought he was about to tell me that, though the show was doing very well and the public seemed to like me, would I possibly mind exiting the elevator at ground level and never coming back.

This would have been fair enough. These people had been more than good to me and they were absolutely entitled to draw stumps on the lark anytime they chose. 'Now what, Baker?' the Gods would have chortled, and I suppose I'd simply have had to feel around inside Fate's top hat and yank out another career rabbit by its droopy old lugs. I sometimes ponder this. It is quite possible that by now I'd have been, if not a leading astronaut, then certainly the chap who pushes the button to launch the spaceship then sits back, feet up, to read a magazine while it wends its perilous way into the atmosphere. All gravy, I've always thought that gig was – and they don't even have to wear ties these days. Anyway, Barry hemmed and hawed about the critical point we were at in the show's evolution – just coming to the end of series one and needing to up the ante for its return – when he lowered his voice further and said, 'Listen, Dan – would eleven hundred be all right for you next year?' I told him it would be all right. Indeed, I may have even expressed a little impatience about how slow he had been in noting my frustration at having to cart home that same old £750 week in, week out. As it was, I was willing to be big about it and, yes, for this kind of dough, I might even consider commuting as far as, oh, I don't know, Alaska.

In truth, I actually got into the lift wondering what the fuck was going on. Why do they keep giving me more money? Wendy and I paid only £28 a week rent at the flat, so I dare say we could even have rubbed by on that distant old five hundred I had so naïvely accepted all those months ago. Besides, a raise – as I understood it from my friends – was usually an extra tenner a week. Sometimes twenty. And didn't you have to lobby for them, go cap in hand or at least employ a little leverage? As far as I knew, nobody else wanted me. In what universe did people, out of the blue, ask your permission to fork another three hundred and fifty crisp ones into an already bulging pay packet every Friday? Why, in eighties media of course.

Stupendous stipend aside, the job itself was turning out to be an absolute pip. The *SOCS* office was freshly stocked with a dozen or so other young prospects who were also at the dawn of their TV careers and had lucked out on to this upbeat immediate runaway hit. People like Paul Ross, Jeff Pope, Charlie Parsons, Ruth Wrigley, Jim Allen, all of whom went on to be enormously successful in the broadcasting game. The hour-long programme was captained by Greg Dyke and the executive producer was John Birt; both subsequently became Director General of the BBC, both now notorious for different reasons. Above all, the atmosphere in the open-plan play-pit of an office was noisy, giddy and wild, with a terrific amount of gallows humour underscoring the worth of much of what was produced. It was one of those smart, cynical pens where the in-jokes, ad-libs and wisecracks came at a fearsome pace – usually at the expense of somebody else's 'art' – where massive buffets of Chinese food and plentiful alcohol would be delivered late at night, and where the show's snowballing success simply intensified the fun rather than piled on the pressure.

The only eventual downside was that most of us who worked there genuinely believed that all jobs in television would be like this and, without letting daylight in upon magic here, let me tell you, they are not. (Many years later, when I first worked full-time at the BBC, I found that the accepted norm for TV show workplaces – even the frothiest ones – was an atmosphere somewhere between a long-haul flight and a suicide attempt in Lenin's tomb.)

The other great bonus of the *SOCS* was that I got to meet, work with and occasionally get to know the kind of recognizable TV personalities that my friends and family would acknowledge as bona fide stars. At the *NME* even my association with Michael Jackson made very little impact indoors. When 'Thriller' became an unavoidable global video sensation in 1983, my old man's initial reaction to it was, 'Is he the turn you went talking to that time?' I confirmed it was. After watching a little more he had another query: 'Is that what he's known for – all the dressing up?' I said something along the lines of how, for Michael, the music always came first, but, understandably during the transformation scene, Dad doubted this. 'You know who used to do that in my day, don't ya? Lon Chaney.'

After this, Spud took to referring to Michael Jackson as Lon Chaney. Every single time. When the first allegations surfaced about what was supposedly going on behind closed doors at Neverland, the old man said to me, not without some relish that one of my supposed idols had become a scandal: 'I see old Lon Chaney's come unstuck

– touching the kids up.' Consequently to this day I still find it hard to think of Michael Jackson as anything other than Lon Chaney and, though less so, vice versa.

Actually, while we're here, I may as well tell you that Dad similarly rebranded Frank Zappa as 'Percy the Tramp'. In 1970 I had put a poster of this icon of the counter culture on my bedroom wall. Not the infamous and bestselling study of Frank on the toilet – I think that's a revolting picture and anyway, the old man would have had that down before the Sellotape had touched the wallpaper – but a simple head-and-shoulders shot of the great maverick with his arms folded. The morning after I had first displayed it, I came downstairs to get some tea.

'That's a lovely picture you've put up of Percy the Tramp,' came a flat voice from behind the *Daily Mirror*.

Percy the Tramp was a well-known, old-fashioned down-and-out whose beat was Deptford High Street. This wildly hirsute local fixture dressed in the classic garb of his social class, right down to battered hat, flapping boot soles and string belt around his distressed old mac. His two signature flourishes were a flamboyant nosegay of flowers that hung from his lapel (and were, surprisingly, refreshed daily), plus a milk-bottle full of tea that would be replenished free of charge by the bloke on the pie stall outside the Deptford Odeon – who I was told was his brother. Percy was completely harmless and once, when I was about five, thrilled me by raising his milk bottle to me as I passed, saying, 'This is the only truth.' Local legend had it that Perce was worth several million pounds but went off the rails when a doodlebug landed on his fiancée. It was many years before I realized that a similar tale gets attached to every district's local eccentric and, while attractive as a back-story, it was very likely bogus. This was pretty much confirmed one night when we stopped for a hot pie at his 'brother's' stall and Peter King asked him if he really was related to the top hobo of SE 8. 'He's not my brother, thank fuck,' snapped the bloke, wiping down his counter. 'And I've got the pox of being asked about it too.' Some of my mates thought such a tetchy denial was proof positive that it must be true, but I think you have to draw the line somewhere.

Anyway, in our house Percy the Tramp became Frank Zappa and then eventually any guitarist whose wayward solo tested the old man's traditional ear.

'Lovely that, boy. Beautiful music. Is it Percy the Tramp again?'

Incredibly – although possibly not to those of you by now inured to the way my life has simply bounced along – within a few years I got the chance to judge the other side of the Frank/Percy comparison in the flesh. I had remained a big fan of Zappa, so in 1980 when Monty Smith, my good friend at the *NME*, landed an interview with him at a London hotel, I barrelled along too. This turned out to be a very poor decision and possibly instrumental in one of the most uncomfortable encounters I've ever had with any celebrity. I must accept the lion's share of the blame with this. Quite what role I thought I was going to play was something I hoped to figure out en route. Frank Zappa was notoriously hostile toward any rock journalist, and especially British ones, so what he made of the pair of us gormlessly loping into his inner sanctum stinking of beer, I'll leave you to imagine. Monty says he heard Zappa mutter, 'Great. Drunk English guys,' as he turned from opening his hotel-room door, but I still think that was paranoia on Monty's part. Whatever the truth, this went badly from the off.

'OK,' Frank drawled, sitting on the edge of the bed and eyeing me venomously as I dragged another chair across to sit beside Monty, 'which one of you is actually asking the questions?' Monty said he was. 'So why the hell do we need him?' he barked, stabbing his cigarette, held tensely between index and middle fingers, toward me like a pistol.

'Oh, we always do it like this,' I frankly fannied. 'We're known for it.'

'*Known* for it?' he replied, dragging the first word out and imbuing it with as much distaste as possible. Then, the coup de grâce: 'Known by *who* exactly?'

At that moment, just to make the atmosphere even more light-hearted, there came a loud thump at the room's door and I rose to let in the third of what Frank doubtless considered to be an endless stream of toxic stooges, the ever-clubbable *NME* photographer, Tom Sheehan.

'Jesus Christ,' dead-panned Frank, 'another one. How encouraging.'

The fact is, we should have arrived together – not that this would have eased the trauma for Mr Z – because all three of us had hitherto been necking down pints in the White Horse pub, a popular venue for rock journalists given that it was virtually next door to Cheapo-Cheapo Records, a tumbledown second-hand shop in Rupert Street that gave music hacks hard cash in exchange for the tons of promotional LPs record companies bombarded you with in those days. Knowing Zappa was going to be a thorny old encounter, Tom, Monty and I had wisely decided to meet there and stun ourselves heavily beforehand. Now bursting into his presence, Tommy – who like me was then a rotund fellow with few emotions outside the euphoric – explained it all in typical fashion.

'I'm not late, Frank. We've been heavy on the old sherbs for a few hours and I stopped off in the lobby for a gypsy's kiss. Could have used yours, but some people are a bit funny about that!'

It was here I swear I heard Frank Zappa growl. Literally growl. However, we knew everything was going to be all right. You see, Tom had brought Frank a present. Armed with this we were confident that before much longer we would all be swapping phone numbers, lacing daisies into each other's hair and laughing about how incredible it was that we had all got off on the wrong foot. The gift was *that* good. You see, through the rock'n'roll grapevine, Tommy had learned that the last time Zappa was in London he'd seen a copy of *Time Out* magazine that featured his face on the cover, cleverly formed of thousands of tiny music notes. Apparently somebody had heard him say he considered it rather good. Acting upon this lead, Tommy had tracked down the original artwork and secured it. This, in terms of the volcanic mood in the room, was to be our get-out-of-jail-free card. Thinking about it, it's a wonder we didn't extend the gag and wind him up further, possibly burning an old tyre in his hotel suite fireplace, just so we could watch the thunderous reaction dissolve into a beaming grin when we handed him the painting.

Tom passed it across and Zappa unsheathed it from the stiffened cardboard holder.

'What's this?' monotoned the maestro coldly.

'It's that thing, Frank,' said Tom.

'Somebody told us about you saw it,' I helpfully chipped in, losing grip on the mother tongue in my enthusiasm.

Frank Zappa gave a short baffled shake of his head and then looked back up to us like someone handed a summons on their wedding day.

'It's that thing you saw, someone said, you know,' came Tommy again, by now selflessly protecting his sources lest they too might get dragged into in the looming bloodbath.

'Ya got me,' sighed our star with renewed weariness. 'I don't know what this piece of shit is.'

Monty, possibly drunker than we two, stepped in to clarify: 'No, not a piece of shit. Nothing like that. You said you really liked it and Tom got it. It's yours – from us.'

'*I* said *I* liked this?' spat Zappa with a disbelieving snort. 'I think you must be confusing me with . . . let's say, a guy like Ted Nugent.[1] I can do shit like this in my sleep.' And with that he threw the thing away, spinning it with such force that it cracked against the far wall. 'Now ask me some goddamn questions and let's get this fucking thing done.'

He was rude and we were stupidly drunk. I should have left it there. I *really* should have left it there. But we all go through a stage of believing that, if we could only spend five minutes with one of our heroes, we could show them that we are nothing like all the boss-eyed bumpkins they usually have to suffer and are in fact exactly the sort of down-to-earth great company they must be starved of in their rarefied fame bubble. We know their humour, interests and their speech patterns. We even know what bores them! In short, we

---

[1] A notoriously unsophisticated seventies hard rock act who later became a right-wing blowhard, famous for apparently wanting possession of firearms to be made compulsory in the US. He is best remembered for his line, when ordering a meal in London's Speakeasy nightclub: 'Honey, I don't care what you bring me – just take off its horns, wipe its ass and stick it on a plate!'.

are their soul mates . . . all bar the trivial matter of never having met. In Zappa's case, I had actually come close to that, sort of, back in December 1971. That was the night he was attacked onstage at London's Rainbow Theatre and hurled into the orchestra pit by the jealous boyfriend of a super-fan. It was an assault that put him in hospital for nearly a year and came close to permanently crippling him. The gift of the painting might have failed, but this memory was going to be my 'in'.

'Frank,' I said, 'you remember the night you got thrown off the stage by that madman?'

He didn't answer, but by the way his eyebrows shot up we may assume he did recall something of the night in question.

'Well,' I went on, 'I had a ticket for the show after that, only it got cancelled! I've still got it somewhere. All my friends went to the early show, but I thought the late one would be better so I got tickets for that. And of course there wasn't one . . .' I finished, or more accurately trailed off with a particularly weak half-smile.

The immediate lesson was, sometimes you really need to say words out loud to yourself in private before offering them up, simply to find if they have even a scintilla of collective worth. Having voiced this bunch, I was pretty sure they hadn't.

There are some people – aunts, sympathetic partners, small children, et cetera – who will kindly overlook the paucity of an anecdote and nobly try to fill the ghastly dead air that ensues after one has laid such a conversational egg. You won't be surprised to learn that Frank Zappa isn't on that saintly list. He was quiet for a while, his clasped hands resting on crossed legs that were vibrating in agitation. Then, glaring at me with a cold rage, my hero spoke:

'OK, I need you to leave – and I mean right now.'

In response to this I smiled at him vacantly like a hundred per cent half-wit.

'And that's all there is to it,' he said.

And in that final sentence the two worlds of Frank & Fred collided. 'And that's all there is to it,' was possibly my old man's favourite phrase, used to double-underline any declaration and regularly employed just in case his audience was under any illusion that he was opening the floor to a conversational counterpoint.

'You're not going out in those fucking shoes – and that's all there is to it.'

'We are not watching *Monty* fucking *Python* – and that's all there is to it.'

'You *are* coming out with us on Saturday to Aunt May's – and that's all there is fucking to it.'

I often think a really strong Prime Minister would use the line at the despatch box:

'We are going to drop a fucking bomb on Finland – and that's all there is to it.'

The moment Frank Zappa said it to me I could visualize the old man sitting beside him, wearing an identical expression and turning to say, 'See what I mean about him, Frank? Silly as arseholes.'

I left the hotel room as instructed. Monty and Tom say the atmosphere remained flatlined, despite their attempts to haul it out of the permafrost. The article, when it was published, made Zappa seem particularly sullen and difficult with no mention of the fiasco that had coloured his mood. Happily, among much of my day-to-day circle, offending the composer of 'Peaches en Regalia' carried slightly less weight than offending the real-life Percy the Tramp.

However – and to return to the point I think I was making – my dad's indifferent reaction to my work changed when TV put me in the orbit of names he knew and situations he understood. While not exactly bursting with pride, he would sometimes obliquely enquire as to whether this unexpected boost to his reputation on the estate was worth getting used to.

'This telly game,' he'd ask as he drove me to work, 'd'you reckon you'll stick it out?'

I'd tell him I reckoned so, and he would pull a face as if to say, 'I'd get stuck in while you can, boy . . .'

Over those first couple of years, the extraordinary popularity of the *Six O'Clock Show* in London took everyone involved with it by complete surprise. Broadcast live virtually all year, it grabbed an

enormous audience every Friday evening. In terms of onscreen confidence and star pulling power, the show was more like a network
Light Entertainment juggernaut than a vehicle for the featherweight
end of local news. I became thoroughly identified with it in people's minds, signifying as it did the start of many a working household's weekend, and I was very happy to go along with every bit
of its broad-brush wide-eyed hoopla. This was easy street. This was
plush. The rising amounts of money that LWT were throwing at me
required but the flimsiest of workloads. Here's how it went, year in,
year out.

I couldn't drive, so on Monday lunchtime my old man would pick
me up in his motor and chauffeur me to what is now the ITV studios
by the Thames. There I'd barrel through a raucous hour-long meeting, during which all the real makers of the show would outline their
simple but inventive ideas for the short film reports around which
that week's show and guests would be hung. As noted, the atmos
phere in the ideas room would be ebullient and competitive – if not
quite up to the unforgiving standard of *NME* editorial meetings,
where you really did need every bit of jousting armour your wits
could muster. What they both had in common was that, once business was concluded and the dead had been buried, everyone went
straight to the bar to guzzle down liquids as if an enormous asteroid
had been sighted hurtling past the moon.

On any of the three days following these team meetings I would
be required to front one of the selected reports, craftily adapted as
they were from an original item spotted in one of the capital's micro
publications. It might be about rag-and-bone men. It might be about
budgerigars. Eccentrics and their inventions was always a winner.
Solid-gold subjects like nudists, improbable ghost sightings and
ecclesiastical fashion shows became our staple fare. Quite often I was
required to dress up and behave idiotically for a gag piece to camera,
emerging from inside a wheelie bin or hanging on a bell-ringer's
rope. On location days, everybody involved enjoyed long lunches in
good restaurants – all cheques picked up by LWT, of course – and
all of us had a fair few again after the final shot. Sometimes well
before it too.

Come Friday, the show would be staggered through once in a mid-afternoon rehearsal then boomed out at six o'clock absolutely live in front of an audience with a top-notch guest joining we regulars to chat breezily about events. By seven it was all done; the audience would applaud wildly and copious amounts of free food and drink would be forced upon everybody concerned.

This light, stress-free schedule was my entire week. So what did I do with the rest of my time? Well, fuck-all. Absolutely fuck-all.

Possibly because I couldn't allow myself to believe that this nonsense would amount to anything, I may have been stockpiling my greater energies for some more tangible toil yet to reveal itself as my True Calling. I knew I was pretty slick at frothy TV, but who wouldn't be? Competent showing off certainly didn't feel like a particular skill or anything I could take elsewhere if they decided to hand me my hat – a prospect that didn't unsettle me one iota. I was very aware that I simply lacked whatever determined, or maybe needy, gene it is that makes show-folk strive. Most new TV performers, having finally got their break, really, really don't want to fuck it all up. After all, this was 'it', the longed-for breakthrough signalling that their career was on the up at long last. The problem was, I didn't come from a background where people had 'careers'. You went to work, you had various jobs at different times, but it was all in a jumble. It did not define you or plot your course in life – and thank God for that. All of us on the *Six O'Clock Show* felt extremely fortunate to varying degrees, but I felt lucky in a different way, like when you find money down the back of a couch or get into the pictures without paying. I certainly never regarded any of this folderol as 'getting my foot in the door'. What door? As far as I could see, I had arrived in Wonderland by accidentally popping up out of a loose manhole cover.

Had I been required to struggle a bit, or even had the tiniest hankering for the media lifestyle, I would have been completely absorbed in how well I was now doing and possibly gone round the bend in an orgy of self-love, like so many do in broadcasting. If I'm honest, I reckon I would have made a first-class media-mad person. We will meet examples of this potty breed as my story unfolds. On the many occasions I got to observe them pout, rant and rave, I always suspected that, given a more insecure nature, a good excuse and a penchant for unhinging drugs, I could have given all them a right old run for their money. As it was, ever since quitting school without so much as an O-level to wave at the hard-knock life, employment had felt like extended lark. Even if it came to a halt in the next heartbeat, I would still have looked on it as an exhilarating suspension of real life. I imagine my wife would have said to me, in the normal years that followed my fleeting fame, 'Do you remember when you used to be on telly a lot?' and I'd say, 'I know!' Following which the pair of us would crease up at the giddy memory of such a preposterous liberty.

Perhaps it is my passport for the years 1978–88 that best sums up my half-hearted commitment to whatever it was I felt I did for a living. In the space on the document marked *Occupation* were written the curious words *Music Writer* – and they were written in my own hand too. When I had filled out the form for this, my first proper hardback passport, I had been writing in fits and starts for the punk fanzine *Sniffin' Glue* – a stapled-together amateur effort sold by myself and a few friends. The idea that I could put 'Journalist' down as my profession seemed hopelessly grand. So I put 'music writer' and toddled off to the official offices in Petty France to hand in the forms, prepared, if called upon, to better explain my fuzzy old line of work. In the event, nobody was in the slightest bit interested in what I did. But when the little book was handed to me, there, under profession, my job was given as 'musician'. I stared at this for some time. Would it do? Did it matter? I figured it might. The reason for me applying for the thing in the first place was that my friend Stephen Saunders and I were selling everything we had to hop aboard Freddie Laker's Sky Train – a new venture by which you could fly to New York for just £60. What if the notoriously cynical cops at US immigration read this 'musician' boast and asked me to prove how I made a crust? At worst they would hand me a saxophone and ask for a demonstration, at best they might casually ask what instrument I played – and you can't answer 'nothing' to that one, unless you're Yoko Ono. So right there outside the Passport Office I took a biro and crossed out 'musician' and wrote above it my original bluff of 'music writer'. I had no idea that doing this was totally illegal. Basically it invalidates the entire document and makes you ineligible to travel anywhere, though I have to say that in the ten years I went around the world on it, only once was I ever questioned about the alteration. Arriving at Los Angeles to interview ex-Motown boss Berry Gordy – who by that time was running a peppy disco label called Solar – a guy at Customs asked if I actually wrote music, 'Y'know, like Beethoven'. I told him that I had changed the words myself and they were just a lie basically. 'I didn't hear that,' he said, handing it back to me with a facial expression I have since come to know as 'the old skunk-eye'.

So there it was. I was in my mid-twenties, popular and successful, hopelessly, happily in love, earning tons of money in a fantastic, easy job on TV that was a real pleasure to do. The form in autobiographies is to now write: '. . . but I had no idea that this idyllic lifestyle was about to come crashing down around my ears and life was going to get very hard.' I fully understand that. It's the kind of thing that gives consecutive chapters some emotional light and shade. 'Ah!' says the reader. 'A reckoning!' As I said in the first book, it might appease certain sourpusses if I eased up on the lashings of joy and light that seems to attend the events in these volumes, but to what end? What I present are the bald facts and we're stuck with them. Indeed, in the current style I should say SPOILER ALERT here, because any readers who could reasonably expect a bit of struggle and darkness from their tomes might want to make for the last bus now because a) I don't get cancer till Book Three and b) Believe it or not, the professional hijinks were only just beginning.

None of the preceding cart-wheeling should leave you with the impression that, even with a hit TV show thundering away each week, I was entirely to the manor born. In fact I could have done with putting on a little more side and taking expert advice in how best to handle this jamboree. Here's a perfect example.

When you first begin achieving any kind of profile through the media, you simply can't do enough to keep up with the schedule such a privileged position brings. You reply personally to the trickle of letters that arrive at the studios. You accept invitations to present cheques in pubs, often many hours from your home. You take part in tug-o'-wars to raise fourpence ha'penny for church-steeple funds. I have even been locked into authentically fashioned medieval stocks in order that people might throw sodden sponges at me for 20p a pop. This, to be fair, can be a lot of fun, so long as people are forming a queue to aim their soggy missiles at you. It is in the longueurs between customers that you begin to question your status as a draw. There you are, in public, your head and hands poking through two tiny wooden apertures that scrape off skin with every attempt to find comfort, arse and legs sticking out behind, inviting stray stones from the younger set, and, worst of all, a procession of indifferent stragglers go strolling by within yards of this ignominy, not so much as glancing in your direction. You've taken a few hits, so the water saturating your hair is now freezing cold and the seemingly incessant rivulets make you blink like a strobe light. Meanwhile, the woman assigned to take the money and hand out the sponges is similarly fed up with being ignored and keeps throwing you embarrassed glances, saying things like, 'Blimey, you're a flop! We had Wincey Willis last year and I'd taken thirty quid by this time.' Of course you can take this information either way. You can tell yourself Wincey is a controversial figure so it's no wonder the crowds flocked to launch their sponges at her helpless head, whereas you are universally loved and simply do not deserve such treatment. But part of you wonders whether it's because the public have no idea who this absurd man in the humiliating contraption is and haven't the least desire to waste 20p attempting to feed his raging ego. The internal debate surges back and forth interminably as the punters drift by, oblivious, ignoring your inane grins that you hope will make you look a bit like someone they'll have seen on television at some point.

Extraordinarily, my mum and dad would treat these low-wattage gatherings as irrefutable signs that their boy was at last on the map. My previous front-page bylines in the world's most read music paper were as nothing compared to being pictured on page 17 of the *South London Press* in a pretend head-lock with wrestler Kendo Nagasaki. Of course, this was understandable. Friends of theirs would shout across the Jolly Gardeners saloon bar, 'Here, I saw your Danny in the

South London yesterday!' Whereas they never came across a single living soul who had seen my rather caustic half-page about Brian Eno in that week's *NME*.

The very first public event I was ever invited to attend as a result of my minuscule public profile was a fête at the Erith & District Sports Centre. I was actually asked to open the affair. It was to be on a Sunday morning at nine o'clock and, suburban Erith being a good forty-five minutes from where I was living, I asked my dad if he'd mind 'running me'. (Nobody I knew ever asked for a 'lift' from the few among us who had cars. You always asked if someone could 'run' you somewhere.) Spud's face as he drank in the info that I was kicking the event off was a picture of wonder and joy.

'How comes they asked you?' he said. And I knew that he'd only asked so he could hear the reply that would confirm his pride.

'I suppose they've seen me on telly and think it'll drum up a crowd. I dunno.'

He drank this in momentarily, then moved on to his inevitable secondary train of thought: 'And are they giving you a nice few quid?' he beamed with a relish signifying my confidential answer would be all over Bermondsey's best boozers later that day.

'No,' I said with as much insouciance as I could muster. 'I mean, leave off, Dad, you do these things for nothing. You know, it's a good cause and that.'

The fascination fell from his face. 'What? Fuck-all? Not even a drink?'

''Course not,' I came back, though by now not meeting his eye. 'That's not the way things are in telly. They're trying to build a new sports hall or something in Erith. You can't ask for money. Anyway, I'm happy to be giving something back.' Even as I said this I knew I might as well have been talking Chinese.

'Give something back! Well, if you say so, boy. But I tell ya – whenever there's pound notes flying about, you better have a fucking good look how much of it winds up in the pot. You'll soon find out who's giving something back! Do yourself a favour – just make a few enquiries when you get there. You find the right bloke and you'll get in the swim – they'll all be at it, don't you worry about that.'

Again, readers of the previous book will already know that, no matter what the gathering, service or enterprise, Spud always believed there was 'a swim' that allowed access to only a golden few. He never, ever had the slightest trouble 'finding the right bloke' on these occasions, because nine times out of ten that bloke would be him.

In the event, on the morning of the Erith & District Grand Fête the phrase 'in the swim' would have another, almost literal, meaning. It was hammering down. Pelting. As we sat about to set off in Spud's two-tone bronze 1976 Ford Granada, neither of us thought the trip would be necessary.

'They ain't gonna fuckin' go ahead with it in this, are they?' he asked, for about the fifth time.

I explained that – cancelled or not – I had better show willing and pitch up. Dad didn't see this.

'Wha'for? Even if the gates are open, you'd have to be puggled to come out in this. Fuck me, boy, people wouldn't turn out for Frank Sinatra in this lot – what chance you got?'

Bolstered by this, I asked him to turn the ignition key and head south.

When we arrived it wasn't raining as bad. It was raining far worse. The venue was an open-air municipal complex, little more than a small reception bungalow, a few changing rooms and then a running track encasing an oval grassed games field. There were about six cars outside in a car park that could've held fifty. Out on the field were three drenched and bedraggled stalls that looked to have been erected and abandoned some hours previously. The long PVC banner announcing the event had come adrift at one end and was slapping against the puddles as the wind whipped beneath it. In the short run from our car to the facility's entrance, my dad and I could not have taken on more water had we gone down on the *Lusitania*.

Bursting breathless and cursing into the tiny concrete reception space, Spud summed up our situation with a surgeon's precision:

'Well, this is bollocks!' he boomed, without the slightest hint of humour.

Far from laying on a welcoming committee for their star turn, there wasn't a soul in sight. Plainly the thing had been called off, but I still needed it confirmed before I would get back in the car and order Dad to find the nearest warm café. I wanted them to know I had at least seen my part of the bargain through like any seasoned pro was expected to in 'my' business. Three options stood before us. The door straight ahead would lead out on to the running track. To our right, a short corridor of changing rooms and showers. To the left, behind a council-blue door with a frosted-glass window, was what we assumed was some sort of office. Dripping a trail behind us, I knocked on the glass. As I did, I was able to make out a few blurry, silent figures within. When a woman eventually opened the door she looked us up and down and said, 'Have you come for the fête?'

'I'm Danny Baker,' I said, blowing a good-sized droplet off the end of my nose. 'I was asked to open the event.'

'You were?' she replied, with, for my liking, too strong an emphasis on the first word.

I nodded.

'Yes, well, that'll have been organized through John Riley,' she barked. 'I'm afraid he's not arrived yet. Come in, won't you?'

Inside the cheerless little room four other people were gathered about a wooden table, trying not to hog a two-bar electric fire that was causing significant steam to rise from sodden shoes and trouser legs. After shaking hands all round, we were offered tea. Some small talk about the conditions ensued, during which I could just about hear Spud behind me, wheezing a low 'fuck-ing hell' in a singsong tone I recognized as both amused and exasperated. Then one of the ladies dropped her bombshell.

'In any case, we will be planning on going ahead on time,' she announced.

She carried on talking, but I was too numb at this news to register anything else. Eventually I managed a small, 'Really?'

'Yes,' she rattled on crisply. 'We've discussed it and there are one or two brave souls sitting out in their cars waiting, and we've got the under-sixteens marching band due at any minute. They've been working very hard, so . . .'

This last revelation struck me as particularly farcical. On a day like this, any marching band, irrespective of what age they were, might just as well have marched straight off the end of Clacton Pier. Naturally, I felt for these poor kids who'd obviously been looking forward to a decent blow as they kicked out the Erith jams, but my plan now was to hurriedly cut whatever ribbon I was expected to and, stopping briefly to deliver a few amusing words for the local free sheet, follow the siren call of that hot sizzling breakfast. Inwardly, I hoped, and hoped hard, that I wouldn't be asked to stick around for the junior swing combo's full honking set.

No such luck.

With mounting horror I was informed that, as far as the Erith & District Events Committee were concerned, no proper Erith & District Annual Fête could be properly pronounced open without the Erith & District Marching Band (under-sixteens) first making one full circuit of the Erith & District four-hundred-metre running track.

OK, so my sausage-and-egg sandwich would be delayed for thirty minutes. This might be something I could just about cope with. There was bound to be some sort of porch or canopy beneath which we dignitaries could shelter while the youth made their noisy wet way around the flooded asphalt. Except it was then explained to me that whatever lucky celebrity been given the honour of opening that year's spectacular would be fully expected to march at the head of this cacophony – trumpets, tubas and drums blazing away – waving wildly at the ranks of cheering spectators (a throng that currently numbered approximately three desolate souls).

As the woman outlined these proceedings, she seemed to pay little heed to the fact that her words were being drowned out by the monsoon raging against the room's sole window.

Sure enough, the band duly arrived, shocked, squelching and bedraggled, and we were soon all jostling for the high ground beneath a small square exterior roof that was our last refuge before marching out into the tempest. There was nobody, *nobody* out there and it was now raining so hard that none of us could even see the far side of the field. Out into the wall of water we went.

Incredibly, the parade could not immediately get underway, as I had hoped, at a lunatic pace redolent of the Keystone Kops. No. First the band had to be physically arranged and lengthily briefed by their sergeant or whoever this cruel martinet was. It seemed to be all about proper distances between marchers and thumbs aligned parallel to trouser seams. All the while I stood patiently about five feet in front of them with not so much as a hat to ward off the continuous assault. Eventually he came over to me.

'I'll instruct the boys when to begin, Mr Baker,' he said. 'When you hear that, start walking smartly – but in sync with the drum at all times.'

'OK,' I gasped, bitterly noting that he was issuing his instructions from beneath a large striped golfing umbrella.

So, there we all stood. At long last he stepped back and barked something unintelligible but military-sounding and the band began to play. I swear to God it was 'The Liberty Bell' – better known as the theme to *Monty Python's Flying Circus*. And off we went, around the six-lane Erith & District municipal running track. Now I pride myself that I can keep a beat pretty well but, probably because my ears were full of rainwater, coupled with an understandable urgency to get the thing done, by the first turn I seemed to have opened a twenty-length lead over the orchestra. To an untrained observer it must have looked as if I was trying to shake them off. Figuring I had better let them catch me or risk appearing even more forlorn and ridiculous, I slowed down and marched on the spot for a bit. Once we were a unit again, through squinting eyes I scoured the few stalls at the centre of our parade, one of which had totally blown over, for any signs of life. Nothing. Out of sight of even the organizers, we were marching around in the storm-tossed wilderness for no apparent reason.

By the time we arrived at the far side of the track – I think the musical programme had segued into 'The Washington Post' at this point – I saw that a line of houses backed on to the facility and at one or two of the upstairs windows, confused residents awoken from their Sunday morning lie-ins by this gurgling din powering toward them, were attempting find out what the hell was going on. What they must have made of the sight of a satu-rated marching band coming a-Sousa-ing around the bend during what was clearly the end of the world, I simply can't imagine. And what, they must have asked themselves, was that idiotic man at the front doing? Shouldn't he be tossing a baton in the air or some-thing? Has the poor fellow just got mixed up in all this? Are those people making that racket just to show him where the local bus stop is?

I have to say I have never felt so utterly ludicrous in all my adult life – and as this book will prove, I have had some cracking contend-ers for that title.

After a single interminable orbit we finally found ourselves back where we started. The music ceased with a lone trombone quack like the last fart escaping from a scuttled submarine and we dashed en masse into the base camp, united in our embarrassment. We were greeted by half-hearted applause from the five or so witnesses who had seen it through. Spud was nowhere in sight. I eventually located him in the small office space where I'd left him, though by this time he was ensconced in one of the two chairs either side of the electric fire and holding a tumbler of Scotch. (When asked if he'd like tea, Dad always said, 'Well, if there's nothing stronger knocking about . . .' and usually there was.) In the other chair was one of the officials who had given the thumbs up for the parade to go ahead, also enjoy-ing a fiery drop. Neither of them had moved a muscle to watch us go round.

'This is Georgie Howard!' boomed Spud. 'I used to work in the dock with his brothers!'

No matter where we went, without fail, my old man invariably met someone who knew someone who knew him, and within min-utes they'd be breaking out the bonding booze.

Then, finally noting my appearance, which was of course now almost entirely liquid, he enquired, 'How'd it go?'

'Terrible,' I whimpered, trying not to overly offend the stranger who had sanctioned my descent into the maelstrom. 'Really, really bad out there. And not a soul to be seen, Dad. Felt a right idiot, going round like that.'

'Well, there you are,' he said with a tickled expression, 'If you will go volunteering for these things.'

Now you may think that was an end to my agonies. However, as I waited for Spud to finish up his drink with his new friend, and as a few towels and warming plastic cups of tea arrived, something peculiar happened. The rain weakened and then stopped. And, as sometimes happens on even the most inclement of days, several glaring rays of sun suddenly shone through the previously unbroken clouds. When this happens at home, one usually calls to one's partner or children, 'Blimey! Have you see it out now? Would you believe it?' At the Erith & District Sports Centre it almost magically signalled the arrival of about fifteen new vehicles in the car park. And where there had been just the mournful sight of a few disparate abandoned stalls out on the grass, the area immediately took on the intense bustle and swarm of a Marrakesh souk in high season.

'Oh, what a shame!' I trilled to the woman in whom I sensed a natural organizing authority. 'If only we'd hung on a bit!'

'Well, actually, could I be very cheeky?' she smiled back. 'Word seems to have got around we are actually open and there are a quite a few more here . . . So I wonder if you and the band would mind . . .'

I didn't hear the rest. The next thing I remember was putting my best foot forward again as the brassy juniors kicked into the theme from *Monty Python* and once more around that fucking running track we set sail for the second time in thirty minutes. With every step I took, the water in my shoes shot out through the lace holes like a surfacing sperm whale.

Dad didn't budge from his Scotch for this lap either. Afterwards we didn't speak much until, as he turned the ignition for the journey home and I buckled up my seat belt, he took a moment before putting the car in gear to say, 'Well, that was a fucking waste of time, weren't it?'

'Yes, it was,' I said, in a voice as cold and flat as my arse at that moment. 'An absolute waste of time.'

Of course I had no idea that that particular mantra would cover pretty much everything else I was to take part in across the following three decades in this relentlessly farcical industry.

Up In The World

Familiar TV face or not, Wendy and I were still living on the nineteenth floor of Maydew House, one of the four landmark Swedish-design council-estate towers that stood overlooking the Thames in Deptford and Rotherhithe. Today I'm sure these flats have been privately sold and resold many times, recognized at last as the stylish apartments in a prime location that they always were. Back in the early eighties, however, nobody wanted to live in this part of South-East London. It was universally regarded as a screamingly unfashionable location, barely part of the 'real' capital at all, despite the borough bordering on Waterloo, Southwark and London bridges. Cab drivers in the West End famously would not go 'south of the river' and, given that it was ill-served by Tubes and overground trains, this could put a crimp in your late-night carousing. It took the eastwards shift of the City into Canary Wharf for the streets in which I grew up to be 'discovered'. Now, even the restructured classroom spaces in my old school require a five-figure deposit. This is a good thing. And yet, on the occasions today when I pass the neighbourhood's upmarket al fresco restaurant tables around which sit four or five City – or media – types braying away another expenses lunch, I do have the overwhelming urge to shout, 'Why don't you lot just fuck off back to Chelsea?' I never will, of course. And even if I did, they would be entirely baffled as to what I meant, so completely redrawn is the map of my youth.

The only real drawback to living in a high-rise flat was the lifts. Unreliable, claustrophobic, dingy and eternally reeking of piss, it could often take more than ten long minutes before the one lift that was working – rarely would it be both – wheezed open in front of you

41

with a metallic shudder. A slow journey up to the nineteenth floor would then be slowed even further because some lousy ponce had purposely pushed all the buttons before getting out and you were now required to stop on every single level. On most of these floors the filthy steel elevator door with its useless tiny wired-glass window that was forever covered in dried phlegm would slide back to reveal identical dismal landings that were made even more sullen because 80 per cent of the overhead light bulbs were broken. On most of the stops you would find a forlorn-looking bloke, broken by the long wait, or an equally desolate mum with a pram that denied her the option of using the stairs, both looking at you with a defeated air before asking plaintively, 'Going down?' to which you would shake your head and break the doleful news, 'No. Up. Sorry.' And the door would sigh shut again.

The lifts at Maydew House could hold, uncomfortably, about ten people. Though there was never a breakdown while I was inside one, they rattled up and down the shaft at a snail's pace as if they might give up the ghost at any minute. Also, as a bonus, back then everybody else in there with you would usually be smoking.

At the base of the rear of the lift was a recess about three feet high. I had supposed this was to help with moving longer items of furniture in and out of the tower, until a caretaker one day explained to me that its primary function was for removing coffins.

These finicky elevators lead us into two notable stories.

One: I was talking to a rag-and-bone man in a café one day – the area boasted many stableyards for this, at the time thriving, profession to house their horses – when the totter, recognizing me from the show, asked if I still lived in the area. When I pointed toward Maydew House, he moved uneasily in his chair and gave it some, 'Don't talk to me about fucking Maydew House.'

It turns out the block had given him one of the worst experiences of his working life. He'd been calling out his traditional cry along the streets one day, a deceptively difficult ululation, when he heard the distant voice of a woman shouting, 'Rag man, up here. Rag man, stop!' Pulling the reins, he brought his horse to a halt and located the plea as coming from a window very close to the top of Maydew House. At first he chose to ignore the woman – tower blocks were the bane of the rag-and-bone man's life, and unless he had good cause to believe there was gold in them thar hills, a seasoned totter would opt to stay on the street. The woman proved very insistent though, so cupping his hands to his mouth he bellowed back, 'Is it worth my while, lady?'

Her reply saw him immediately reaching for the horse's nose bag: 'Oh it is!' she yelled. 'I've got something special for you here! It's all yours!'

Arriving at the notorious Maydew lifts his hard-working heart sank right down into his manure-flecked wellington boots: out of order, both of them. The woman had informed him that she was in flat 121; scanning the corroded metal sign that adorned the space between the lift doors he could see that her lofty drum was stationed right up on the twenty-first of the sky-scraper's twenty-four floors. Many a lesser rag man would have baulked at such an epic climb but, as he told it, 'It was about fakkin' two o'clock be then and all I had on the cart was a couple o' bits of shitty aluminium, a few bottles and an old R Whites sign. So when she says she's got something special, I think, "Fuck it, there's me beer money, I'll go up."' And up he goes.

I can tell you from bitter experience that there are four long flights of cold grey concrete stairs between each floor in Maydew House. Each flight has fourteen steps and the levels are arranged in an odd-number sequence: 1, 3, 5, 7 and so on. Thus our man had to slog up 560 unforgiving elevations in full winter work gear – including, remember, wellington boots – while carrying a cumbersome sack. In my own attempts at this feat I found that, even allowing for one being a few pounds above optimum fighting weight, you would definitely have to lean heavily on the stair rail for a bit of a blow after floors 5, 9, and 13. By floor 17 this regime would expand to sitting down for a minute on the piddle-smelling stone landings provided at the turns. I can assure you, by that point, the spectacular views across London available through the stairwell windows would count for nothing, because they would be seen through eyes now popping out of your pulsating head and stained blood-red by the sting of a torrential sweat.

With this punishing struggle finally behind him, our intrepid rag-and-bone man arrived on the twenty-first floor. Doubled over, gasping for air like a gaffed salmon on the towpath, the heat of his thickly socked feet causing spirals of steam to issue from the turned-over tops of his wellington boots, he steadied himself with one hand on the corridor wall and staggered his way along to number 121, the last door but one. Summoning up a final iota of strength from some deep inner reservoir, he managed to press the bell. From behind the frosted glass he could see the figure of a woman making her way to the front door. When she yanked it open, he could she was gripping a small child by the hand. The red-faced toddler had tear-stained cheeks and had plainly just been having a bit of a tantrum. Seeing the clapped-out stranger on his doorstep, his mouth fell open in shock. Looking triumphantly at the stunned boy, the woman announced: 'Here he is, what did I tell you? And unless you start behaving your-self today, next time I WILL give you to him!' She then turned to address what was left of the totter:

'Thanks for that, rag man – he's a little effer some mornings.'

And with that she promptly shut the door again.

'I fuckin' stood there – I couldn't get angry, I was too fucked,' the shabby tradesman concluded. 'I opened up the letter box and tried to shout through: "Thanks a lot, you potty tart!" But nothing come aht! I couldn't face going back down again, so I just slumped down next to her milk bottles. Next thing I hear from inside is the pair of them, fucking singing along with the telly! And I'm out there fucked – totally fucked!'

And that, understandably, is why you should never talk to him about Maydew House.

The second of the tower block's lift stories concerns my life-long friend Peter King. Pete, like me, had attended West Greenwich sec-ondary school and left without gaining a single certificate. You just did in those days – and still can, of course. Despite what anyone might try to tell you, it usually turns out really well.

People insist that times are radically different nowadays, but if you are truly bright and peppy no amount of A levels ought to be needed to convince some dull-eyed job-Caesar on the other side of a desk that you will be just great to have around. Besides, if everyone has dozens of A levels, doesn't that make them worthless? I mean, if you have ten A levels and Victoria over there has eleven, shouldn't that mean she will always get the gig? If not, then as I suspect, these certificates are as worthless as Deutschmarks after the First World War. Frankly, too much studying and exam sitting makes youth jittery and subservient – which is the point, I suppose. Of course if you subscribe to the view that it's vital to attend university, you will be required to jump through those dreary academic hoops. Personally, I consider university to be a fucking nonsense three-quarters of the time, unless you are after something genuinely quantifiable like engineering or medicine. Middle-class parents seem to be convinced that a child who winds up at university is the rubber stamp on good parenting, but you know what, kids? Fuck that. Sod the gap year – have a gap life.

The real killer is that we have only a handful of real and satisfying jobs today – certainly for working-class children. All the traditional industries have vanished – steel, cars, coal, docks . . . right down to proper shops, chocolates, print and television – and all we are left with are millions of mimsy office jobs, each with some windy meaningless title invented by a team of real drags seeking to elevate their vacuous positions. They wasted their teens getting paper vouchers that say they listened well in class and now they insist you to go through that too. Everywhere you look it's the choking revenge of the suited dullards on the carefree crowd, and nowhere is this con more visible than current TV. TV used to be fronted by popular entertainers happily giving away cash, caravans and white goods to ordinary folk, who by and large lived unexciting lives. Now somehow the star prize is a desk-bound job in Alan Sugar's boring old office block. Boy, do they make the kids eat shit for that privilege! Dragon's Den *– suited money-men sit in grim judgement on those who actually create. Then there's* X-Factor *– the biggest star in British TV is a fucking 'music executive' waving his hand like an emperor over desperate kids hoping he will run their entire lives! Rock'n'roll! When I was fourteen,* Monty

Python – *indeed, all comedy shows – routinely portrayed bankers, businessmen and accountants as the cautious, office-bound bores they invariably are. Now the world has been turned on its head and we are led to believe that these are 'playas' who for some reason simply must have their own round-the-clock TV channels. (And if I didn't have to haul this back to Peter King's Maydew House lift fiasco, I'd also get right after the dozens of specious, solemn, puffed-up rolling news networks that exactly NO ONE asked for, yet are apparently above ever getting axed the way regular TV shows do – and being axed from the schedules is a subject I have about ten thousand A levels in, as you will eventually find out.)*

Pete and me, though we had enjoyed our time at the old alma mater, dropped out of school so fast that on our last day, like the Roadrunner, we both left behind a dust outline of where we'd previously been standing. I headed into the record shop that altered my whole life while Pete took a job with his dad's mate on a local milk round. This was a sweet berth. Not only would he be finished by eleven every day, he also got to plug the line of idle milk floats into the mains socket at the end of each shift – a duty I imagined would be both satisfying and amusing. I saw them all being juiced up together once, a static parade of those funny little craft that at this particular dairy had coned frontages like sawn-off aeroplane heads. Each of them was connected to the electricity by a long thick cord as if they were busy sucking milk straight out the system.

'How comes milk floats always have to be electric?' I asked one old stager.

'Because they just fuckin' do,' he helpfully explained.

Pete had planned to be the sort of milkman that after twenty-five years of dedicated service is given his own cow. In the event, he lasted two days. Once again it was the treacherous lifts of me and Wendy's future home in the sky that did for him. What happened was that, now his dad's mate had a float co-pilot in young Pete, he assigned him the part of the round that he looked forward to least – the twenty-four storeys of Maydew House.

'What you do,' the veteran milkie said that breaking dawn in 1972 as an awestruck Pete gazed up at the never-ending edifice, 'is get all your crates to the lift first. Then, when it comes, you load 'em all in and take it floor by floor. Now then, here's the clever bit . . .'

At this he held before Pete a single matchstick.

'See this? You take that and jam it into the little gap around the "Open Door" button, got it? Wedge it right in there when the lift door opens on each landing and that will keep it open while you drop off yer bottles. Don't just stick a crate down to block the door sliding shut, because that sets the alarm off and that WILL make you popular at this time of the day. Now, I'm warning ya, always use a new match for each floor, 'cos otherwise they get too squashed, fall out, and the lift will fuck off without ya. You got that? Good. Unload what you need and I'll meet you again in Abbeyfield Road.' With that he threw Pete a full box of matches.

Well, what, as they say, could possibly go wrong? To be fair to Pete, anyone living on floors 1, 3 and 5 actually did get their daily pints as per usual. It was on floor 7 that his matchstick fell out. Why did it fall out? As he tells it, he clumsily dropped the prescribed Bryant & May matchbox down the side of his crates on the third floor, and after straining to reach it – followed by a failed struggle to manoeuvre the load over to one side – he settled for sticking with his existing wooden wedge. Apparently it did a hero's job on the fifth. However, after about thirty seconds on the seventh it gave up the unequal struggle and plummeted to the floor. At least, Pete presumes it did, because at the awful moment he heard the distant sound of the lift door shuddering closed he was halfway down the landing, putting a couple of cold sterilized on to someone's ragged old welcome mat.

Frantically he raced back to the stairwell and began shoving at the call button like a madman, hoping that his load would be instantly revealed but all he was rewarded with was the little light inside the control dimly glowing to let him know that the car had departed and the next available one would be arriving soon. Of course, this being a council flats lift, 'soon' actually meant 'some time before Christmas'.

His brain whirling, Pete knew he had to make a vital decision. Did the lift containing his seven full crates of milk and orange juice go up or down when it left him?

Deciding that the call had most likely come from somebody leaving for work as opposed to a night-shift bloke arriving home, Pete careened out on to the stairs and bounded up the four concrete flights to the ninth. Nothing. So off he went again, up to the eleventh; still no sign of milk. By the time he reached the seventeenth he was in such acute physical distress that he was sure his head was going to implode like one of those cooling towers you see being demolished. On the twenty-third he almost caught up with the tormenting carriage. Despite his exertions creating a din in his inner ear akin a raging Niagara, he could just hear above the torrent what sounded like an elevator full of milk bottles juddering to a halt. Unfortunately by this time he was gaining altitude at barely a shuffle, and with two entire flights to go all he could do was plaintively call: 'Hold the lift! Please hold the lift!' Although what actually came was something closer to a hoarse wheeze: 'Hole a liff . . . psss . . . hole . . . a liff . . .'

Broken, Pete arrived on the twenty-third minutes too late to arrest his roving cargo as it plunged, full throttle, back down the shaft.

My friend Peter King never did catch up with his milk and orange juice. Every time he summoned the lift, the wrong one would arrive; every floor he looked in at he was merely taunted by the receding jangle of bottles in crates. Eventually he did what anybody would do in the circumstances and went and hid in the local park until it got dark.

His dad later received an understandably irate call from Pete's brief boss saying that he waited nearly an hour for 'the little fucker' before heading off to investigate. Naturally when he called the lift, the correct one showed up almost immediately – in a state that might best be described as ransacked. People had helped themselves. Whole crates had been liberated and the couple that remained contained nothing but a few empties – which at least shows a degree of social responsibility.

'You wouldn't think so many people would be up and about at that time,' offered Pete's dad lamely.

'Don't talk bollocks,' came the unequivocal reply. 'Soon as word gets out there's freeman's to be had it gets around this estate like fuckin' measles. Eighty quid's worth of stock gone in a fuckin' flash! Didn't even get the crates back!'

For what it's worth, I can still recite the number plate on the float Pete rode during his short and disastrous career. It was XMT 426. I know this because, to this day, whenever life deals Pete a raw hand, he will sigh and mutter, 'This is XMT 426 all over again.'

I think the point I was hoping to make rather more crisply at the top of this chapter was that, despite my apparently glitzy job, we were still living on the Silwood Estate where I'd spent my entire life. Indeed, from our front room, I looked straight down on to my mum and dad's flat in Debnams Road. But now Wendy and I wanted to start a family – couldn't wait – and both of us realized that, lovely in design though our place in the sky was, losing crates of milk in those lifts would be as nothing to the thought of chasing up and down the stairs after a runaway baby in a pram. Therefore we decided to buy a house. The only problem was, we had not a single shekel in savings and neither of us – nor anyone in our extended families – had a clue how you went about implementing such a crackpot decision.

Thank God then, for *Carry On* star Kenneth Williams.

Veterans of these tales will know that the universe has been terrifically, almost perversely, kind in laying fate's fast track before the locomotive of my life and, inevitably, here we go again. Because when I examine the extraordinary circumstances that led us to suddenly owning a beautiful Victorian house bordering on a lovely London park, it really is Kenneth Williams that I should thank first for making it possible. We will come to that fortuitous whim of the cosmos presently, but first here's how I came to meet the brilliant public persona and private man of letters in the first place.

A feature of the short filmed items that peppered the *Six O'Clock Show* was that they usually had a well-known face pop up at some point to give the package a bit of a boost. In the voice-over I would say something like:

'Another person who remembers the war-time blackout beetroot thief of Balham is actor Donald Sinden. He recalls one night when he almost came face to face with the purple-fingered fiend . . .'

Upon which Sinden, voice rich as a plum cake, would give us a juicy sound bite from his 'childhood memories'.

We found most celebrities would rattle off a bit of overheated hogwash for us, provided we sent a car and offered expenses – particularly if they were currently appearing in an underperforming farce at the Whitehall Theatre. We would show them walking past some obviously placed posters for this doomed production seconds before they coughed up the necessary light anecdote and thus show-business honour was satisfied all round. Nowadays every branch of the media is so stuffed with monotone-grey lunatics whose sole job is to make sure nobody is falsifying anything that even fanciful stories about wartime beetroot thieves would be decried as the greatest deception since Watergate. Consequently nobody in broadcasting has much fun any more and rotten plays featuring nudists in suburbia close months before they otherwise might have done.

During the very first series of *SOCS*, the star-turn on a piece I was fronting was to be Kenneth Williams – a prospect that thrilled me even more than the thought of palling about with Frank Zappa. Some of my more hipster friends might find that hard to understand, so let me explain. One was Frank Zappa. The other was Kenneth Williams. And there you have it in a nutshell. Even in terms of songs listened to and LPs bought – a process by which I weigh most things in my life – I was a fan of Kenneth Williams long before the Mothers of Invention advised me that all the smart set were doing sardonic these days. His album *On Pleasure Bent* was a delight I had learned by heart since it first popped up in the Spa Road record library just a cat's whisker before the summer of love changed my shirt colours from pale to neon, although rather presciently it did have a psychedelic cover. Two songs in particular on the album left their mark: 'Above All Else' – a yearning lilt worthy of Noël Coward that told the story of how a computer fell in love with a weighing machine – and the raucous rasp of 'Boadicea',

> So if you look around the place
> and see a Roman nose upon an English face
> Oh, Boadicea, she's got a lot to answer for!

I will to this day eagerly perform both tracks in full should anyone be good enough to drop a hat – so don't talk to me about *Hot Rats*. And there was one other track, 'Spa's', a monologue played by Williams as a spluttering hypochondriac crone, during which an endless stream of ailments were all followed by the phrase 'My Iris will tell you . . .' that I could also rattle off in character and verbatim. Almost beyond reason, it was to be this long-dormant and seemingly superfluous morsel of salted-away brain matter that was to see *Carry On* Kenneth Williams open the door to me and Wendy's first married home. Here's how.

The item we were filming that day – let's say it was about the sad disappearance of coal deliverymen from the London scene, it very often was – had not been going well. Interviewees delivered hesitantly, working horses refused to thoughtfully munch their nosebags on cue, nostalgic mountains of coal adamantly declined to be photogenic and, most crucially of all, whoever had worked out the day's timings and locations had obviously mistaken the map of London with one of Beccles, Norfolk. Consequently, as it stood, we were finishing one section of our opus in a coal yard in Stepney and then had then about ten minutes to get to our next set-up at somebody's backyard in Hayes, Middlesex. For those of you who don't know the distances involved, it is the equivalent of leaving yourself the duration of a Ramones record to get from your bedroom to the moon. Thus when we came to set off for out last rendezvous of the day, a meet with Kenneth Williams at the Albery Theatre, St Martin's Lane, we were running approximately one hour late. Again, for those of you unaware of the geography, the Albery is in the heart of London's West End. Or to give it it's full and tremendously accurate title, London's *busy* West End. We were slogging our way there from Poplar in East London. Even if there had been mobile phones then it is extremely unlikely Kenneth Williams would have had one. Besides, such was his reputation for insisting on punctuality that none of us would have had the guts to ring it if he had.

Given the circumstances, we made pretty good time getting across town. When we arrived at the theatre – the staff had arranged for someone to open the doors for us late afternoon – we were only five minutes shy of being two hours tardy. The upside to this was that there wasn't a chance Kenneth Williams would be there and so at least we would be spared the full-flared nostril wrath as we weakly explained ourselves. So as we bundled into the dim Albery foyer, the plan was to apologize to the few staff around and, simply by showing up, show that our nightmare tale was the truth. At first nobody could be found. It struck me that to leave a West End theatre entirely unguarded was a tad cavalier. In the days of strolling players it would have been an absolute gift of a squat.

Eventually, after a wandering the deserted corridors and calling a few muted 'Hello's?' a woman emerged from a small office at the rear of the deserted stalls. Before we could speak, she asked, 'Oh God are you here for Kenneth Williams? He's been sat downstairs alone in the bar for hours. I keep checking on him. He was in a filthy mood an hour back – Christ knows how he'll be now. I pity you lot, that's for sure . . .'

I'll be honest with you. Our crew that day included a hard-bitten, seen-it-all director, a cameraman who had covered football riots and a sound engineer who had been in Belfast for Bloody Sunday. And we all wanted to run away.

Nobody said a word as we heavily descended to the gloomy half-light of the lower bar, which was of course closed. I remained at the back of the group because, as I say, I adored Kenneth Williams and I thought it would be a shame if he killed me before I could tell him how much I liked *On Pleasure Bent.* Just before the storm broke I glimpsed him about to explode, sitting cross-legged on a bar stool, his cream-coloured mackintosh belted, his face pinched and thunderous, his mouth tightened into a terrifying moue.

Our researcher had barely set foot on the final step when Williams flew into a fury that had been stoked and carefully worded over the long wait. He began, wonderfully, incorporating a phrase that was almost a catchphrase:

'Oh – now you fucking arrive! Well, it's a dis-grace!'

As he bellowed those last two syllables, I swear he sounded EXACTLY like Kenneth Williams.

'If you think I have nothing better to do than to sit here while you moronic Neanderthals sit in the pub counting your money and chucking it down, then you can stick it up your arse! I am not giving you a word, do you hear, a word! I only hung on and hung on so I could tell you straight that I will be making a serious complaint to whatever boss-eyed twerp runs your otiose little outfit and hopefully get the lot of you sacked! I came here on the bloody bus, through the rain, as a favour, because YOU asked me, and then you leave me here in this gloomy pisshole for TWO hours?! I won't have it!'

It was as he paused for breath – or dramatic effect – that I said something that was possibly the last thing Kenneth Williams was expecting:

'My Iris will tell you,' I piped up.

I had not planned on saying anything. It had been reflex, pure nervous reaction to a horrible atmosphere, but man alive – talk about your silver bullets!

Kenneth Williams' expression went from the outer reaches of austerity to the warm core of elation in less than one second.

'How do YOU know that!!?' he bellowed through a smile as wide as the coal chutes we'd hoped he would wax nostalgic for. It was as if the very walls of the bar had suddenly exhaled. 'You're far too young to know anything about that!'

'Not at all, Mr Williams – it was a staple in our house,' I said, making my way over. 'I know every word of that LP: "Pardon Me, Sir Francis", "Boadicea", "Above All Else" – it's like Noël Coward for me.'

I know, I know. Obsequious little runt. Note the 'Mr Williams' due deference too – but Jesus Christ did it do the trick. Returning to his former frostiness in instructing the crew they could 'get set up now and be bloody quick with it', Kenneth led me to a corner table and proceeded to tell me expansively all about the record and how he felt he never got the opportunity to break out into some of the personas it allowed him. Incredibly the one track he prized above all others was 'Spa's', and though he hadn't written it he had contributed the phrase 'My Iris will tell you', of which he was very proud. Of course, it probably didn't hurt that I was a fairly good-looking bit of rough then too. When, eventually, I tried to explain why we were so late, he lowered his voice and with a conspiratorial smile said:

'Oh, fuck that. It was a bit of a performance that. I've been shooting out, going round the bookshops – it's been nice. Quite peaceful down here, actually. You know I've got bugger all else to do – but don't tell this lot that – let 'em stew in it.'

I rolled my eyes in sympathy. *Yeah, bloody telly people.* It was really quite frightening how readily I formed an instant artist's bulwark against my still-cowed colleagues. To be fair to them, they knew that that one verbal punt had pulled everyone's arses out the fire and understood all this haughty horseshit was absolutely essential, and of course I was revelling in every second of their agony.

We got our Kenneth Williams remembers the coalman footage, complete with evocative anecdotes and funny voices. In the forty minutes or so it took, Kenneth never once spoke to or even acknowledged anyone else there beyond the most minimal of responses. It was as if these dreadful plebs were eavesdropping on a conversation Ken and I – as performers and fellow lovers of the arts – were enjoying and which they couldn't possibly understand. When the PA flagged him down a cab, he only said goodbye to me.

'I've seen you on that Aspel's show,' he said as we shook hands as warmly as Kenneth Williams ever did any physical attachment. 'Can't bear him, the dreary queen. Can't you slip something in his Sanatogen and take over?' Then almost seductively he purred, 'Bring your LP next time we meet. I'll sign it for you. Something filthy . . .'

And with a salacious wink, off he went. I know many of you may now be flagging up a rampant narcissism here, similar to when I suspected Kate Bush of flirting with me in the previous book. In mitigation I would direct you to Kenneth Williams' posthumous diaries.

There you may note this entry for 21 February 1986, one of our many subsequent meetings:

. . . left for LWT to do the *Six O'Clock Show* with Michael Aspel, Gary Wilmot and Danny. It went OK.

No surname you'll observe – just 'Danny'. When I first read that, I confess I was thrilled at the affection such familiarity from so famously cold a figure implies. It may be that he didn't recall my full name, but it's unlikely given we had done quite a few TV shows together since that initial fraught encounter at the Albery. So affection I'll take from it. And right back at you 'Kenny'. *On Pleasure Bent* indeed.

Walk Between The Raindrops

My early encounters with the famous in TV, though usually effervescent and mildly bonding affairs, never evolved into anything approaching friendship. Once the light entertaining had been delivered and a few green-room cold drinks had been sluiced in high spirits, I hadn't the faintest wish to belong to any social society of showbiz pals. I somehow doubt they were bursting to jot down my home number either. For example, in the six and a half years that I worked week in, week out with Michael Aspel, I never met him outside work other than a drink at his house once after he'd asked me to help him with an auction at his local school. I certainly knocked about with the noisy young gang of foot soldiers who created the programme each week, though I had no thought that they would ever go on to be famous names themselves. I have somewhere a wonderful piece of video where I am filming an idiotic sequence being ad-libbed by future media ever-present Paul Ross in the *SOCS* office. I was recording this shameless mugging on one of the earliest video cameras available to the public, a huge contraption that came in a massive steel suitcase hired from one of the high street electrical shops like Granada, DER or Radio Rentals. These were the days when even TV sets would be leased to you on monthly payments. Anyway, as Paul was hamming it up, most likely with lots of swearing which was still then a real thrill to do in front of a camera, some oaf walks right into shot, obscuring Paul's uproarious mumming.

'Excuse me, mate,' you can hear me say, 'we are trying to film something here, could you get out the way?'

The interloper meekly does, with many apologies. Paul Ross raises his eyebrows at camera and asks if he should start again. Then he says to the scene-spoiler off camera, 'You fucked that right up. Just sit over there for five minutes.' Turning back to camera he sighs resignedly, 'That was my brother Jonathan. College boy. Fucking nuisance.'

Of course, cut to a few years later and I would be working for that same photo-bombing wonder-kid.

The majority of my social hours were still spent with the same crowd I had always beetled about with in the countless pubs of Bermondsey. Never having just one regular hang-out we would usually visit two or three different boozers in a typical night and even this trio of venues would vary depending on mood, day of the week or things like local snooker tournaments. Arrangements were vague, mobile phones a future fantasy, and so the form was that you'd simply try to find each other. Quite a sizeable part of any evening would be taken up walking from pub to pub and sticking your head in the door to see if anyone you knew was inside. Most pubs would have at least a dozen people in and chances were, if you drew a blank and one of your lot wasn't inside, somebody who knew one of your lot would be, even if it was only the barman.

'Phil,' you'd shout, half in, half out of the saloon, 'any of our lot been in?'

'Not as far as I know,' might come the flat reply from some tubby host mid-pint-pull. 'I think I heard Stevie Driscoll say he was meeting Lenny Windsor in the Red Cow later.'

So off you'd ankle to the Red Cow, putting your head in at the Gregorian, the Rising Sun and the Lilliput Hall on the way. At the Red Cow it would be disco dark and packed even on a Tuesday and you would prise your way through the dense throng hoping to glimpse the top of a familiar head. Assuming there was still no luck, you might find a friend of a friend's sister was working behind the jump that night so you could bellow at her above the sound of Tavares' 'Heaven Must Be Missing an Angel':

'Kim! Kim!! KIM! Where's your Joey and that lot gone?'

'Eh??'

'Your JOEY? Where gone??'

'They're dunfla Hurrk Pakaver!'

'WHAT?'

'They're down fuckin' Southwark Park Tavern!' The shriek causing her to fumble the glass she was holding under a gin optic.

Forcing your passage back out again, away you would go at a quickening clip similar to Dick Emery's Mandy character, on to the Southwark Park Tavern, while pausing to check The Horns, The Fort, the Colleen Bawn, the Blue Anchor, the Ancient Foresters, the Raymouth Tavern, the Stanley Arms and several other hostelries en route in case they had decided to nip in there for one. Quite often a mate would turn up, angry and partially collapsed, just as a pub was ringing last orders.

'Here you are, you bunch of cunts!' they'd yelp accusingly as though uncovering a plot. 'Been looking for you lot all fuckin' night!'

With the tiny amount of pubs that live on in Bermondsey today, no such confusion could ever arise.

It was while we were in a funny old boozer that was on the very outskirts of our regular circuit that one of the strangest events of not just the early eighties but of my entire life unfolded.

The pub was called The Antigallican in Tooley Street near London Bridge. Never a popular place with the younger set, it was the kind of down-at-heel dockside dump that was left beached once industry on the Thames began to decline and then vanish. People like to romance these long gone quiet local inns and yet the truth is that for decades they were depressing little lounges whose chief problem was that they were *so* quiet they lapsed into torpidity. Heightening this state would be the frowsy threadbare décor, revolting toilets down steep stairways, sickly lighting and a strobing fruit machine whose cheerless electro-gurgle gave you a headache. A possible plus might be that they had a bookies or cab office next door, but actually the true attraction of these grim parlours was that you could invariably get 'a late one' from their indifferent, often alcoholic hosts. Because of this, a mournful premises such as The Antigallican – the name means 'Down With France', by the way, and was once one of the most popular pub names in London – would hardly take a ten-pence piece till about 10.30 p.m. when groups of blokes began to pile in, well aware that the mandatory eleven o'clock curfew on selling alcohol would be allowed to sail by no questions asked. The landlord's only concession to the law would be to turn out all but a few low lights behind the bar and request that any conversation be tuned down lest the police came knocking – and, hard as it is to conceive of this now, the Old Bill really did raid pubs that they believed might be dispensing beer at eleven fifteen or, surely even more remarkable to today's drinkers, still taking orders at ten past three in the afternoon.

Everyone knew the half-dozen or so pubs in the borough that would oblige with what later came to be called a lock-in, but sometimes you might just stumble across a place that, even though it had rung the last bell, had yet to put the tea towels over the pumps. (This last bit of semaphore was universally understood by all to mean 'That's your lot'.)

One of your crowd might idly check their watch as the lights started going out and find that it was five past eleven. Scoping out the bar discreetly from beneath their eyebrows they would search for any signs of liquid movement. Having determined sufficient evidence, they'd then break into whatever burble the others were engaged in by quietly saying, 'Keep it to yourself, but I think they're still serving . . .'

A genuine thrill would zip through the company at this. Regardless of whether or not you'd been gasping for another pint, your tongue would be hanging out. Next came what for me was the dreadful price to pay for this erstwhile bonus. One of you would be nominated to go to the bar and find out whether there was any truth to these suspicions about extended licence. I hated doing that. It was OK if you knew the pub, but in a strange venue, for me, this pleading enquiry always carried with it the humiliating whiff of Oliver asking for another scrape of gruel. Should it be decided it was my turn, up I'd reluctantly get, the scrape of my chair announcing my intention with a noise like an anvil being dragged over a tin bath, and with heavy legs I'd make my way toward the dim point of sale where it suddenly seemed the publican and his two best mates were simply enjoying a late but legal nightcap.

There I'd stand. Perhaps more truthfully, there he'd make me stand. I mean, it was gone eleven now, what could this desperate wraith with his empty pint pot possibly want from a tapster at the end of his shift? This lonely agony, however, was all part of the required dance. Eventually he'd break off his quiet chat with the regulars and look across at my pitiful pleading stance.

'Yes?' he might bark, fully aware that the recently acknowledged customer–publican axis had now shifted entirely in his favour.

'Erm . . .' I would begin weakly, realizing that to embark on further syllables would mean no turning back. Then, after an agonizing pause during which he and his company eyed me as if they'd just caught me washing my pants in a barrel of bitter, I would grimly take the plunge: 'Are you . . . still serving? At all?'

Cue a draught of air sucked in over his teeth like a wave receding across the sand. Then a quick look down at his watch.

'It's ten past . . .' he'd offer in a vacillating tone similar, I imagine, to that employed by Roman emperors deciding which thumb to give a floored gladiator.

Nothing more to add, I would smile pathetically, my mouth closer to a cartoon wavy line instead of actual upturned lips. It was usually at this point, during the horrible hanging hiatus, that I would be most in awe of the way my father handled this most delicate of public negotiations.

Though I'd never been around him at closing time, I can't believe he varied the approach much. On the occasions I'd been with him during a midday session, even on unfamiliar ground, the instant the pub clock registered the first seconds beyond the legal close of business at three he would, while remaining seated at the table, boom across the boozer, 'Chas! Don't pull the plug on us now for fuck's sake – we're all gasping over here!' Far from prompting a sharp intake of breath followed by a lecture about the law, this had the landlord scurrying to remove the tea towel from the pumps. I've even seen publicans bring the drinks across to him.

Anyway, back at the Antigallican, pantomime performed and loss of status granted, the pissed old alehouse governor had his moment then grunted, 'Go on then . . . wotcha want?' and we all settled in for what my friend Johnny Summer used to refer to as 'a sensible drink' – a term that meant just the opposite, of course.

Wendy was staying over at her sister Carol's that night and so I had no reason to get home at a reasonable hour. Against this, I have always had a sort of inner regulator that flags up the very moment to stop drinking and I rarely pick up a glass again once I've noticed the first creak of crumbling motor skills, though happily, an inherited capacity for alcohol means it can be many hours before I do pull stumps on a thundering good night out. Even so, I was the first to quit the session that night and to the usual jeers of 'lightweight' I announced I was heading out into the damp dockside shadows for the thirty-minute walk home.

'Sit down! Give it one more and we're *all* going,' was the general consensus from the table. I knew this to be hogwash of the highest order, given that once you enter a pub the number 'one' takes on an almost infinite quality. So I began walking toward the door. The landlord and his two, by now, sensationally sozzled companions bade me a short fractured noise that I took to mean 'goodnight'. Then our host said something else, quite clearly, and with a mischievous smile:

'Careful you don't run into Davey.'

'Davey who?' I answered brightly, as though his warning had been the set-up for a knock-knock joke.

'Davey the dwarf,' one of his wretched chums managed to articulate, completely without humour.

With no further punchline forthcoming I reacted to this fantastical non sequitur as might anyone – with a simple baffled grin and a wave of the hand. On the whole, I'm all for private jokes and will happily play the stooge for one if it helps a party go with a bang. But then my friend Paul Baldock chipped in from across the darkened bar:

'Davey the dwarf? Blimey, is he still about? Oh fuckin' hell, I will have one more then . . .'

My friends all groaned comically then started to low-talk again with renewed animation. Now I had two choices before me. One: I could go back to the table and see why the mention of this alliterative little person had set them chattering so, or Two: open the door and just go home.

I chose to head home.

Tooley Street, on which our tale is set, runs down from London Bridge to Tower Bridge Road and has, like all the sprawling square miles around it, been transformed beyond recognition over the last thirty years. During those early hours when I set out in the drizzle to tramp along its broken pavements after departing the Antigallican, Tooley Street was a poorly lit thoroughfare hemmed in by the railway arches on one side and abandoned warehouses on the other. Even when it wasn't past midnight and raining, the looming Victorian brickwork about you would be dark and damp, seeping fusty reminders of the thousands of cargoes the walls had stowed or the countless railway carriages the arches had borne. Today the location is as good, or bad, a testament to the power of capitalist investment as you will find anywhere in Europe. And yet one feature of the area hasn't changed. Indeed, can't be changed. The arches that lie beneath London Bridge Station and that connect Tooley Street to the rest of Bermondsey are long and narrow, and no matter how many light bulbs the authorities place along their snaking length, they will always appear dim and ominous for pedestrians. Any modern business high-flyers that, as night falls, choose to haul their own suitcases from the river jetty toward the famous gleaming Shard would certainly think twice about the shortcut these tunnels offer before opting to walk the longer way around instead. Not for nothing was the original London Dungeon horror museum built within the neglected empty vaults these subways cut through.

Crossing the road, I entered the longest tunnel at a brisk pace, hands in pockets and head down, inwardly wishing, as I invariably do, that I had left much earlier and so might be in bed asleep at that moment. I had gone only a hundred yards into the cavern when I heard a pained exhalation as if somebody had been punched in the gut. At first I looked behind me, because it had seemed to come from close by. Then peering ahead I saw through the pools of weak yellow light falling from the intermittent lamps a sight that immediately reduced my clattering gait to an almost complete halt.

On the other side of the narrow road that ran through this

subterranean hollow, some distance ahead, was a figure so tall he had to lower his head lest it scrape along the arched ceiling. Delivery vans passed through here so I assessed that he stood, or rather lurched, at well over eight feet in height. With every strange, stiff-legged step he made the giant would groan and then stand still, seemingly gathering his strength while leaning heavily against the damp, soot-encrusted walls. As he rested he formed low and grievous half-sentences like someone who had just received the most awful news. I had never seen anything like this in all my life and there was no one else around, no passing traffic as his sobs and moans echoed down the tunnel. You don't run away at times like this as you might see in a creepy film, which of course I'm aware this entire implausible incident must read like. I found myself almost involuntarily walking at a casual pace toward the figure, as if by carrying on reasonably the whole outlandish event would root itself in normality. I didn't stare at him continuously but checked on his progress toward me with frantic turns of my head in his direction. With quickening breath I could hear myself whispering, 'Fucking hell . . . fucking hell' over and over. I was absolutely terrified.

When he was less than thirty yards from me I could make him out at last. Apparently oblivious to me, I saw a man whose face seemed to place him in his forties. His expression matched the agonized cries that punctuated his slow progress along the narrow pavement. Every now and then he would stop and bury his face in a handkerchief he held in one hand. Whether this was to soak up his sweat or his tears, I couldn't tell. He wore a thick, dark woollen suit that appeared to be tailored on the army 'demob' style – with one bizarre modification. The trousers were colossal, the belt buckle securing them at the waist higher than the hair that was now standing up on my head. They encompassed towering and apparently useless lower limbs that swung out in a broad arc with every heavy, laboured stride he attempted. Whenever his thick shoes found the uneven ground once more he would let out one of his guttural wails. As we passed he never once looked in my direction. It was as if he didn't know I was there or, more probably, didn't care. I could only stop and stare as this poor tormented soul made his tortured way on toward distant

Tooley Street – not for the ghoulish spectacle, but so I could say to myself repeatedly, 'This is real. I am not dreaming this.'

I picked up speed again and made it swiftly through the rest of the arch. Even as I turned into Druid Street at the far end I could hear those terrible groans billowing through the damp night air.

The next morning I knew that if I rang my friends babbling about seeing a distressed giant so soon after their dire warnings about malevolent dwarves I would be exposing myself to a torrent of wounding comments. Anyone else I might mention it to would naturally view my account of events as coloured by the fact I had just left a notoriously accommodating alehouse. However, you can only sit on such trauma for so long and when I did start raving about what I'd witnessed in the eerie arches under London Bridge few seemed sceptical.

'Yeah, that's Davey the Dwarf,' Paul Baldock confirmed, hardly looking up from the hand of cards he was playing. 'Frightens the life out of ya, don't he? They reckon he lives in that estate off Crucifix Lane. He's well known – I'm surprised you didn't know about him; walks around Bermondsey in the middle of the night. Porky Vincent's seen him stacks of times. Never says nothing to no one, he's harmless . . .'

The story runs that Davey, anguished by his dwarfism, used to roam the lonely streets in the small hours experiencing a twilight life as a 'normal'-sized person. Over the years, this tragic yearning lapsed into hopeless obsession and the stilts he used to achieve his longed for assimilation became grotesquely elongated and unwieldy. The cries and struggling I witnessed that night were but a terrible symptom of his nocturnal madness, the bizarre extended suit of clothes the shield of his suffering.

Had I known as we passed that night that what I was seeing was based in the psychological rather than the spectral, I like to think it would have made a difference to the sheer terror I experienced. As it was, I just recall running home to Maydew House, jumping at every shadow and, not wanting to hang about for the lift, making it up those notorious nineteen flights of stairs in about thirty seconds flat.

*

South-East London had a lofty living legend in Davey the Dwarf and I had seen him with my own eyes, but over in West London I learned they had their very own illusive sensation with which to spook out the youngsters. This was the Brentford Gryphon, a top-notch mythical creature with the head and wings of an eagle but the body of a lion. After a vote during the *Six O'Clock Show* weekly meeting it was overwhelmingly decided that this fabulous beast knocked poor old Davey and his stilts into a cocked hat and so in May 1983 I was dispatched to file a report about it for that week's programme.

Obviously, the main problem with filming an item about a magical beast – particularly a mythical one – is that you cannot just dial up its agent and arrange for it to be under the clock on Waterloo Station at two the following Thursday, spruced up and bursting with usable anecdotes. This is what differentiates a gryphon from, say, Gyles Brandreth. Such details rarely threw the *SOCS* team once an enjoyable yarn had been decided upon, so a few malleable souls were lined up to tell us they had seen the gryphon perching on neighbours' roofs and rifling through builders' skips and suchlike. A couple of wary local historians were also interviewed and then edited to make it appear they believed in the glorious old brute, and I stopped a succession of passers-by and asked for their own stories about it.

Now I have completed thousands of vox-pops, as this process is called, and earned a reputation for being just about the best in the business at them, but let me tell you, on the scale of life-affirming pursuits I put the practice on a par with sawing at the skin between my toes with a breadknife. Even in the days when the chance of appearing on TV still had some novelty value, the only people who would happily stop for roving reporters were maniacs, meths drinkers and puffed-up local councillors – who I'm convinced spent their entire working day searching for such opportunities. It's laborious work and can take hours to get a handful of coherent replies from the indifferent masses, even when the question being put is as broad as 'Do you think we've had a lot of rain recently?'

The only person I know who hated vox-pops more than me was Janet Street-Porter, my boss on the very first TV show I had fronted,

Twentieth Century Box. Strange then that it was her insistence that we include tons of these ad-hoc contributions on some of the shows that almost led me to throw her from a tenth-storey window and curtail my fledgling television career in that one rash action. In the event, it was me who ended up in hospital.

I was in the Aldwych, central London, doing some deathly survey at her request about 'Should Teenagers Be Paid More?' or some similarly earnest bilge that was too often the show's stock-in-trade. After an hour we all felt we had landed the three serviceable answers we required for the item and so our director took to the giant car-phone every TV crew proudly boasted back then to ask Janet if any other general shots would be needed. When he came back from speaking into the mammoth instrument he said that Janet felt we should do another half-hour of vox pops. Now I am my father's son and, as future events would repeatedly testify, I have never been one for the traditional office politics of complaining quietly to friends in the corridors. Very few people argue with Janet Street-Porter, even to this day, but I am told by those who were present that as this news was relayed I made a noise like an old-fashioned factory whistle blasting the start of the working day.

'No!' I roared. 'Let me speak to her! Let ME speak to her!'

With the help of two bearers, I managed to lift the 1983 state-of-the-art handset to my ear while several others dialled.

Once connected, I leapt straight in, shrieking at light speed about the appalling randomness of her decision. It's all very well being back at the office balancing spoons on your nose to pass the time, I thundered, but out here at the sharp end we're on our last legs, awash with withering glances, sneered at by school kids and with our confidence lower than this bollocking basic wage that nobody seems to give a flying fuck about. We had got the required desperate sound bites in the bag and, as far as I was concerned, that was that.

Throughout this tirade, Janet remained ominously quiet. Then she spoke.

'Listen, Dumbo,' she said quite calmly, 'I am the producer on this show and if I say—'

I didn't hear the rest. I bolted from the car interior, out into the traffic, and steamed full-tilt toward nearby Waterloo Bridge upon whose far side were the offices of London Weekend Television and JSP. I ran and I ran, my rage increasing with every beat of my shoes upon the concrete. I could not fucking believe this. It might be the norm for Janet to talk like that to these cowering college kids who cling to their media posts like limpets, but she would find that she'd come unstuck trying it on with me. I still had a real leather-jacket job over at *NME*, which I considered my true place of work, so fuck TV, fuck underpaid teenagers and fuck this master–serf bullshit. I was going to sort this out NOW.

Turning left off Waterloo Bridge into Stamford Street, I sincerely believed the pavement was riding up behind me – something I've only ever seen happen in *Road Runner* cartoons. By the time I scorched into the reception area of LWT I knew I was giving off so wild and manic a vibe that I just couldn't be near people. Heading for the stairs – yes, stairs again – I bounded up them four at a time like Jason King with a good lead on his missing milk. Emerging through a fire door on the tenth floor I bellowed 'Where's Janet?!' and, noting the alarmed faces of those in the office, was hastily pointed toward the meeting room where she was mid-conference. Striding across and taking the door handle in an iron grip, I flung it open dramatically and stood there huffing, puffing and with teeth bared like Jack Nicholson in *The Shining*.

I pointed one stiff arm directly at Janet like a tank commander signalling the way forward.

'You! If you [huff] If you [puff] you EVER [huff] speak [puff] . . .'

And then I fainted.

I promise you, there and then I actually, and for the only time in my entire life, passed right out. As comedian Arthur English used to say, 'A proper collapse too, lady! Ace, jack, king, queen on the deck!'

When I came round, Janet was forcing my face into a paper bag, urging me to breathe normally, while Kate, the office secretary, was calling for an ambulance.

'Don't, don't . . .' I spluttered through loose lips. Looking at my feet in confusion I seemed to be somehow wearing four shoes. 'No ambulance . . . I'm all right . . . I'm all right,' I wheezed unconvincingly then, rising to my feet too quickly, promptly fell over backwards, hitting my head on the door frame.

Everyone sort of screamed, but strangely the blow seemed to focus my thoughts. Rubbing the back of my nut, I said to Janet, 'What just happened?'

'No idea,' she replied with some concern. 'I was in a meeting, then you flung open the door, pointed at me and fainted. You looked like a completely mad person.'

Giving orders to cancel the ambulance, she got me to my feet, gave me several plastic cups of water and then, putting on her jacket, took me down in the lift and walked me along the South Bank to St Thomas' Hospital, where she insisted they check me over. My temporary collapse was unsurprisingly diagnosed as the effects of hyperventilation. Following some routine tests we both toddled off to a wine bar where we talked over the evening's ridiculous events, probably blaming other people for the whole affair.

It remains the only falling out Janet – who, after all had brought me into television in the first place – and I have ever had. Many years later, when I was the subject on *This Is Your Life*, she came out from behind the sliding doors and it was this story of two very similar temperaments winding up in A&E that she told in what might possibly have been a tribute.

So, anyway, the Gryphon of Brentford.

I mentioned earlier that when vox-popping you can have a dry old time even in getting responses about as universal a subject as the weather. So I think you can imagine how far and few between are the helpful voices when the question before the public is, 'Have you ever seen something half-eagle, half-lion around here?' Quite what we thought we were going to get in the way of replies I cannot fathom from this distance, but probably it was the kind of impossibly efficient dialogue that looks good on a pre-shoot script:

The fantasy: 'Oh yes, just the other day the Gryphon flew down into my garden and carried off ten rabbits. I thought at the time it was some sort of advert for the Midland Bank!'

The Reality: Silent, sour glances interspersed with the occasional, 'Don't talk daft, son, I'm busy!'

Of course, it was also extremely common to walk up to people with a playful grin on your face only to be told to 'Fuck off out of it' before you had the chance to utter a single word. This is the true voice of the people.

On that day in Brentford High Street we were getting nowhere. Unless we managed to drum up a few independent voices confirming the local legend as advertised (by us), the whole piece was going to look thin and flimsy. Imagine that! Then I had a brainwave. Instead of one or two lunatics saying they'd seen it, how about if *everyone* had seen it? So here's what we did. Keeping out of camera on one side of the busy thoroughfare, I hailed passers-by on the other side of the road and, though we didn't record the sound, asked them where Brentford Football Ground was, where the nearest Tesco's might be, and from what direction did planes from nearby Heathrow Airport fly over. What we captured then were scores of shots of people pointing wildly in all sorts of directions. Cutting these together back at LWT, all that remained was for me to record a voice-over that said, 'It seems everyone in Brentford has spotted the Gryphon at some time or another, and locals were only too keen to let us know where it was . . .'

Absolutely outrageous, admittedly, but this wasn't exactly *World In Action* we were making here. Later on in the piece we went even further. Pretending that one resident, who did not wish to appear on camera, had actually recorded the sound of the Gryphon flying overhead, we held our boom mic next to an old umbrella that I then opened and closed swiftly and repeatedly. You would be surprised how that noise, when played back over a black screen emblazoned with the phrase 'Actual Recording' can sound exactly like a mythical creature in full flight. All in all, it was a terrific item that is still mentioned on many of the websites now devoted to Brentford's fabled beast, and I'm happy to report that it wasn't even the most preposterous thing we ever concocted on the *SOCS*.

The reason I draw particular attention to that little film above all others is because it was directly after I had returned from filming it and barrelled in the front door of 113 Maydew House full of bubbling brio and insisting that we go out and spend a lot of money on a magnificent dinner, that Wendy suddenly cut through my frothing.

'Dan, I'm having a baby,' she said.

I immediately stopped my babbling and felt an intense surging wave of impossible jubilation rise from my feet to crescendo in my head. I can still see the both us staring transfixed into each other's wide eyes, just a few yards apart and yet entirely as one, exchanging between us the overpowering force that this moment would for ever hold. Then we held each other tightly, before starting to dance slowly, in small circles, to an invisible heavenly music.

Now all we needed was a beautiful old house to live in. And, as happened so often in my life, almost instantly wonderful old drum fell right into place, bang on cue.

Growing up, nobody in my family had either owned or expressed any interest in owning their own property. None of my friends lived in a house either, except Tommy Hodges and his was above his parent's sweet shop on Rotherhithe New Road, so that didn't really count. True, both my brother and sister had married and moved out of Bermondsey to live in small homes of their own, but I hadn't a clue how this had come about and frankly the day I find myself so lost for conversation that I talk about such rot is the day you can screw the brass plate on the lid of my box. However, something had to be done. I was going to have to address the dreaded world of conformity for the first time in my life.

My first stop was my dad – a bizarre choice, given that he had even less experience of sensible money management than anyone since Sergeant Bilko.

'Dad,' I said over a soothing half in the Jolly Gardeners, 'I'm thinking about getting a house.'

Arms folded, he threw his head to one side and straight away went into a sort of lament. 'A nouse!? . . . fuuckin 'ell – what ya wanna lumber y'self with one of them for? You're having a baby, aintcha? Where's all this a-pence gonna come from?'

All monies to Spud were either 'a-pence' or 'wedge' in the same way individual coins were 'sprarzis' and 'tosheroons'.

'Well, that's the point,' I soldiered on. 'We can't have a baby up on the nineteenth floor of Maydew.'

'Well, get a transfer to a flat with a garden. Blimey, I can sort that out.'

He could have too. The only reason we had the high rise on the park in the first place – where I'd always wanted to live – was because, following the offer of a couple of dreadful dumps near Peckham, he'd 'straightened' a bloke at the rent office.

'No, me and Wend really want to buy somewhere. I'm earning a nice few quid, it makes sense.'

'Yeah, well, that nice few quid will suddenly become fuck all with an 'ouse – you watch. Besides, you can't move out like Sharon and Michael. Your work's here, smack on top of ya.'

He had a point there. In the whole of Bermondsey and Rotherhithe there were so few private houses they bordered on non-existent. And, kids, I know this sounds like absolute science fiction, but I cannot think of a single estate agent with an office anywhere in our corner of the capital.

'There's some houses up the top of Southwark Park Road,' I said weakly. 'And a few near Tower Bridge.'

'Yeah, and fucking people living in 'em, Danny! What you gonna do – go and turf 'em out because you're earning a few quid? For now.'

Those last two words were said with a timely raise of his Guinness and a glance from the corner of his eye as if to shed doubt on the longevity of my 'stardom'.

Ignoring the implication, I got to the real point of my raising the matter in the first place.

'Anyway, if we do find a place . . . what do you do then, Dad? Say you see somewhere for sale when you're out – how do you go about buying it off them?'

My old man did not hesitate to impart the full sum of his knowledge of the subject.

'Fucked if I know,' he said.

Wendy and I took to walking the streets looking for 'For Sale' signs. Surprisingly, there were quite a few more dwellings that had been spared by the Blitz and urban planners than I had previously

71

thought. Not a glut, by any means, and none that could be classed as 'well appointed', but it was odd how I had totally filtered these places from my map of the area. As I say, I knew nobody who lived in them. Besides, not a single one was on what passed for the Bermondsey market. One day we walked to the far end of the Silwood Estate to where the flats suddenly stopped and gave way to a no-man's land of abandoned railway sidings, long-vacated businesses that had once occupied the archways and general open ground. On the other side of the railway lines that bordered this wasteland was Cold Blow Lane, the notorious home of Millwall Football Club.

Wendy, not from the area, was unimpressed. 'Blimey, Dan, where are we?' she said. 'Hope you're not thinking of somewhere around here.'

I wasn't, but we were heading in the direction of an old row of houses I dimly recalled alongside a tiny park right on the border where SE16, Rotherhithe, met SE8, Deptford. Leading my disbelieving, pregnant wife across the kind of shrubby, deserted, broken-bottle terrain that would have brought a location scout for *The Bill* to orgasm, we eventually emerged into civilization again via a small alley that ran behind the Rose of Kent pub.

'What are those trees over there?' she enquired hopefully.

Scawen Road, Deptford, looked like a mirage as we wandered into it that bright summer's day. Built around the minuscule Deptford Park, it was the sort of pretty late-Victorian square that Mary Poppins might have been blown to directly after all her good work with the Banks family in the film. We didn't speak much as we ambled past the proud bay windows set behind gates and privet hedges, but we both knew this was it. This was the perfect, hidden little Eden we had imagined. The houses looked inviting enough, but to be facing on to a park was almost too idyllic to be true.

'Did you know this was here?' she asked me eventually, and I think I said yes, but the truth is I hadn't been in Deptford Park since I played a five-a-side football tournament there in 1968 when I was eleven. I now realized what an idiot I had been back then. Instead of loafing about on the grass between matches, sucking on frozen lemon ice-poles, I should have been busy leafleting all these beautiful homes asking if they were considering selling up in fifteen years' time. As it was, there was not a single sign to suggest any resident had the slightest desire to move out of, what appeared to us, a glorious oasis. The consequence of our extended walks up and down the road was that now we just didn't want to look anywhere else – but what to do?

A week later, the phone rang in our flat on the nineteenth floor. It was my sister, Sharon. Sharon worked in Lewisham Hospital and told me that earlier in the day she had been taking down details from an outpatient who gave their address as Scawen Road, Deptford, SE8.

'I told them that was strange because you were going on about it last weekend, weren't you? How lovely it is, how you wanted to live there.'

I said yes very quickly, hoping against hope that this coincidence wasn't the entire conversation. It wasn't.

'Any rate, she said houses NEVER come up down there, but just by chance . . .'

'Yes . . . yes . . .' I urged her on with a dry mouth.

'. . . she reckoned that one was going to come on the market. An old boy who'd lived down there for ever has passed away or something. She didn't know who's handling the sale, but I've got the number of the house from her. Do you want it?'

I wrote it down, stared at it and wondered what the hell to do next.

When Wendy came in that day I couldn't wait to show her my piece of paper.

'There's a house. In that street. They're selling it!'

'Oh! Incredible!' she beamed, then, just as I feared, got straight to the practical: 'Who's selling it?'

'I don't know,' I admitted, as brightly as I could, but even so I could sense the air was being let out of the moment.

'So what do we do now?' my wife pressed.

Again, I said I didn't know. It was beginning to sink in that simply having a bit of paper with the number 46 written on it would not be considered a firm offer by most vendors.

What we eventually decided to do was walk down there the following morning and put a note through the letter box asking whoever found it to give us a call. When we arrived at the address, we were thrilled to see it stood almost exactly in the middle of the terrace, virtually opposite the park gates. Opening the small metal gate and walking up the short black-and-white tiled path, I took our note and slipped it through the letter box.

We were just turning to go when we heard a voice from inside say, 'Hello?' Wendy and I looked at each other. We felt like we had been caught doing something wrong. What if my sister had made a mistake and this house wasn't for sale? What were we thinking, bothering total strangers who had probably just bought a new sofa and bedroom suite and asking them to 'give us a call'? Maybe we should just stick with the council rent book after all. A moment later a white-haired man of about eighty opened the door and said, 'Can I help you?'

I shook hands and explained about the note and the old gentlemen asked us in. Once in the hallway it was clear that, despite the net curtains at the windows, the house was completely vacant. Our steps echoing across the floorboards, the three of us walked into the two front parlours that were separated by a large set of Victorian pine doors, currently folded back. In both rooms were open fires surrounded by grey carved marbling and large decorative tiles. It was clear this sturdy old place hadn't changed in a hundred years; the atmosphere that enveloped us was one of overwhelming peace. The old fellow introduced himself as Mr Reynolds and began to explain why he was there. As he did, Wend and I touched hands as the extraordinary inevitably of *things meant to be* made itself abundantly clear.

'This was Mum and Dad's house,' he began. 'I was always going to have this place. At least, that was the plan. I didn't know Dad would live to be a hundred and one and I'd be eighty before I got it! I live down at Worthing now and none of my lot want to live up in London, so we're selling. Do you know Deptford at all?'

I told him I was born just a few streets away and he smiled broadly.

'Well, that's nice to know – and isn't this funny,' he went on. 'I wasn't even going to come up here today, but then I thought I should pop in and collect any mail and so forth that's gathering behind the door. I've only let myself in ten minutes ago and I was just leaving again when I heard you at the letter box! I thought it might be the estate agent. I think the board goes up outside tomorrow.'

At this I started to panic slightly. 'I'll be honest, I've never bought a house before. I'm not sure what's next.'

Mr Reynolds carried on smiling. 'Well, I've never sold a house before, so we've got that in common too. I suppose I tell you the price and then you beat me down and we shake hands from there is the form!'

Wendy squeezed my hand even tighter. This was starting to become dreamlike.

'How much is it?' I managed to gasp. At that exact moment I had approximately ninety pounds in my bank account.

'Don't you want to look around?' he said. I said we didn't. This was it.

'Well,' he went on, 'there's three bedrooms upstairs. The big one looks right into the park. But there's no bathroom and only really a scullery out there. Oh, and an outside how's-your-father in the garden. I'm afraid Mum and Dad rather resisted modernization. There's a few old gas lamps here and there too! Anyway, they have instructed me to ask for twenty-nine thousand.'

This meant absolutely nothing to me. All I could say was, 'So . . . what's that?'

He shrugged. 'Well, I suppose that means I should accept twenty-eight!'

And I just said OK. And that was it. We bought the wonderful house off him there and then, less than ten minutes after turning into the street with our hopeful little note in my pocket. Exactly as had happened in the case of moving into Maydew House, against all odds, Wendy and I were home.

Walking around it with him afterwards, it seemed to us an enormous old place but absolutely calm and welcoming in every room we arrived at. There were curious old alcoves and wonderful aged but robust cupboards everywhere. The ceilings were moulded and edged with sculpting. As we walked, he told us that his mother had died at the age of ninety-nine and her husband, at one hundred and one, had followed just a few weeks later. They had been married for eighty-two years.

So now I feel I must address a question you are no doubt very keen to hear answered. How on earth, if I had less than one hundred pounds in the bank, was I going to give the fantastic Mr Reynolds his twenty-eight grand? Well, as Wendy and I walked out into the charming little back garden of the premises and Mr Reynolds momentarily left our side, that was the very first thing my wife put to me.

'Ne'mind about that,' I said, putting my arm around her, reeling with giddiness at the thought of the coming years. 'I'll sort this out. It can't be hard. It's gonna be wonderful – you watch.' And I wasn't lying. I knew it *was* all going to be totally 100 per cent wonderful. As usual, I hadn't the faintest idea of how it could actually happen. I just had total conviction that happen it would. And, of course, it did.

'You have to go to a building society, or a bank, and ask them for a mortgage and then they see how much money they'll lend you to buy a house, once you've found the right one.' This was my sister explaining to me, patiently, later that day what I now needed to do. 'But they don't just dish them out,' she went on, sensing I wasn't grasping the overall gravity of what is for many people A Big Step. 'Don't be like Dad, who thinks you can give a bank manager a drink then ignore any other payments.'

Apparently, he really did this once. Needing a grand in a hurry, whether for a family wedding or a certainty in the Cheltenham Gold Cup, a friend of his had recommended that Spud open a bank account for the first time in his life and then, after securing a loan, 'just knock 'em for it'.

This made exciting sense to Dad, who had no fear whatsoever of any subsequent bailiffs' visits or county court judgements against him. During the interview he was granted with the branch manager at Barclays, Dad apparently interpreted what the official outlined as interest due on a one-thousand-pound loan as a coded message to bung him a 'drink'. I understand their final exchanges went like this:

Spud: 'So if you give me the grand, what are you, y'know, like *YOU*, looking for on top?'

Manager: 'You mean the interest?'

Spud: 'Interest – call it what you like.'

'Well, I'm not sure, but let's say eighty pounds . . .'

Spud: 'Eighty quid, eh? All right, say I can lay me hands on eighty quid this afternoon – I slip you that, then we say no more about the other bit.'

Manager: 'Other bit?'

Spud: 'The grand. We can just drop that out then, eh?'

My mum told me that Spud arrived home furious, tearing off the tie he had donned especially for the meeting, shouting, 'Fucking waste of time! Different breed, that mob – he didn't seem to know what I was talking about!'

I too had never had a single meaningful conversation with anyone in the banking business. The huge cheques that I was paid by LWT went into a joint account that Wendy and I had opened with the minimum of fuss and contact a year previously. All I did was thoroughly knock out what was deposited via a series of cheque books that seemed to require constant replenishing. For the house money we set up an appointment at the nearest building society to where we lived and went in literally hoping for the best. Even before we had sat down it went well.

'Oh, I wondered if it was you!' said the chap, clearly thrilled that Danny Baker Off The Telly was here for a chat. 'We love your programme in our house. I was watching that thing you did with Kenneth Williams last week. Oh, he's funny, isn't he? I would LOVE to meet Kenneth Williams – what's he like?'

Well, I ask you. On another day I might have been allocated some sour old gherkin who never watched TV and kept a special tin of fleas to put in the ears of presumptuous oiks who didn't show due respect. Instead I had chanced upon the financial sphere's equivalent of a stage-door Johnny. Immediately truncating Williams' name to Ken for added familiarity, I confirmed what a true waspish genius he was, who, despite his reputation, actually loved meeting all sorts of people. In fact, now that I think of it, next time

Ken was on the show, why didn't my new chum from the building society come along for a few drinks and lots of laughs in the green room?

The mortgage man lit up with delight. 'Are you serious?' he said. 'God, I'd LOVE to do that.'

Ladies and gentlemen. Let me say I entirely understand if the bumptious good fortune that has been continuously heaped upon my life is starting to make you feel a bit sick. Even when we got off the subject of Kenneth Williams and on to the matter in hand, my new friend acted as though we were just nattering on the back seat of a charabanc to Margate. When he asked what amount of mortgage I required, I misunderstood what this meant, and said, 'Twenty-eight thousand pounds' – the price of the house.

Without undue surprise he clarified for me. 'So you want a 100 per cent mortgage?' This was said in a tone signifying such a trifling request was just about the very least he could do for me.

I was a little fuzzy as to what a '100 per cent mortgage' might betoken, so I just yelled at him, 'Yes, that's it – 100 per cent! Or 200 per cent if you like!' It was as though we were now partners in an up-and-coming new double act.

At one point, almost with embarrassment, he did enquire if I had brought along any contracts I could show him as a security. Trying to hide my distaste that he had sadly introduced so unworthy a note to our hitherto sparkling tête-a-tête, I told him I would post him something later that, though it only covered the next few months, was simply the latest in a blizzard of such cast-iron documents that would undoubtedly keep piling up as the years went by. He said he didn't doubt that and swiftly moved on to ask who was going to be on the show this week. This was extremely decent of him because the truth was I had no real clue as to whether LWT would keep paying me beyond that coming July. I mean, the show was doing well and I *presumed* they would have me back, but even I suspected building societies don't just dish out houses to people simply because a chap likes to look on the Sunny Side.

Anyway, never was a 100 per cent mortgage more happily dispensed and – despite a flurry of phone calls from the estate agents, who were livid we had, albeit unconsciously, short-circuited their system – 46 Scawen Road was very swiftly all ours, lock, stock and outside how's-your-father.

About a year later, old Mr Reynolds called by to see how we were doing. He seemed to rejoice in finding the place alive with noise and babies again.

'Did those people that I approached to sell this house bother you?' he asked. I told him they had, at one point even telling Wendy and I angrily that we shouldn't 'get our hopes up just yet'.

'Yes,' he went on, 'they called me too. Said they had a long list of people who were promised first dibs on anything in this street – including a barrister and some high-ups over at Goldsmith College! Already had 'em lined up to view. Insisted I could get up to five grand more if I reneged on you. I let them speak, and then quietly told them, "My new friends are a young local couple, they are having a baby, I like them very much and we have agreed a price – goodbye." Then I put the phone down. Furious, they were, absolutely furious.' And he chuckled and sipped his tea.

They Might Be Giants

Bonnie Rae Alice Baker was born in Guy's Hospital – right at the heart of Davey the Dwarf's beat – not long before three in the afternoon on Halloween 1983 – a Monday. I was present at the birth, of course, dressed up in the required theatre greens like Jack Klugman in an episode of *Quincy*. Handed my daughter for the first time, I naturally felt obliged to say a few words and I managed a teary, 'Hello, mate' – an introduction that I have found to be the mot juste whenever I am first introduced to my children.

The *Six O'Clock Show* ran on like a bullet train through the majority of that decade, hundreds of shows with just about every major British star spending at least one of those happy hours with us; plus a handful of truly global stars too. I had actually met Mel Brooks before, when I was at the *NME* and had become fed up with talking to rock'n'rollers. Though we had only spent half a day together in 1981, I had every reason to think he would remember me when he came on to the show several years later. When we had first been introduced at Claridge's Hotel, he spun round in exaggerated shock – or at least what I supposed was exaggerated shock.

'Wow! You're kidding! YOU'RE Danny Baker?!' he boomed, now gripping my arms as if I were a long-lost son. 'Seriously, DANNY BAKER – that's you?' Notorious for being 'always on' I figured this was a bit of explosive business he routinely employed just to get a laugh from all the raw chumps a little over-awed to be in his company.

'I cannot tell you how THRILLED I am to meet you!' he chuckled, looking genuinely excited I had walked into his life. 'Danny

Baker! Do you have any idea why this is such a blast for me right now?'

I momentarily thought that he might have really enjoyed my recent *NME* cover story on the Village People, but surely the chances of that were remote.

'OK, come and sit down. This is amazing to me.' And arm around my shoulder, Mel Brooks, who I'd hoped I would catch in a good mood, marched me into the hotel's ultra-fancy restaurant. We sat down and he pointed straight at my face.

'The very first thing I ever wrote for TV wasn't a hit, but I loved it. Do you know what that was?'

I knew he'd created the spoof spy series *Get Smart* quite early in his career and it was one of my favourite American shows as a youngster. But Get Smart *had* been a hit, so I just shook my head.

'It was called *Inside Danny Baker*! Aired in 1963. It was about a dentist and everyone hated it, nobody picked it up, never been seen. And do you know why I chose the name Danny Baker, Danny Baker?'

It takes a lot to shut me up, but I was being magnificently stunned here so I simply registered incomprehension.

'I chose that name because it was THE MOST GENTILE NAME I COULD EVER CONCEIVE OF! There has never been a Jew called Danny Baker, I stake my life on that! So now – if you tell me you're Jewish I'm gonna have to kill you with this bread knife!'

Cupping his hands together, he exploded with laughter and rocked back and forth in his plush dining chair. Across the tablecloth, I did too. Indeed, we got along tremendously all day. I eventually tagged along to Harrods and several art galleries with Mel and his manager, Jo Lustig, until the early evening. Every time someone approached him, he would immediately tell them the story of who I was and how it struck him as incredible that we should meet. It must have been five years later that I walked into the make-up department at LWT and there he was, getting prepared for the show, issuing specific instructions on how to apply the items he'd brought in his own personal kit.

'Hello, Mr Brooks,' I said, while a woman layered his famous old hooter. 'We have met before.'

Now I am well aware that 'We have met before' are four of the most chilling words in the English language, but seeing the momentary confusion on his face as he struggled to place me, I knew I had a knockout punchline to banish his discomfort.

'I am Danny Baker,' I said.

Mel Brooks rose smartly from his chair, the protective make-up gown still tucked in at his neck.

'YES! You are! Danny Baker. Everyone THIS is Danny Baker. Let me tell you all something . . .'

And Mel Brooks once again loudly regaled everybody in the room – and quite possibly people in the corridor outside – to what I fancy might even be one of his favourite stories.

It was in that same make-up room that I witnessed a very different kind of celebrity explosion. Frankie Howerd was the kind of comedian who, certainly at that stage of his career, tied himself in nervous knots before any performance. In the run of the *SOCS* we had done a few of the filmed items, but he had never been the studio guest before and clearly the sound of our four-hundred-strong audience filing in was adding to his apprehension. Looking into the make-up mirror he was ostensibly addressing the woman dabbing at him with powder but, sitting alongside him in the next chair, I could see that his monologue was chiefly for his own benefit. 'Don't know what I'm doing here, honestly. I've got nothing to sell! I could be at home, but no. Why I'm putting myself through this, I can't think. Nobody's told me when I'm on or what they expect me to say. I don't know where the man who brought me in has gone – he seems to have deserted a sinking ship . . .' And on it went, punctuated by tuts, heavy sighs and periods where he shut his eyes tightly at the horror of it all.

I had seen this same self-lacerating routine at a previous meeting with Frankie. It had been an item we were doing about the boom in 0898 numbers – a novelty then, where you might ring up the advertised connection and hear all manner of recorded nonsense from songs to recipes and, yes, even sex chat, although this was well before the entire racket became synonymous with such greasy fare. The latest innovation was that for a pound a pop you could now call one such number and hear Frankie Howerd tell you a joke. On the day he was he was due to lay down his various 'oohs', 'ahs' and 'no don't, missus' for the service, we went along to the studios. Frankie was already extremely gloomy when we arrived. Arms folded, perched on the edge of a desk, he hardly bothered with any hellos. 'Come to film the execution, have you?' he flatly joked. As the crew set up to record a short interview between the two of us, he began rolling out the dozens of reasons why he shouldn't even be there at all. Then he turned to the interview itself:

'I mean, what are they expecting me to say to you?' he pleaded, eyebrows raised in alarm. 'I've got no interest in selling this. I get paid and it's over for me. I haven't got a piece of this, they don't give you a piece. I can't pretend it's the bloody Palladium, can I? So what the hell can I say to you now? I'm so glad to be here? Because I'm bloody well not . . .'

I listened with lots of sympathetic nodding and then, as if the thought had only been born because of Frankie's reasonable doubts, said, 'You know what could be an idea? What if you say, "You might think it's all a recording, but I actually have to sit here all day and night answering the bloody phone." Something like that.'

Frank furrowed his brow and put his hand to his chin. 'No, no, not that,' he said pensively, then, after mulling things over for a few seconds: 'How about, "You might think it's all a recording, but I actually have to sit here all day and night answering the bloody phone."'

'Even better!' I beamed, and he seemed quite bolstered by this line he had just come up with.

Before long though he was back to the muttered gripes and I thought the recording was going to be quite hellish. But man alive, literally as soon as the director said, 'We're rolling, in your own time, guys . . .' Boom! He became Frankie Howerd. Once that red light sparked up, he was magnificent. I had hardly got the first few words of my initial question out before he was turning full on to camera and saying, 'Ooh, doesn't he go on? I can't make head or tail of any of this, can you? We could have got Robin Day for the same money!' He did 'his line' magnificently, and lots more business besides – mainly on how low Francis had fallen to be doing such a ridiculous job. It was pretty much verbatim what he'd been saying so funere-ally only a few minutes beforehand, but in full-on Frankie mode he was every bit the comic giant in full flood. As soon as we stopped the tape his sparkle vanished again and back came the worry-worn pessimist, now greatly concerned that his driver would have gone without him.

So as I sat alongside Frankie Howerd in the make-up room that evening I searched my brain for a similar gambit to the phone gag that might ease his thrashing nerves. But before I could offer even the mildest titbit, the poor woman attending to him made one of the biggest gaffes of her life.

First let us establish this. Frankie Howerd was bald, probably balder than I am now. We will never truly know, because Frankie hid his hairless crown under possibly the worst toupee in show business – a field where the competition for that title is at its fierc-est. Quite why he persevered with what looked like an abandoned seagull's nest up top I cannot fathom, but then again why anyone does it is beyond me. If a bald man walks into a pub, nobody bats an eyelid. If a man in a wig enters right after him, people nudge each other and say, 'Don't make it obvious, but have a look at the syrup that just blew in.' I've long held that if even Frank Sinatra couldn't get a decent rug, what chance have the rest of us got? I understand that Frankie Howerd purchased his faithful old Irish in 1956, so as I tried not to stare at it in make-up I was silently awestruck that it was older than I was. In the fleeting moments I did dare snatch a peek at it 'head on', so to speak, I couldn't help but notice it was more pissed than usual. Frankie's wig always listed a little, but on this night it was looking like the *Titanic* after all the rockets had been launched. The make-up woman couldn't possibly send him out to face an audi-ence like that and so she leaned close in and said, discreetly:

'Do you want me to tease the wig out a little, Mr Howerd?'

Frankie Howerd tore the tissues away from his collar where they'd been protecting his shirt from any fallout and shot to his feet.

'WIG!?' he bellowed. 'WIG!? What are you talking about, you blessed creature? Wig? I've never had that from a make-up person in thirty years. How dare you! I've got a good mind to go straight home!' And he stormed out of make-up, fuming and threatening all kinds of retribution.

The poor young woman who had made the enquiry stood shaking and confused. 'But it *is* a wig, isn't it?' A more senior colleague pulled a face and said gently, 'I think it's always safer to refer it as "hair", June . . .'

Of course, Frankie betrayed no sign of the eruption on the show, and as usual brought the house down. He didn't stay for a drink in the bar afterwards but went off home, where he undoubtedly removed his battered old toupee and lay dejectedly on the bed wondering what it all meant.

Another towering comedy colossus, Tommy Cooper, appeared on the show only once. Tom was due in the building at four that Friday and I grabbed a seat in the narrow gallery directly behind where the production team directed the show. Like 90 per cent of the people there that afternoon, I was simply hanging about waiting to meet the genius in the famous fez. At exactly four o'clock the phone in the gallery rang, which usually meant one of our guests was in reception waiting to be shown where to go. My good friend Jim Allen – then just a researcher on the show but now apparently in control of most of the world's TV output – answered it. After a brief exchange he replaced the receiver and, nodding toward me with a huge smile, announced, 'It's Tommy Cooper!' Off he went to fetch him.

Of the countless encounters I've had with famous names over the years I don't think I was ever as excited as I was while waiting those few minutes for Tommy Cooper to join us in our snug retreat. When he finally arrived in the doorframe I was astounded to discover how big a man he was. He had his jacket over his arm and, in shirt and braces, his shoulders seemed to be roughly the size of the Cotswolds. Into the room he came, and all of us there, roughly ten people, tried to remain professional by mouthing a short hello before pretending to take a keen interest in what shots were being lined up on the other side of the large window overlooking the technical team. There were one or two spaces on the bench seat that ran along the length of the space, but Tommy seemed unable to make up his mind which one to occupy. So far he hadn't said a word and the mounting tension as we waited to hear that gravelly calling card was acute. Seconds passed. He sniffed and looked from one gap on the velveteen pew to another. Still looming over us, he cleared his throat a couple of times. This may not sound like much but it was exactly the sort of non-verbal punctuation we had heard hundreds of times as he pondered which bit of a lousy magic trick should come next, and the anticipation was by this time choking us all. Then, pointing to an opening next to me, he said,

'Do you mind if I get in there?'

I went into such a giggling fit at that mundane enquiry that I had to put my hand over my mouth while wheezing, 'No, not at all.'

Still he didn't sit. He turned to Jeff Pope, who was on the other side of the gap: 'What about you – do *you* mind?'

And then Jeff went as well. Now you may have heard the tired old tribute 'He just had to speak to make you laugh' applied to many half-talents and acquired tastes over the years, but here was the living proof that such a boast can be absolutely valid – and also a terrible curse. As he plonked himself down beside us, we were so desperate not to let him see we were helpless with laughter that everyone's eyes were watering. It was just like being in a classroom directly after the teacher has said, 'The next boy who laughs will be caned' – which inevitably leaves you in the grip of a sort of mania.

Tom cleared his throat again. He gave a sort of half sigh. Then, turning to look right at me, he gave a short sniff and said, 'I ain't half got a bad back.'

Well, that did it. Every person in the room absolutely collapsed. The laugh was so loud it even made the producers outside what was supposed to be our sound-proofed booth look round.

Tommy Cooper, of course, looked entirely bemused. All he'd done was alert us to his physical pain and we had reacted as if it was the pay-off to some wonderful sketch. Realizing this was not a normal reaction, we struggled to gather our wits, but none of us could control ourselves enough to offer the correct sympathetic rejoinder. And the second our giggling died down, he ignited the riot again.

'No, really. I have!' was all he said, but whoosh, we were away again.

Even as I engulfed myself in guffaws, a voice at the back of my head was saying, 'God, this must be absolutely awful for him.' He wasn't trying to be funny but, then again, Tommy Cooper didn't have to. He can't have been offended, though, because what he did next was exquisite. He had been carrying with him a strange sort of bright yellow attaché case that now, when seated, he just held directly out at arm's length. He began turning his head from left to right, as if searching for somewhere to set it down – again accompanied by the sniffs and throat clearing. Then, noticing the long shelf that ran beneath the viewing window upon which were various polystyrene cups, he said, 'Is that safe?'

'How do you mean?' I managed to choke out.

'Well, this is very valuable, you see. And if I put that on there, I want to be sure it won't fall off.'

'I think it's fine,' I found myself squeaking in a pitch several octaves higher than my usual voice.

He turned to Jeff. 'Shall we give it a go?' Jeff could only manage to nod vigorously.

'You'll all be my witnesses if anything goes wrong, won't you?' he boomed with gravity.

By this time we were all aware we were being given a private performance.

Raising the attaché case carefully, he set it down on the shelf two feet in front of him. As he let go of the handle, the entire thing collapsed into a tiny heap. It had been brilliantly, ridiculously, made from the flimsiest thin rubber, although this was undetectable until it was required to stand under its own weight. It was a tremendous effect and Tommy looked around as we bust a gut, clearly delighted.

'That's good, isn't it?' he beamed. 'Smashing prop, isn't it, that? Just got it. I might use that on the show!'

But he didn't. Whether he forgot about it or changed his mind, I have no idea. It is entirely possible that he brought it along as a private gag to break the ice. In the event, he did that simply by entering the room.

A couple of other comedians now referred to as 'legendary' appeared on the show at various times. Ken Dodd surprised the hell out of us all by being among the more 'clubbable' attractions to bolster our on-screen sofa. By this I mean while most stars would have a few glasses of wine in our green room after the programme, Ken would loosen his tie and get stuck into the pints of lager, particularly if the conversation was about long-vanished music hall acts – a subject I could certainly hold my own in. Let me state that while his on-stage work speaks for itself, the record should also state that Ken Dodd is stupendously good company away from the spotlight.

I can remember his anxious assistant, who probably knew the signs of when Ken was up for the cup, coming over repeatedly to our little gathering in the bar:

'Ken, if we leave now we can get the seven thirty-eight from Euston,' she cajoled hopefully.

'Oh, not now, my love,' Doddy demurred. 'The lads here have just brought up the Great Frank Randle! We'll get the one after . . .'

As it happened, I think he even missed the 12.20 and eventually took an ITV car all the way back to what I like to think was Knotty Ash.

Spike Milligan was something else again. The first time I worked with Spike was over at TV-AM, the station that had just been stopped from disappearing down the television toilet by Greg Dyke. Greg basically transformed the grim, ailing news outlet into an extended version of the *Six O'Clock Show* that he'd recently quit in order to take on the desperate task. Nobody believed he had a hope of pulling it off. Indeed, at his leaving do from the *SOCS* I stood on a chair and read out a poem I had specially composed for the occasion. It went:

There was a young fellow called Dyke
Who pretty much did as he liked
He went to TV-AM
And was never heard of again
Fucking well serves himself right.

Pretty soon after taking control of the moribund breakfast franchise, Greg asked me to begin fronting up the kind of preposterous light reports I had been already been knocking out for several years. I cannot recall a single one of them today, although I have a nagging recollection of standing in a diver's wet suit somewhere with Ernie Wise. What I do recall clearly is the exhilarating rush I experienced when Greg asked me to sit on the settee with Spike Milligan. I just knew we would get on well – and we did. Aware that the old Goon had a deserved reputation for being 'difficult', I figured the one thing Spike hated more than meeting new people was meeting new people who told him how great he was. Many years after our first encounter I was at the after-party for a BBC one-man show called *An Evening With Spike Milligan*. This was arranged to be nothing less than a full-tilt celebration of the man's genius – a word that gets thrown about these days like a Frisbee and now carries about the same weight. Spike Milligan, however, was the genuine article. But on the night of this salute he thought he'd performed poorly. So much so that when the celebrity audience rose for the necessary standing ovation at the end of the show he bade them to sit straight back down. Asking for his mic to be turned up, he said to the crowd, 'I wasn't any good tonight. So why are you doing that?' Everyone laughed uneasily because his face showed he wasn't joking. A section started applauding again and he turned on them. 'No, stop it. It was no good. Don't thank me for bloody crap, man.' And he walked off. At the rather muted affair afterwards I was sitting with him at his table. Because of the relationship I had with him, I told him he'd really soured the moment and been rude to people who just wanted to thank him for many other things. Rather admirably, he stuck to his guns.

'Couldn't care less. I wasn't going to stand there and be bloody

patronized, Danny. It was a bad show and they were a bunch of pho-
neys for lapping it up.'

At this exact point, across to our table came a man who today is
one of Britain's best and most-loved performers. I dislike memoirs
that play coy with their information, but in this one instance I am
going to protect the victim because he didn't deserve what happened
and it was mortifyingly awful. The chap was just starting to gather
a reputation at this stage in his career and we had met a few times
before. Putting his hand on my shoulder, he asked quietly, 'Dan, do
me a favour, introduce me to Spike . . .'

'Spike,' I said brightly, hoping he would trust me with the kind
of interaction he loathed. 'This is —— and he is brilliant. You'd like
him, Spike, he's one of the good ones!'

Milligan looked up at my pal like he had just come to repossess
his teeth.

'I know you don't like this sort of thing, Spike,' began the comic,
'but I couldn't let this moment pass. You are my absolute hero and I
just wanted to say hello.'

With no attempt at a handshake, Milligan continued to grimace
toward the hapless fan. Then he replied:

'All right. Now you've met me. Fuck off.'

My chum puffed out his cheeks, clapped me on the shoulder and
strode smartly away.

'Why did you do that?' I said to him. 'He's a good bloke, he is. He
only wanted to acknowledge what you've done for him.'

Again, Spike would have none of it. 'Danny, man, don't start all
that. These people are pests. The next thing you know they'll be calling me a fucking genius. It bores the piss out of me – if you want to
talk, talk. Why do they debase themselves and crawl around my feet
– who wants that?'

It was an intuitive feeling I had about Milligan's attitude to fame
that obviously helped when we first met.

I had already done one spot on the programme and then made
my way into the TV-AM green room where everyone was asked to
wait before going on. Milligan was already there and sitting alone. I
marched right across to him.

The only known photo of the whole family together: Mum, Dad, me, Sharon and Michael. Norfolk Broads, 1963.

First photo of me. I'm on the right, playing with Stephen Micalef by the rubbish chute in the flats.

Debnams Road, where I lived until I was twenty. Ours was the first door along.

(*above*) We were big on blue in my set. Spud can be glimpsed here employing a shop-bought saveloy as a comic phallus. My father, folks.

(*right*) Mum and Dad: Bet and Fred.

Spud typically enjoying both life and the Courvoisier. My brother's picture is beside him.

Outside the caravan shortly before shattering my legs in the ill-advised Dr Syn fiasco.

Dad and me at the 'van. It was twice runner-up in *Horse & Hound*'s Britain's Most Luxurious Dwelling poll.

Michael Aspel and me on *The Six O'Clock Show*. Or possibly *Waiting for Godot*.

This was how I fed and clothed my loved ones for six years. Note the Taser he's holding to force me into such public ignominy.

(*above*) Wendy holding Bonnie in Deptford Park. Our house is roughly centre in the row behind.

(*left*) At work with Bon-Bon, 1985.

(above) 46 Scawen Road, Deptford.

(left) I forced Sonny out to make his own way in the world when he was three. I presume he's doing OK.

(top right) When you enjoy a short rest at Christmas, possibly after a Tio Pepe or two, somebody will always take your photograph.

(*above*) Twizzle confined in his alley. You can just glimpse the gate on which he hanged himself – before resurrection – at top left.

(*right*) Twizzle again. We never suspected he was mad.

(*above*) The only picture I have of my time in panto. Here I am appealing for any loose change.

(*left*) The cover of the programme from The Great Dick Whittington Scam.

'Spike Milligan,' I said with some surprise. 'Still alive?'

I knew it was a line he himself had used when greeting old friends on shows like *This Is Your Life* and, as with Kenneth Williams, it turned out I couldn't have said a better thing.

He crumpled with laughter and rocked over to one side.

'Yes, man,' he chortled, 'still here, but the suit gets cremated in the morning.'

I introduced myself and said we would be on together later in the show.

'Sit down with me,' he said, banging the cushion beside him, 'before another bloody producer asks me if I'm OK. OK! It's a TV show, for Christ's sake, not bloody Anzio. Here, did you just say on there you're from Deptford?'

I had.

'You know I used to live in New Cross, don't you?' he said chummily.

'I do, mate. And that's why they had to close it down.'

Boom. You have to concede – I was getting quite expert at this.

Possibly the most famous visit of the many Milligan made to the *Six O'Clock Show* was one that has now passed into backstage lore. Claiming a migraine on arrival, he made straight for his dressing room and asked not to be disturbed until it was absolutely necessary. 'Don't bother me with bloody forms to sign or fucking make-up,' were his instructions as he disappeared inside his darkened sanctuary. What happened next almost took the entire network off the air.

Having apparently settled down to try combat the noise in his head with a period absolute silence, Spike gradually became aware of, and then totally enraged by, the constant ticking of the second hand on a clock on his dressing-room wall. With a momentous yell he stood on the provided couch and yanked the tormenting timepiece from its moorings, hurling it at the floor with such force that it shattered into its component parts.

Now then. This act of pique might ordinarily be overlooked in the highly strung world of show business. What gave it wider significance was that all the clocks in London Weekend Television at that time were connected and synchronized. When Spike Milligan tore the fixture from the wall it immediately stopped every other clock in the circuit, including the ones in studios 1, 2 and 3. As you can imagine, if you are minutes away from broadcasting live, having no working clocks around you tends to make things a bit messy.

Nobody could understand why the failure had occurred and while frantic calls to engineers and electricians reverberated around the building Spike himself showed up in the gallery. Having either calmed down or possibly been struck with remorse, he asked the line of seated production crew who was in charge. The producer, Maeve Haran, made herself known.

'Yeah, well, I owe you for one clock. I just demolished it in my dressing room. Why do they have to tick so loud they keep you awake? It's madness. Madness!'

Of course when it came to a little madness, Spike was most decidedly your man.

Jesus Was A Cross Maker

L ife, or at least my working life, had become, in the nicest way, routine and comfortable. To be honest, I did sometimes miss the zippy unpredictability of the punk and *NME* years, but thankfully I could also appreciate that as I approached thirty, it was perhaps for the best that I no longer lived for power chords, gigs and a life in the leather jacket. There were odd moments when the wilder ways returned, such as the time actor Christopher Walken came on the show and then afterwards asked if we could take him to some 'real' London pubs. In fact I took him around most of the better ones in Bermondsey that night and, in tribute to his Russian Roulette scene in *The Deer Hunter*, invented a game called The Beer Hunter where six cans of lager were purchased and then one of them would be vigorously shaken up in secret. The players then had to select a can each and open it right next to their face. The one who chose the shaken can – and thus got covered in boozy spray – was the loser. I had little inkling that in another decade I would professionally be coming up with lots of games like that, as well as being hurtled right back into the rock'n'roll maelstrom during the glorious years on *TFI Friday*.

Yet, despite the regularity of the work, in the mid-eighties I still felt as if it was all a larky distraction before I would return to writing of some sort. Or something. Fact was, I hoped I would never have to confront this dilemma – at least not in the next hundred and fifty years. This nebulous career plan was brought into clearer focus one day when I read a description of myself in a newspaper as 'an old person's young person'. That'll give you pause, I can tell you. Another phrase that seemed to routinely be tagged to any press I got was 'professional cockney'. I genuinely never understood what that was supposed to mean. I might concede to it if I were, like so many in the media, hiding some kind of public school background or an upbringing in one of the leafier parts of Surrey, but that not being the case I recognized it for what it was: the superior sneering of a relentlessly privileged middle-class industry. It's a form of control, pure and simple. What they meant by 'professional cockney' was actually just 'cockney', and they really didn't like the uppity working classes anywhere in their game unless they were in the canteen, post rooms or maintenance. I'm not sure if it has changed that much today. Even the most liberal university types go on the back foot when they meet someone who has simply got by on their wits, and they tend to feel threatened if that person is actually brighter than they are. So they resort to suspicion and the curled lip, attempting to denigrate this intruder by suggesting the whole 'working class' thing is an act and, really, all these 'chavs' have to offer is an accent. Thus even now you will read that someone is a 'professional Geordie' or 'professional Scouser'; back in the eighties, you'd even come across a 'professional black person'. Nobody who has come through the correct middle-class upbringing with the benefit of a few quid in their family coffers will ever be so disparagingly described. No, you'll find they will simply be 'professionals'.

While we're here, I may add that, far from being a typical working-class 'bloke', I could never claim to be even marginally competent in the traditionally masculine field of home improvements. Away from a typewriter, latterly the computer keyboard, I am not only a disaster at DIY, I fancy I rather stand alone as the most clueless exponent of the handyman's skills. This is another area where I am totally my father's son. Though Dad was a terrifically hard worker, whether in the docks, clearing railway arches of rubble, or as part of an early morning office-cleaning gang, he could not for the life of him build, repair, install or decorate anything. Despite this, during the sixties he was given little choice in the matter, being required by Mum to wallpaper the front room in our maisonette roughly once a year. The rest of the family soon learned that it was absolutely essential for us to retire to another part of the house and cower in safety until it was all over. Like me, Dad had no finesse, no patience and genuinely believed you could inflict pain on any particularly finicky inanimate object that pushed you too far. I've no idea how many rolls of wallpaper it took to cover our small living room. Let's say it was six. Dad, knowing how these affairs went, would order ten. This was because when a patterned section he was holding folded in on itself or refused to match up with one already in position, he could only achieve catharsis by furiously mashing it up into a ball, screaming 'You dirty bastard!' at it and throwing it across the room. Sometimes Mum would hear this happen four times in as many minutes and call out from the other side of the door, 'You all right, Fred?' to which he would explode, 'No, I'm fucking not!'

The rest of us would then have to make sure our inevitable gig-gling fit didn't make a sound, which could really hurt your lungs sometimes. The worst rage he ever flew into was when he couldn't get his plumb-line – those weights on strings that are supposed to show a decorator where a true straight line falls – to stop swaying back and forth.

'This is fucking impossible!' we heard him storming to himself. 'Bastard thing won't keep still! How the fucking hell you supposed to do this?' A moment later we heard, 'Oh, this is just BOLLOCKS!' and then an almighty shattering of glass as he launched the plumb-line straight through the window out into our garden.

Mum, obviously alarmed at this devastation, then broke the unwritten rule by hurrying into the room.

'Fred, what the bleeding hell was that?!' she asked, not unreasonably.

'Bet. Just. Go. Out. Leave me alone when I'm doing this!' Spud bristled.

Mum saw the almost cartoonlike jagged hole in the glass pane.

'My God, Fred. Why have you smashed me windas?'

'I did me nut, all right? It's enough to drive you round the twist, having to do this. I wasn't having it.'

Mum decided to keep her own fury in check and just heave an exasperated growl as she made to leave the scene of the crime. Before she closed the door, though, Dad said with as much contrition as he could muster,

'Bet. Just go out in the garden and make sure I didn't hit Tom the Tortoise with the fuckin' plumb-line, will ya?'

Fortunately no such tragedy had occurred.

Having inherited this same lack of practical expertise, the few times I did have a go at becoming master of my surroundings the resultant element of farce was actually heightened because Wendy, youngest of ten children, came from a background where all the boys and even the brothers-in-law could turn their hand to absolutely anything. They were effortlessly outstanding at every aspect of do-it-yourself from carpentry to brickwork, from installing white goods to finished decoration. Indeed, Wendy's closest brother, Rod, was a pro at interiors and is still hired by stores like Fortnum & Mason to take care of their window dressing each Christmas. Me? Not a clue. Worse, my inability to do it myself was fatally combined with a total disinterest in learning how it was done.

I really believe there is something in the universe that controls these things. I remember trying to prise the lid off a tin of paint once. I had put newspaper down so as not to get any drips on the front-room floorboards but, try as I might, the screwdriver I had wedged under one edge of the lid would not free it from the glossy mother ship. So I thumped my fist down on the screwdriver handle and the lid promptly flipped off, sailing high in the air like a coin tossed to determine head or tails. Had it just gone up and down again, I think I could have contained the splatter. Instead – and I am pretty sure in defiance of all the laws of physics – it went up and out, coming to rest – paint side down, naturally – on our Liberty settee. Taking a leaf out of the old man's manual here, I just stood there and shouted, 'Oh, for fuck's sake!' And do you know what? Wendy blamed me anyway.

'You're supposed to do that outside, THEN bring the paint in! That's ruined that cushion. I'll never be able to turn that over, will I?'

On another occasion we bought a small bedside cupboard that 'required some assembly'.

'Dan, why don't you just leave it until Bill can come round and put it together?' said Wendy wearily after I asked where the claw hammer was kept.

'Wend, mate,' I shot back, a little tetchily, 'I'm not a complete washout. Look, there's only five bits to it!'

But I *am* a complete washout when it comes to these things. The sort of washout that even Noah might have deemed a corker. I won't go into detail about my bedside cabinet fiasco, but I will say that I completed it in very smart time, had no bits left over and it looked exactly as it did on the box. Still seated beside my undoubted triumph on the floor of our bedroom, I called out to Wendy, and did so frankly in a tone that suggested here at last she would have to eat her words.

She came in, looked at it and gave a surprised hum of appreciation. 'Blimey,' she said. 'I take it all back.'

As admissions go, 'I take it all back' is the one I find husbands most like to hear from their partners. But as I stood to put the brilliantly assembled piece of furniture into position, I noticed one of my legs wasn't playing ball. This was because I had somehow screwed one of my socks to the bedroom floor. I promise you, that's what I'd done and I fancy that's a trick even Frank Spencer missed. I hadn't felt a thing and it had gone straight through the wood, into the flappy bit of sock up by my toes and right down into the carpet. In my defence, let me say that the screws shouldn't have been long enough to do that, should they? That's a design fault, in my book. We were lucky I didn't just plough on till I'd gone through a gas main or something.

This humbling moment was then made even worse by Wendy sprawling helpless on the bed while I, now in a terrible mood, had to sit there and unscrew my sock. Then I had to re-screw the fixture properly, sans my sock, although this time it simply wouldn't anchor itself in the required hole and the entire cupboard developed a bit of a list. I insisted it was nevertheless fit for purpose and stuck it by the bed, where it remained for about a month. Every time Wendy placed so much as a magazine on it, it slumped over to the right.

My lowest moment as Man of the House happened when I said I would paint the ceiling in the little back bedroom. This was while we were in Maydew House and so it really was a little back bedroom.

Once again, Wendy implored me to let Rod or Bill or Brian do it, but this was early in our relationship and a chap has to try and keep the lustre of love and admiration at maximum levels during this honeymoon period. I said I would get it done while Wendy was out at her sister's one afternoon. As soon as she had gone, I carried the paint tin down to the tiny room and had my usual difficulty prying off the lid. I managed it on this occasion without ruining a thousand-pound three-piece suite, but didn't know what to do with the dripping tin Frisbee once I'd freed it up. Figuring I'd put it, for the time being, in the bathroom sink, I carried it back up the stairs – the flats were of a curious but wonderful design – and plonked it down beneath the taps. The paint on the lid seemed rather fluid and lush to me and I thought, 'I bet that will eventually run off there and on to the white porcelain of the bowl.' So, and I know you are going to think I must be several layers beyond moronic here, I turned on the tap to wash it off. I know. I can't explain what made me do that. And it was so much worse than you can imagine, because I gave the tap handle a right good turn, causing the jet of water to spurt out at about ten thousand gallons an hour directly on to the slightly concave upturned lid. It went *everywhere*. I often marvel at how, even when you've only left the dregs of some wine in a glass, should you then go and kick it over it seems to issue forth like Lake Windermere bursting its banks. Well, this apparent smear of paint on the underside of the lid appeared to multiply its mass until Wendy's pristine bathroom looked like a troupe of old-fashioned clowns had been rehearsing in there. In case you're interested, it was a small, classically white bathroom and the paint was a shade of blue that edged toward the turquoise. If we'd stuck with our original plan of doing the little room ceiling a delicate cream, I insist the splatter flecked across my wife's tiles and towels would have been that much easier to disguise. But that's Wendy for you – always changing her mind.

Swearing furiously, I stood stock-still for a few seconds. I was wringing wet from head to toe. When I took off my spattered glasses to wipe them on my sodden T-shirt, the paint spots simply smeared across my lenses and, even though I gave it a go, made even partial vision impossible. This was not going brilliantly, I had to admit. Figuring I would now need to do some clearing up before I could even get down to the real task of the day, I went in search of the Flash or Ariel or Mr Sheen or whatever it was that Wend seemed to buy by the bushel and constantly clean things with. Ours wasn't the biggest flat in the world. This stuff couldn't be that hard to hunt down. I must have stood for about half an hour at the open doors of the food cupboard, straining my gaze beyond tins of beans and packets of pasta, hoping to catch a glimpse of something caustic. From there I began feeling round the back of the dinner plates stacked up alongside the cups and bowls. I mean, really, what was the point of secreting this stuff away? These are the sort of tools one needs in an emergency and they ought to be stored somewhere obvious. As it was, it struck me as akin to the boss of a fireworks factory just leaving a few hints as to where the fire extinguishers might be. After about ten minutes of cursing and carrying on a salty monologue at high volume, my eyes fell upon possibly the most secretive of all places in the modern home: the small door beneath the kitchen sink. I may have even said, 'Aha!' out loud. But after getting down and opening this mysterious portal all it revealed was a rubber plunger of the sort comedians used to get stuck on their face, a plastic washing-up bowl filled with parched J-Cloths, a small bottle off Zoflora disinfectant (hyacinth) and, right at the back under the pipes, a lone potato that in the darkness had sprouted some impressively curlicued tendrils.

Rising, defeated by this underwhelming cache, I was further buoyed to note some of the blue paint that had been on my jeans had now transferred itself to the kitchen floor. The only conclusion I could arrive at was that Wendy must have taken all the cleaning stuff with her – not the loopiest of hypotheses, given that she rarely entered a café or train carriage without saying, 'This needs a bleeding good clean in here.'

I went back down to the little bedroom, popping my head in at the bathroom on the way just to see if it had dried out a bit in the meantime. It hadn't. If anything, it was looking even more Jackson Pollock than previously. Gazing up at my overhead task, for the very first time I began to wonder how on earth you actually painted a ceiling. In the first of these books you may recall that a few years earlier my hapless flatmates and I had disastrously painted a large council flat kitchen with black gloss, including the floor and Ascot water heater. The ceiling had been the responsibility of my friend Steven Saunders, who completed the task by standing on a table at one end and then just moving it along till he arrived at the far side. This worked very well, although for some time afterwards Steve's right hand predated Michael Jackson's single black glove look by several summers. I didn't have a table or even a broad enough chair to gain the required altitude, but the room did contain a single bed. I decided to use that. Hauling it into the centre of the room – I planned to do the edges last – I clambered up on to the mattress holding the tin of paint in one hand and a brand-new broad brush in the other. To put the method to the test, before putting brush to paint, I straightened my arm to make sure the bristles would get a firm connection with the ceiling. They did, but only just. What I was after was a firm slap that would slather on the colour in long strokes. So, dipping the brush into the mix a full three inches, I placed the tin back down on the floor and began energetically bouncing off the bed, hitting the target above me in a series of wild arcs. After a minute or so I stopped and, panting a little, leapt off the bed to see how it looked. It looked absolutely fine, I thought, and what was more this was great fun. Yes, my exertions had caused some of the paint to fly off on to the walls, but that was all right, they were being repapered next week anyway. I carried on with my improvised trampoline act until all that remained to do were the edge areas, as per plan. Then, it being a Saturday afternoon, I decided to take a bit of a break and go upstairs to see how the football was getting on.

Two hours later I was still lying full-length on the sofa when Wendy came home.

'Blimey, it stinks of paint in here,' she said immediately, as though, when a man has been straining every nerve in his body refreshing the entire look of a nearby room, it shouldn't. This was followed by, 'Dan! It's all over your hair and hands, don't lay on the settee like that, it'll get everywhere!'

I must say I wasn't expecting her to place a garland of gardenias around my neck and coo 'My hero' by way of gratitude, but I did think her tone was a bit off in the circumstances.

'I have just this second sat down,' I replied with some steeliness in the voice. 'No paint could possibly have got anywhere.'

'Well, it has because I can already see a smudge on the arm from here.'

Turning, I could just about make out this almost imperceptible speck if put my nose virtually against the fabric, yet somehow she could see it from way across the apartment. Wives, I have found, can do this. I was of course all too aware that the carnage in the bathroom was going to go over big now and so I thought I would get in early and lay the blame exactly where it belonged.

'I had a bit of a nightmare in the bathroom earlier. I did try to clean it up but there wasn't any proper stuff in the house. It held me right up, actually.'

'Stuff?' she said sharply. 'Stuff? You mean that entire shelf full of cleaning things in the kitchen?' And she turned to hotfoot it toward the proof. I knew I was expected to follow.

Arriving at the big cupboard where I'd spent so long gazing at all the bags of rice and peaches in heavy syrup, she pointed to a compartment down at floor level. There I could see the massed ranks of every kind of spot remover, stain soaker, vanishing foam and emergency rinse available on the modern market. It looked like the kind of inventory they keep in coastal warehouses in case oil tankers split in two and threaten the beaches. I swear it hadn't been there when I had absolutely scoured the area earlier.

'Anyway, what do you mean you had a nightmare?' she snapped, heading off swiftly to answer her own question. I stayed where I was and yet heard her cry of horror as distinctly as if she had been at my side. Then she said something I will never forget.

'Oh fucking hell! It looks like *Psycho* in here!' There were several 'Oh no's' followed by an 'I don't believe this!' and a volley of 'What the bloody hell has happened's before I heard her make her way to the bedroom that, if I'd had a chance to say it, I would have pointed out was still very much 'mid-project'.

It was as she first looked upon my labours here that for the one and only time in my life I heard a person say 'Eek!' like in a sixpenny comic. Now I was happy to concede the bathroom, but this seemed too much and so I strode down the stairs to put the case for the defence. As I arrived next to her in the doorway, where she stood with both hands up to her face in shock, I found that her 'Eek' had been expertly chosen. Something seemed to have happened to my brushwork since I'd left it. Instead of the lush uniform colour that I was convinced had covered the ceiling almost to the boundaries earlier that afternoon, up there now was a multitude of jagged slashes that ranged in hue from deep turquoise to an insipid eggshell blue, many of which seemed to peter out less than a foot from the light fitting at the centre. While wet it might have deceived the human eye, but once dry it bewildered the human mind.

After a series of almost frightened swallows, Wendy gathered her thoughts and came up with an outlandish theory:

'I've never seen anything like it. It's insane. It looks like you were jumping up and down on the bed trying to do it. What *did* you do?'

And at that point we will leave this abject tale. It can do no good to dwell on the decades of ridicule I have suffered over these honest attempts to muck in with the manly responsibilities. Indeed, I may have revealed too much already and am starting to understand why so many show business autobiographies draw a veil over the home life, choosing instead to gallop through encomiums received and charity golf matches taken part in. All I wanted to point out was that, though I was no match for my dad in most fields, when it came to fixing up the hearth and home I could effortlessly eclipse even his ineptitude.

So you can imagine what sort of tasks the pair of us were allowed to undertake when it came to renovating our new home in Scawen Road. In short, we were only permitted to be basic labourers for my wonderfully gifted brothers-in-law. Whenever things needed clearing, smashing out, dumping or lifting, we would be given the chore. Nothing as chancy as knocking down walls, but as Dad brilliantly described it, 'Anything that requires getting covered in shit.'

It was while we were finessing one such duty in the house that a really strange thing happened, one even hardened cynics couldn't pass off as a good omen.

You may remember that the place hadn't been altered since it was built – a circumstance that had both positives and negatives. All the sturdy Victorian features remained in place, which sounds great, though this meant that the only bath in the building was a peculiar tank-like affair in the small kitchen. A lid covered this rudimentary fixture to make it serve as a worktop.

On the day in question, Dad was helping me clear everything out the old scullery, and this included pulling up an expanse of ancient lino that looked as if it had been on the floor since Edward VIII abdicated. As we tore up the oilcloth in great jagged sections, I noticed that some newspapers had been laid under it, possibly as a primitive underlay. Like most people I find old papers mesmerizing things to pore over and so, as my old man heaved what we'd already removed to the skip outside, I sat on the floor reading the ridiculous old ads and stiffly worded stories about long-forgotten aristocracy. I looked for a date on this edition of the *Daily Express*. It said 26 May 1951 – 26 May! That was Dad's birthday. There was another edition of the same paper spread out a little further away. I picked up a page. This one was dated 22 June. My birthday.

When Fred bustled back in I was dumbfounded.

'Dad, look at this! It's incredible. The papers under that lino – one's your birthday and, look – the other's mine!'

Getting his nails under a long strip of the floor cover, he yanked it up.

'Yeah, well, don't sit there reading fucking papers all afternoon – we got upstairs to do yet.'

I couldn't believe he wasn't as astounded as I was. Or even a tad astounded.

'Don't you think that's weird?' I gasped, trying to get some sort of acknowledgement for this phenomenal coincidence. 'Of all the dates these could have been, they're our birthdays! I think that's staggering.'

'Yeah? Well, I notice I'm doing all the fucking staggering at the moment, son – out to that fucking skip. Now grab a load and take it outside, will ya?'

And with that he scooped up these, in my opinion, profound documents and shoved them into a rubble sack.

And that was that.

King Of The Mountain Cometh

Sonny Michael Rodney Baker was born on 10 December 1986. Now we had two children, the house was humming along, there seemed to be a family party about every three days and we all took a couple of good holidays a year – at least one of them at sumptuous top-notch resorts in America. Given my job, the bank allowed us a whopping £6,000 overdraft and we caned every penny I earned to make sure we were right up against that and quite often beyond it. Overdrafts have always struck me as tremendously mad things. My philosophy, handed down from Dad, is that financial responsibility doesn't really exist, it is just another form of control. If you are any kind of a live wire you will generally find ways of grabbing hold of a few quid. When a bank says, 'On top of your own conker pile, you can have this amount of ours too,' I believe you should just head for the far end of that amount and keep on shoving. People will wag a finger and talk about 'rainy days' and 'bank charges', but I have to honestly say I've refused to acknowledge either of them. If an accountant – something I never had in those days – had said, 'Do you realize you paid £2,100 in bank charges last year?' I would have had to reply that I didn't feel a thing. The storm of cash going in and straight back out was a fantastic way to live, untainted by any arbitrary cautions agreed upon at some dull fiscal meeting I must have missed. I'm aware there is a sizeable contingent of citizens that resent such gormless good luck, but I say it again: I cannot temper the facts of my story with a more popular philosophy or a fake retrospective unction. Utter recklessness has worked for me and, grate as that might, here we all are.

As a sop to those who might require the whisper of A Reckoning, let us now turn to how, in 1988 at the age of thirty-one, I went absolutely tits-up skint and became jobless for the only time in my life.

The *Six O'Clock Show* had been on air for over six years and toward the end of its run was caught up in what some might call a revolution in TV, others an ageist pogrom. Back when the show began it was understood that mass audiences of TV programmes were at least the peers of the onscreen talent and often old enough to be their parents. Today, if you go on YouTube and check out a show from the period like Yorkshire Television's *3-2-1*, it is hard to concentrate on the weak shenanigans of host Ted Rogers and Co. because the studio audience appears to be comprised of a phalanx of ancient old waxworks and assorted gargoyles seemingly tipped out of the care home for the day. Even the contestants, repeatedly described as 'young couples', look to have missed the advent of pop culture altogether and adopted a style so beige and acquiescent that society seems to have reverted to that pre-rock'n'roll era when teenagers dressed like their school teachers.

At a point just after the mid-eighties all this began to change rapidly as thrusting, monied young professionals – yuppies was the ubiquitous term – began taking over the vacant sites upon which had once stood traditional manufacturing industries and opening up thousands of businesses – most based in selling property and moving money, but a good deal of them creating and exploiting a new youth-dominated media era. In a neat little irony, many of the junior staff from the *Six O'Clock Show*'s early days had gone on to become altogether bigger players in the TV industry and now they found themselves in a position to slip a noose round the show's neck and shove it off the precipice.

The *SOCS* was deemed too comfortable and corny – two of the traits that had made it such a success in the first place. Certainly I, so identified with it that I had no hope of surviving any rebirthing, could have no complaints if they decided to replace this 'old person's young person' with the genuine article. Which is exactly what they did –by the power-suited, padded-shouldered, big-haired bushel.

When the show came to the end of its final forty-four-show run in 1988 it was announced that a brand-new, relevant, hard-hitting news show was to come roaring in to take its place. This show would not concern itself with the folksy, the silly and the intrinsically local. This show would reflect a New London: urgent, dynamic, young, going places. The very title was a statement of its vitality: *Friday Now!* That exclamation mark was actually part of its title, as if to proclaim, 'Stand back, old timers, the future is here and *you're* in the way!'

In September 1988 *Friday Now!* was unleashed upon this perceived Brave New World and went straight down the toilet. The programme managed to struggle on for an entire year, presenting its happening, go-getter face to a frankly aghast public every Friday, and it was during this period that I finally had my Mr Micawber philosophy put to the test for the very first time since leaving school. In short – now what?

My chief problem was that I had never taken on an agent. True, I had never needed one; LWT seemed happy to chuck a number at me in the company elevators once a year and away we'd go. I certainly didn't want someone to find me other work while I was rattling around this playground. Other work would have meant *other work*, and at least 50 per cent of that phrase struck me as vulgar. However, when I realized that, against all odds, the day I handed in my hat on the *SOCS* there would be no long queue of other programmes willing to cram cash through the letter box, I did ponder whether I ought to have taken more notice of how the industry operates. The question was, did I want to carry on doing this for a living? I mean, what did I even do? The generic term for it was 'presenting', but what's that? Jugglers juggle, magicians do tricks, singers sing, but presenters . . . present what?

It wasn't long before I was given a vision of what my future could hold, disastrously 'presenting' on a thing that, without doubt, and in the teeth of stiff opposition, remains by far the biggest stinker I have ever been involved with. And agent be damned, this shocking outrage of a vehicle came looking for me.

I was sitting at home one day, flicking playing cards into a top hat, when the phone went. It was a producer I'd worked with at LWT who said he'd had a call from someone at Thames Television who wanted to know who 'represented' me. Well, for a moment I did toy with doing what I like to call the old Russ Conway. Popular pianist Russ was a huge star in the sixties but, as I hear it, could be rather eccentric. For a period in his career he was exclusively represented by Trevor Stanford and anyone wishing to talk turkey with Russ simply had to go through Trevor first. OK, that is par for the course when dealing with celebrities. The twist here was that Trevor Stanford *was* Russ Conway, so when interested parties would call Russ' business number – coincidentally identical to Russ' actual home number – the following conversation would ensue:

Interested Party: Hi there, who's that?

Russ Conway: Trevor Stanford.

IP: Hi, Trevor, I need to speak to Russ about that lighting change he wanted at Bridlington.

Russ Conway: Is it anything I can help with?

IP: No, I said I'd get back to him direct.

Russ Conway: OK, I'll just get him.

[Sound of phone being placed on side table, followed by a few footsteps.]

Russ Conway: Hello?

IP: Is that Russ Conway?

Russ Conway: Yes, it is.

And so on. Frankly, I think that's a tremendous way to carry on. Even though everyone claims to have been aware that they were speaking to the same person both times, the business just went along with it.

After toying with the notion of hiring my alter ego, I eventually plumped for just passing my number on to the person at Thames. At a pinch, maybe my wife could take the call and say I was in conference but could spare a few minutes if they were brief. In reality I would have been two feet away with Bonnie and Sonny on my lap, watching that day's gripping instalment of *Button Moon*. Anyway, Thames did call and ask me to attend a meeting they were having about a new network series. I stress the word 'network' here, because up until now nothing I had done on TV had made it out of the London area. This meant an exciting opportunity for me to be disliked nationwide and I was thrilled at the prospect.

The series turned out to be a misbegotten heap of cock-eyed ordure called *The Bottom Line* – a consumer watchdog show, no less! Plonked into a big-shouldered suit, I joined three other shame-faced confederates – Emma Freud, Janice Long and Michael Wilson – and ran in a studio each week so that I could pretend to give a flying fuck about people who had not had their greenhouses delivered. And when I say 'ran' into the studio, I mean exactly that. At the top of the programme we were required to dash on to the set as if we were being chased by thousands of angry hornets. I think the idea of this pointless animation was that it would somehow con the audience into thinking we were so busy fighting for their rights out on the high street that we barely had time to deliver the show itself. The pounding theme tune went, 'It's the Bottom, it's the Bottom, it's the Bottom Line!' which, after first hearing, we naturally transformed into: 'It's the bottom, it's the bottom, it's the bottom of the barrel!'

This clunky look at low-level cons and sellers of stolen goods even boasted a studio audience – poor souls must have written in for tickets to *Benny Hill* and got lumbered with us as a booby prize. Worst of all, given the programme's brief, how long would it be until my own father popped up on the agenda?

The show tanked after just six episodes, but as you're probably anticipating, if I hadn't donned that cape and fought for truth, justice and a temporary pay packet, then my subsequent career in broadcasting might never have happened. First off, I got myself an agent: Alex Armitage of Noel Gay Artists, under whose umbrella I remain to this day. Second, while lying about in Emma Freud's dressing room, the pair of us having the usual clandestine fits at the piss-poor fare we were about to drop on a public who had done little to warrant such a rotten trick, Emma mentioned that she'd been asked to expand her role at GLR, the BBC's local radio station for London. Having previously done two shifts at the week-end, she would now be taking over a daily slot.

'You should come on one of them, Dan. Talk about music and that. You'd be good on the radio, you would.'

I filled Emma in on the only radio show I'd ever haunted, a woeful guest spot to promote my first television show *Twentieth Century Box*. The full and terrible details of that fiasco can be found in *Going to Sea in a Sieve*, but suffice to say I had taken to the medium like a duck to . . . well, *radio*. I literally thought no more about it but, happily for the upward arc of this story, Emma did.

Once the *Bottom Line* sank out of sight like a barge full of clinker, I had absolutely nothing to do and absolutely no money in the bank. I penned a few pieces for various publications but all the time letters would arrive from Barclays pointing out that no substantial deposits had been noted for some months now and could I pop in to see them? In fact, these letters were a salvation in themselves because they were written by one Mervyn Willcock, who is the sort of bank manager I suspect only I could run into. Mervyn was an extremely funny and accommodating man. His letters were always inventive, always amusing and, most crucially of all, always hinting that if I wanted to extend the overdraft a little further, that'd be OK with him. I think he must have found my bullet-proof optimism both refresh-ing and somewhat admirable, given the prospects facing me. His letters would be longish affairs, plainly typed out for kicks between a welter of more formal admonishments, and I was overjoyed to find when looking for photos for this book that I'd actually kept some of his riper missives. Typically, he would ramble into a fantasy world where everything was plainly his fault, but if I could at some time pop by his padded cell and remind him of his former life and cor-rect him on some of the illusions he'd formed about our relation-ship, he would be eternally grateful. Another one, addressed entirely to Wendy, he wrote as a condolence letter following my death. This he had concluded would be the only possible reason I was ignoring him, and he closed it by saying, 'If there is anything I can do at this difficult time then please leave a lamp in an upstairs window so I may see it from across the Thames. Alternatively, could we think about some kind of séance whereby I might speak directly with your late husband to hear his views about reducing your facility with us from beyond the veil.' In yet another, he contrasted with supreme wit the circumstances that had led him to be shivering in his office at Holborn with the colourful postcard I'd recently sent him from Estepona in Spain, where I was holidaying.

'Factually your card is a little incorrect in that the manager of our Estepona branch is a Mr Charlie "The Mad Axeman" Smith and I have written to him thanking him on your behalf for the superb service you are receiving . . . If, and here I have my doubts, you do have any potatoes or traveller's cheques left, please let me have them and I will be only too willing to place them into your account.'

Can you imagine such a magical human being working within the banking system today? But there he was and it was purely through his generous, dotty nature that I wafted along on little but fumes for a considerable period in the late eighties. I sincerely don't remember feeling any pressure because my theory that you can continue to live well, albeit at a reduced rate, and wait for the next currency boost to reveal itself lived up to the test. Thus I would call Mervyn and say, 'If you were to go right round the bend, how much could you free me up at this moment?'

'But I raised the overdraft last week,' he might say. 'Has this film you were talking about directing fallen through?'

'Film, Mervyn, film?' I wailed, reminding him to keep the conversation respectable. 'Must you always be thinking about work? I'm planning a short break soon so I can come up with hundreds more ideas – but I can't do that if you're forever nagging me about old motion picture projects. I need £300 to get away on the Norfolk Broads for a bit – £300! My God, you've probably got that in your hat band right now!'

And off to the Broads we all went. While we were there an incident typical of my relations with Barclays occurred, and again I wonder whether it would be given any credence today. We arrived at one of the smaller outposts on the riverways and after mooring up the boat began a pleasant, if longish, walk through the woods toward the village. Here in one of the antiques/junk shops Wendy saw a couple of things that would look really terrific in the beautiful old dresser we had in our dining room and there was a clutch of old LPs that I certainly wasn't going to leave behind either. What was needed now was the cash because we had no chequebook with us, and even if the hamlet had a cashpoint you couldn't reason with a machine like you could Magnificent Mervyn. Bowling over to a phone box, I rang him in London.

'Mervyn,' I began brightly. 'Baker here in sunny Norfolk.'

He may have groaned theatrically.

'I need an emergency fifty in cash.'

He pointed out that there was that amount available in the newly restructured overdraft.

'I know that,' I impatiently shot him down, 'but we're in some thimble of a village and no chequebook or card with us. There is a little Barclays though. Could you ring them and have somebody fork over the necessary?'

Weighing this, he said he probably could, even if it meant legging it out of some important meetings concerning international consortiums investing in Dubai. I think he was being sarcastic. The only stipulation would be, he averred, they would require some form of identification.

'But I don't have any,' I stressed, and it was true. I didn't drive then and had figured that Norfolk, though it has its own definite ways, wouldn't require me to produce a passport.

'Well, is there anything I can tell them to ask for?' he pleaded.

I mulled on this then, looking down, I had it. 'I'm wearing fake leopardskin shoes!' I announced brightly.

A heavy sigh came at me down the line before he said, 'All right then. I'll tell them to look out for you.'

Marching along to the adorable little branch I joined a short queue and waited for the single window to become available. About five minutes later I stood facing a woman in her fifties who regarded my smiling face with a curdled interest.

'Yes?' she asked.

Slipping off my right shoe I held it beside my head and said confidently, 'I think you're expecting me. I'd like fifty pounds please!'

She had no idea what I was talking about, but I insisted that if she just made a few enquiries she would find that everything was in order. She got up and went to talk to somebody in a small office behind her. All the while I stood there with my shoe high up, facing front. Within thirty seconds she came back and without any further discussion, squinted at my animal-print brothel creeper for a moment, then said:

'How would you like your money, Mr Baker? Tens all right?'

As I left the place I like to believe that the old man who was in the line after me went up to the same woman, took off both his shoes and said, 'In that case can I have a hundred?' but we can leave that to the sketch writers. The extraordinary truth is that this was the kind of financial fairyland I inhabited during my skint year.

And then things became *really* critical in what I believe is often referred to as 'the dark before the dawn'.

I mentioned watching *Button Moon* with the kids earlier, and I suppose I had become rather expert in the minutiae of toddlers' TV, what with hanging around our new house all day. It was a time when ITV really led the field in this genre and I had tremendous affection, as well as some strict opinions, about the shows that ruled the designated lunchtime spots for under-5s. Today, looking back and without undue nostalgia, I should say that the top six programmes were as follows. In reverse order:

6. *Orm and Cheep*
5. *Tickle on the Tum*
4. *Emu at the Pink Windmill*
3. *Allsorts*
2. *Button Moon*
1. *Rainbow*

Some may raise an eyebrow at the omission of *Sooty & Sweep*, but you must remember this was before Matthew Corbett had resuscitated his father's brand and the team were very much between projects. By the early nineties when they were turning out episodes like 'Super Sweep', 'Burglar Box' and 'Cousin Scrappy Comes to Stay', I would have no hesitation in including them in the top three, but I have to keep this journal true to the times.

Anyway, it was while I was watching a corking edition of the number three on that list wherein Spike, the secretly talking dog, had been playing a practical joke on Jiffy, his keeper, by progressively hiding all the things he was laying out for their day at the beach, that the front door bell went.

Taking Sonny off my lap and placing him inside the upturned box that had once contained our washing machine but now Bonnie liked to use as a sort of Second World War coastal lookout through which she would watch her shows, I went to answer the door. Two men stood there and asked me to confirm who I was. There may have been other chit-chat between us, but I can't recall any details. What I do know is pretty soon they got down to the reason for the visit. They asked me if I had £15,000 to give them. I remember the amount very specifically, chiefly because it was *fifteen thousand pounds*. They may as well have asked me, 'Do you think if you flap your arms hard enough you could fly to the moon?'

These people were from the VAT office, a branch of government that I'd only previously encountered via their signs in London's electrical retailers where they claimed not to apply to foreigners. From their tone as they stood on my doorstep I ascertained they didn't consider me a visitor to these shores. But fifteen thousand pounds? Were they entirely sure? Was there not a chance that somebody up at their HQ had accidentally nudged the old abacus as they passed, causing one of the beads to slip along an extra zero? Mind you, that would still be fifteen hundred pounds, and even Mervyn at the bank wasn't going to OK that with a light laugh, no matter how many shoes I showed him. Fifteen thousand! Our house had only cost twenty-eight. I did toy with the idea of asking them if they were fans of Kenneth Williams.

Once I had patted my pockets a few times and looked under the Welcome mat, I told them that I couldn't quite guarantee the sum they were looking for. To this they said they would come back at five o'clock that afternoon and if I failed to provide the full amount they had licence to start carting off house contents in lieu. Closing the door on them again I went back into the front room and tried to pick up the plot on *Allsorts*.

'Daddy, why is Spike hiding Jiffy's bucket and spade under the bed again?' asked Bonnie.

Even though I like to think I am there to answer all my children's questions in life I have to say I didn't answer this one. In fact I mutely watched the rest of the episode in something of a daze. It was twelve thirty by this time; when Wendy came back from Sainsbury's I waited till she had put down the last of the bags and finished her usual stream of cathartic outbursts about how many 'barmy people' there are out there before I told her it probably wasn't worth unpacking all the steaks, vegetables and bottles of Comfort because the carrier bags would make it easier for the VAT people carry them out again just as they were.

People who learn of my cavalier attitude to finance often tend to assume that my wife must be the wise old head in the relationship, who, while indulging my extravagant ways, actually makes sure that at least one of us keeps our head out of the clouds. Not a bit of it. Wendy can burn through a pound note at a rate almost the match of mine. In a way, it's her unbending resilience in the face of a problem such as we had at that moment that is the ultimate expression of her faith in me. Her first reaction is to go on the attack.

'Fucking bastards, ain't they, some people? When you think about what they get up to in the City and Margaret Thatcher's fucking mates.' Steam let off, she set about devising a solution.

'Well, you'll have to ring Rodney and get it from him for now,' she said, starting to put away each piece of shopping with a punctuating thump.

Rodney, Wendy's nearest brother in age, headed up a small but hectic business out of a couple of railway arches in Herne Hill. Here, along with the designs for department store windows, he and his team also made props for various exhibitions and even feature films. One of the first times I met Rod I went back to the fantastic flat he had in a condemned yet still sturdy old council block and found his hallway difficult to pass through because it was totally dominated by one of the huge Jabberwocky monsters used in the film by Terry Gilliam. Rod had also made all of the terrifying tableaus on display in the London Dungeon. He'd either personally created or supervised the authenticity of every single sore, boil and bubo in the building, along with all the racks, thumbscrews, gibbets, coffins and gallows. During this mammoth task he had gently press-ganged all members of the family into having their faces 'life-moulded' so as to provide the array of different heads he'd need. For this process your entire face has to be covered in a thick warm pink goop for about fifteen minutes with a couple of thin cardboard cylinders placed up your nostrils to allow you to breathe. Once cool, this is then peeled off to form the vessel from which a new mannequin's face can be cast. Even when my children were very small, they would never be truly alarmed when visiting the Dungeon because they recognized Auntie Maddie was the witch being burned, Uncle Brian having his fingernails pulled out, Cousin Sean dying of the plague and, why, there's Daddy in a cauldron being boiled alive. It was tremendous fun to do and a rollicking in-joke on the many occasions I strolled those grimy chambers with friends. Wizard with his hands though Rod is, he too has never been one to knuckle down to sensible fiscal planning. When the London Dungeon was being created, the owners offered him a share in its future profits in return for agreeing a reduced lump sum for his work. He declined and took the pretty modest payment in full. Today, whenever he passes the famous attraction, as he has done for almost thirty years, he looks at the long lines of tourists patiently waiting to get in and says, 'Yep, that's me. A regular Richard Branson.' Nonetheless Rod's business always had a steady turnover and so it seemed possible I might dip into his till for a loan. I rang him and after a few chuckles and 'fucking hells!' he said I could go straight over and collect the required sum.

At five o'clock the doorbell went again, right on cue. I opened it smartly and before a word was spoken shoved the cheque out toward them.

'OK?' I said brightly.

They took it, looked at it and said OK back to me. I closed the door swiftly and that was the end of that.

Talking to my dad the following day he of course thought I'd caved in needlessly. 'First off,' he began, 'you don't open the fucking door to 'em. If you do, size 'em up and see if you can tell which one of 'em is the most approachable, then get him away from the other one.'

Approachable was Dad's word for 'bribeable'. In his world, everyone had their hand out. I attempted to explain that above all other branches of authority VAT inspectors had a cast-iron reputation for utter probity, but I didn't get to finish the thought. Eyes closed, shaking his head, he knew he was dealing with a complete novice in these matters.

'Ne'mind about reputations – everybody's on the lookout, don't you worry about that. You shoulda rung me up. I'd have come round and straightened one or the other. When there's two of 'em you can guarantee if one's a ponce the other will be one of the chaps. Every time. You just need to give a tug to the right one. Have a look at the motor they come in. If it's an old banger, ask whose it is. Then ask the other one what he drives. If it's a fucking Rolls-Royce – that's yer man.'

There may, of course, be something in this, but to put it to the test you have to have the sort of brazen fearlessness my dad displayed in all his dealings with authority. While hardly one to embarrass easily, I have no such nerve when attempting to circumvent the system.

The breathtaking extent of Dad's boldness was brought home to me when I was no more than seven years old. Very early one Sunday morning there came a repeated rap at the door. From Mum and Dad's bedroom window you could look straight down at the street door and, ascertaining the caller was wearing a tie, Spud figured he was after a payment of some kind; possibly a loan club, an insurance man or hire-purchase recovery. I imagine, as he walked around to my room to wake me up, he would have said, 'Fucking cheek, this time on a Sunday morning . . .' Rousing me from my dreams of Dusty Springfield, he told me to go down and tell the man he wasn't in. I'd done this many times before, but perhaps not quite so groggily. Taking the chain off the door, I opened up to him.

'Is your father up yet, son?' enquired the chap.

Waggling my little finger in my ear, I sleepily told him Dad was out. He seemed not to buy this. Plainly this was not his first time being fobbed off at our place, hence his unusually early start.

'Now look, boy, I know he is and you tell him that unless—'

That was as far as he got. Spud came thundering down the stairs and roared up to the front door.

'Listen, you big ponce!' he shouted, causing the man to back off into the square. 'That's my son you're talking to. He's seven years old and if he says I ain't in – I AIN'T IN!'

With that he slammed the door and went back to bed, leaving me to admire the extraordinary Wonderland perfection of what had just occurred.

There was no way of disabusing Dad of the notion that this was the way everyone carried on, so you didn't try. You just let him roll with it, generally with a growing realization that he might be right. He did suspect though that this method of defying the storms of working-class life, the ducking and diving as they say, was in the process of dying out. He was also aware that I was not quite constructed of the same intrepid, confrontational timber.

'So what you gonna do? How're ya getting Rod his few quid back?' he asked, intrigued.

'I dunno yet,' I replied. 'But it'll be all right.'

'Course it will,' said Spud, without a trace of doubt, adding as he turned to the racing pages of his paper: 'We can always forage, us lot. There's always a way.'

I'd heard him say this countless times when I was growing up, and it is such a fantastic trait to have had passed down to me. On the surface it appears to have no basis in reality and can seem little more than denial. Yet if you have it, you know it trumps anything as intangible as mere hope and defines almost every action and situation you face. When we eventually arrive at the moment I was told I had cancer, you'll see it kicks in rather well there too.

Anyway, about two days after the VAT men had pitched up like the broker's men in a panto, Emma Freud rang. She said she'd told them at GLR that I ought be on the radio and now they wanted to see me. 'It's absolutely shit money here,' she chirped, 'but you will be so good at it.'

So. OK. Radio. Let's have a bash at that.

Call Any Vegetable

The huge advantage I had when striding along Marylebone High Street toward Greater London Radio's studios to meet the controllers was that I had never really been a radio listener. Having no car in the family when growing up I had no experience of long holiday drives with familiar DJs thrashing their way through the Top 40, or even the usual tale of taking a transistor radio to bed to listen to a far-off friendly voice deep into the night. I had heard John Peel quite a few times, but he was nothing like the fixed date he was in most of my contemporaries' lives. I had heard some of Kenny Everett's invention-filled broadcasts too, but again they would have just been on in the background in a café or round someone else's house. In my own home as a kid it would have been the staid and reliable sounds of *Two-Way Family Favourites* and *Housewives' Choice* that Mum would have on to accompany the housework. The most evocative radio memory I can muster would be the intro to *Sing Something Simple* that filled our house every Sunday teatime while Spud prepared the shellfish supper. Actually, let me elaborate on that a little.

Sundays in Debnams Road – and I fancy in 95 per cent of working-class homes during the sixties – followed exactly the same routine every week. The day began fairly early with breakfast (the only time in the week that meal would be eaten). While a stack of kippers was not unknown, this would normally consist of a fry-up of sausages, bacon, eggs, beans, tinned tomatoes, fried bread, bread and butter and a big old teapot of tea. This sizzling repast would be served up one plate at a time to whoever claimed they were starving the most. None of the plates ever matched on the kitchen shelf and the flatware – 'eating irons', as Dad called them – was another conglomeration of misfits all mixed together in a drawer. The metal-and-Formica kitchen table never had a cloth on it and I never saw both of its fold-down sides extended at the same time. Rather than all get around it at once, and thus completely block off access to one side of the small room, you ate in shifts. The tea was never-ending, made with actual tea leaves in the pot, and the milk sat in its bottle, never decanted into a jug, smack beside the red and brown sauces, the sugar bowl, butter and tea strainer, all crowded into the centre of the narrow eating surface. A plate of fried breakfast, though mainly eaten off the plate, was good for at least three mid-meal sandwiches too. Laying a thickly buttered slice of Mother's Pride bread right next to your grub, you would lift piles of the hot mixture on to one end of this and then just fold it over. Chomping your way through this oozing bulging creation, you'd arrive all too soon at the last bit of crust, which would then be mopped into the pools of beans and tinned tomatoes for a final succulent mouthful. Having consumed at least half a loaf in this manner, you'd top up your mug of tea, rise up and say, 'What biscuits we got, Mum?'

At around eleven, after doing the washing up – 'Everyone fuck off out of it while I do this' – Dad would commandeer the bathroom for the elaborate Sunday-morning ablutions he employed prior to the Jolly Gardeners sliding its bolts off at noon. One of the few ter-rifying sounds I can recall from an otherwise idyllic childhood is my old man thundering: 'Who turned the fucking immersion heater off! Water's running stone-cold up here!' Fortunately, these explo-sions were rare, and as soon as he emerged from the bathroom Dad would get dressed up in full suit and hat with shoes that he had previously polished to army standards, rounding off the immacu-late vision perfectly. Quite when this ritual became the norm among working men I have no idea, but up until about 1975 the pubs on Sunday lunchtimes in those areas that housed factories, docks and heavy industries were jam-packed with blue serge, silver mohair and 100 per cent worsted, mingling in the combined mists of Old Spice, Brut and strong drink. And the pubs were packed. All of them.

Upon leaving the boozer, Spud, toting a carrier bag containing a few bottles of Guinness to have with his dinner, would head straight for the rickety shellfish stalls that were plonked on the pavement outside most public houses. There he would select from the various bowls of seafood, bagging up pints of prawns, cockles, eels, winkles and whelks, as well as a large pink-and-pale-cream boiled crab that would be our teatime centrepiece.

Then it would be home for the Sunday roast that Mum had down to a fine art. So much so that my abiding image of Bet on a Sunday is of her on the settee in our front room, legs tucked up beside her on the cushion, reading the *Sunday Mirror* while various pots and saucepans bubbled away in the kitchen beyond. Between one o'clock and three, the air along the communal landings on council estates hung rich and heavy with the smell of a thousand roasts wafting from open kitchen windows. It was an olfactory fog of gravy, Brussels, cabbage, carrots and trays of potatoes browning off around resting joints, stuffing being spooned out of tender chickens. By the time you got home from a drink, though it had been barely four hours since the hearty breakfast, you were *ravenous* and desperate to get among it.

Then everyone would have a bit of a kip.

At about six, people would start to rouse themselves. Mum and Dad would do all the washing up, then Bet would go upstairs to get herself ready for the upcoming night out. While she did, Dad would decant all the seafood from the sodden, yet famously hardy, small brown bags in which they were dispensed and start the laborious process of preparing our next meal of the day.

As with decorating, this was an activity which required Spud to be totally isolated, as though he were working with high explosives (which, given his temper, he was). Preparing shellfish for the table is just about the most labour-intensive task in the entire culinary canon. It is fiddly, smelly, messy work and can be very disheartening when you finally see the amount of edible return weighed against the mountains of shells, husks, bone and poisonous detritus the process produces. Were this not so, I maintain that the winkle sandwich would be as popular in Britain as the egg or sausage variety. A canopy of winkles, each one freshly disinterred from its black shell with the aid of a safety pin, sprawled over a slice of thickly buttered bread, splashed in vinegar before being concealed beneath the upper slice and squashed down, is as near ambrosia as any fare gets. On the down side, to liberate enough winkles for a single sandwich takes about two hours. Is it worth it? Yes. Do I want to do that? No. But for my old man the ritual had an almost sacred quality on Sunday evenings, and so we'd hear him out in the kitchen swearing and huffing, providing himself with a running commentary:

'Where'd that one go? It fell on the floor, where is it?' Or the constant refrain, 'I'm not doing this bastard job no fucking more!'

This was merely the build-up to the most difficult of his duties: prising every last bit of meat from a hard, unyielding crab. Today there exists an entire range of tools designed for this specific task, but back then Dad simply set about it with a hammer. The heavy thumping that boomed from the kitchen sounded as if he was mending his boots rather than preparing a meal.

Once the last bit of white flesh had been sprung, the final prawn peeled, each whelk separated from its tail and all the winkles winkled out, we would be summoned to make short work of the bounty. Mum, half made-up, would add a tin of salmon and an angel cake to the spread, and there, ladies and gentlemen, I would feast upon the finest food I have eaten in all my life. Dad, strangely, would never join in. Every week we went through the same conversation as he, shirtless, in a white vest and suit trousers with the braces dangling, made his speedy exit from the kitchen.

'Dad? Ain't you having none?'

'I'm all right. I'm going upstairs to have a wash. I'll pick on what's left, just leave a bowl of eels, that'll do me . . .'

Today, on the few occasions I try to recreate this banquet, I have to admit I cannot conjure up such noble discipline. The only thing he did take away from the room would be the small Sanyo transistor radio that peculiarly he would not have on while he was up to his elbows in crustaceans. Only when he retired to the bathroom and set about refreshing himself for the second pub session of the day – the Duke of Suffolk being the required step-up in venue when Mum went along too – would the transistor come to life with the lilting intro to 'Sing Something Simple' by the Cliff Adams Singers and a glorious secure calm would settle over the house. The tune retains its power to lull me like a narcotic to this very day.

None of this Proustian preamble was of any assistance to me as I arrived at 95 Marylebone High Street for my 'quick chat' with the GLR controllers, Trevor Dann and Matthew Bannister. The interview, such as it was – for I do rather tend to take over in these situations – went with a definite swing, I think, although I am under no illusions that it was my recent reputation as a London TV 'face' that they believed would give the local station a boost rather than any untapped broadcasting potential. For a network that called itself Greater London Radio, the place was noticeably lacking in people who sounded like natives of the capital. I was offered a three-hour breakfast spot at weekends starting at 6 a.m. I took it. Actually, I took it even before Matthew uttered a phrase that was starting become a refrain where this gig was concerned:

'The money's not great, I'm afraid,' he said with a guilty look toward his shoe.

And it really, really wasn't. I was offered £70 per show. Not per hour, not per record, not per word – per three-hour show. This was and remains the fathomless canyon in finances between national and local BBC services.

I took it all the same.

Arriving home, I bounded in, announcing to Wendy that I was back in the media business at the very highest level and we should immediately haul the kids home from school and all go out to celebrate. Overjoyed, she never thought to ask me how much I was getting for it, and I certainly wasn't going to spoil the moment by pointing out that this proposed meal would in itself eat up my first month's wages.

'Radio though, eh?' she said with a trace of scepticism. 'Do you know anything about that?'

The honest answer was 'Not a God Damned thing.' This guileless state of grace would turn out to be the greatest boon imaginable to my subsequent life at the mic.

However, I am not sure whether the bosses at GLR were aware that I had literally zero experience in their medium, beyond one catastrophic appearance on the show *Jelly-Bone* where, for the only time since Sumeria in 55 BC, someone's tongue really did cleave to the roof of their mouth.

I was due to start in two Saturdays' time and they asked whether I would be able to pop in again before then to 'get acquainted with the desk'. This desk, should you be unclear, is that thing you often see DJs sitting behind that features about the same amount of dials, knobs and meters as *Apollo*. By nature I am an extremely confident old horse, but in the days leading up to this proposed 'run-through' I started having definite anxiety dreams. I remember one in which Paul McCartney asked me to join him onstage at an imminent Wembley Stadium concert but asked if I could have a couple of sitar lessons first. My wife tells me I awoke from that one wailing like Oliver Hardy getting a thousand volts sent through him.

I went back to GLR on the Thursday before my programme was due to start. It was lunchtime and Emma Freud was on the air. Trevor Dann thought it would be a good idea if I went in to her show so she could unveil me before GLR's modest audience. This peppy five-minute exchange saw Emma and I cooing at each other a good deal before she finally asked me to introduce the next record, which I did in the style of an old-fashioned Radio 1 jock, right down to getting the name of the track and artist out just before the first word of the song kicked in. When I emerged from this spot Matthew Bannister was beaming. 'You did that well enough!' he said, chuckling. I laughed too. Yet at that happy, relaxed moment, neither of us could have had a clue that over the next twenty-five years I would never do such a conventional and routine thing again.

From there he led me to a dim, vacant studio and sat me down in front of all the forbidding technical hardware.

'I take it you'll not be driving yourself at first?' he said. GLR, with its minuscule budgets, preferred all presenters to manage themselves.

'Not at first,' I trilled, setting him up for the punchline. 'I think I'll only need help until the oceans boil and the sun turns to blood.'

With another snort of comforting laughter Matthew walked across to a short row of grey house-phones perched on a shelf.

'Hi, mate,' I heard him say quietly into one after a few moments, 'I've got Danny Baker here. I wonder if you've got five minutes to brief him about the desk? Great. Thanks.' Putting the receiver down, he made for the door.

'I've got to get back to it,' he said, exiting. 'Somebody will be up in a moment to take you through it.'

Sitting alone, I marvelled at the array of gadgetry packed tightly on to the wood-framed board. I recognized the long thin slits with plastic squares that slid along their length as the 'faders' you dragged up and down to make records play. But there were about twelve of those here. What did they all do? As for the legion of other knobs, switches and buttons, the contraption looked exactly like a Moog synthesizer, the monstrous and complicated instrument that in my early teens I had literally dreamed of owning one day. Idly, I twisted something at random. Had I just turned up the broadcast volume of the whole station? Had I put the news woman on air just as she was in the middle of swapping a juicy story with her colleague? Curiously, an excited imp in me hoped that I had. I must have remained alone at the controls for about five minutes, when suddenly the studio door sighed open and in walked a gangly youth wearing Buddy Holly's glasses and Ivan the Red's spare hairpiece. I was later to learn that he had not been in London long, arriving down from Manchester too late to marvel at the tail end of my *SOCS* tenure. Thus he had absolutely no idea who I might be, just as I had no inkling that this kid, whose energy levels instantly struck me as rivalling the nation's finest, would come to be like a younger brother as we tumbled toward the millennium.

'Hello!' he barked, striding toward me, hand held straight out for a vigorous shaking. 'I'm Chris Evans.'

Baby's On Fire

Though by 1988 the switch from LPs to compact discs was in full flood, a substantial part of my record collection was still in that old – and these days happily revitalized – vinyl format. Much of the stock liberated from the record shop where I had once worked had remained in my old bedroom at Mum and Dad's council flat, simply because I had never lived anywhere that could comfortably house such an impressive library. Now that I had a job where I would need them all again, I set about uniting the old favourites under one roof – or to be precise, in one cellar at Scawen Road. Two incidents that happened while attempting this seemingly straightforward task nearly killed me.

The first was when I called round to Debnams Road to box up all the hundreds and hundreds of albums that had lain undisturbed since I'd bid adieu to that period in my life when every music release seemed vital. Or at least that's how I perceived it then. When you fall in love and have children, your wild dancing years appear suddenly juvenile and, like the memory of a distant old playground, while the affection remains, you find it hard to conjure up the potency the attraction once held for you. Happily, for me this turned out to be but a temporary amnesia and before long I'd be climbing back over the park gates to ride on those noisy swings and roundabouts all over again. Indeed I believe that my mania for music began to reboot itself that very evening as I sat packing up all those rediscovered LPs from my teenage bedroom floor. Then again, had I not lovingly lingered over the richly evocative album covers, track listings and long-forgotten liner notes, I probably wouldn't have been there when the explosion happened.

Real-life explosions, I have found, do not always resound with the ear-shattering edge they display in feature films, where an increasingly jaded audience require more bang for their buck. The one that I registered as I sat looking at the small print on Curtis Mayfield's *Sweet Exorcist* album – *all selections arranged by Rich Tufo except * arranged by Gil Askey* – was more of a muffled 'dooomph', like somebody striking a bass drum while secreted beneath a tarpaulin. Nevertheless, you are immediately aware that all is not well. There is something in the tone of the thing that lets you know that this is not simply a hat stand falling over and you really ought to go and see what that was. So I did. As I emerged from my old bedroom on to the small upstairs landing my mum was already at the bottom of the stairs looking up.

'Was that you?' she said, as though Curtis Mayfield albums had the habit of exploding unexpectedly.

Before I could say no, I smelled something acrid and intense. Standing stock-still I just let my eyes swivel left and right, looking for the source, and calmly said, 'Fire.'

Perhaps because of the soft way I had said it, Mum failed to grasp the urgency. 'Fire? Don't say that. What d'you mean, fire?'

'Something's on fire!' I underlined, this time with added alarm to let her know I wasn't just ordering troops to discharge a cannon. Bolting across to their bedroom, I flung open the door. Now every know-all will tell you that if you suspect a room is ablaze the last thing you should do is open the door to find out, but the trouble with know-alls is they haven't ever had to put this lofty theory to the test while their entire LP collection might be about to melt like a field of Dalí clocks. As soon as the bedroom door got halfway open it almost blew itself shut again as a rush of searing air bellowed out. Stopping this action with my foot, I could see the whole far side of the room was rippling with flame similar to those upright grills they have in kebab shops. At this point I started shouting 'Fire!' repeatedly like Clive Dunn in *Dad's Army*.

Now here's a strange thing. As I slammed the door shut again, not so much as a sensible precaution but more in the hope it would just go away, one image filled my head. Wendy had had a fire at her house when she was young and her father, the pipe-smoking, utterly bald Jim, had attempted to put it out himself. As he aimed buckets of water at the blaze, the heat, having risen to ceiling level first, made the plastic shade they had around their central light-fitting turn molten and it plopped down in one on to his hairless head like a scalding turban. Apparently he dashed about screaming, 'Me nut! Get it off me nut!' Though his sons subsequently swiftly dealt with the flames, the scars to his bonce remained for the rest of his life. Nobody ever told this tale with the slightest sympathy for the old father-of-ten and even he used to chuckle as he recounted that he had to hold his head under the bathroom tap to cool the mass down, whereupon it set hard and had to be removed at the local A&E. This was the only thing running through my mind as Mum now ran up and down the stairs shrieking, 'Oh my Gawd! Somebody help us!'

Dad meanwhile had legged it past her in the passage downstairs and was banging on the neighbour's door, shouting at them to dial 999 – our own phone was an instrument only intermittently connected, depending on Dad's willingness to pay the bill on time. Incredibly a fire engine came flying down the turning within a couple of minutes because somebody in the block opposite had seen the curtains burning some time before and, believing there might be no one home, had raised the alarm. The upshot of all this was my parents' bedroom was almost completely gutted, but the rest of the home remained untouched.

So what had happened? Well, those of you whose lips purse at my father's deviance from the straight-and-narrow norm might find some succour in the fact that this fire came as a direct result of Spud being 'at it'. Having had one of his occasional 'burglaries' a few weeks before the conflagration, he had asked friends and neighbours to harbour some of his household goods while the insurance inspector made note of what had been 'taken'. This was a very common favour across the estate and quite often as a child I would come home to find we temporarily owned all manner of extra TV sets, radiograms, clothing and canteens of cutlery. I remember we had to 'look after' somebody's Bontempi home organ once and my brother and I became really attached to it while this monster dominated our front room. Neither of us could play it and we weren't allowed to even plug it in while Dad was home.

'I've got to give that back to Alfie in a few days. If it's fucking out of tune when I do, he'll go wild.'

I never figured quite how it could go 'out of tune', but there it is. Anyway, after salting away some of the more valuable things he possessed, as well as inventing quite a few he didn't, Dad struck on the idea that it would be entirely feasible if the thieves had carried off his and Mum's very latest addition to the home and hearth: a tumble dryer. For some reason he thought he could just hide this in one of the rooms 'the burglars' hadn't touched, and so with his mate Paddy Buckingham assisting, the pair of them hauled the bulky bit of white goods up the stairs and into the small main bedroom. Just in case the insurance assessor was 'a nosy bastard', Dad stuck it right in the corner and put an angled tallboy wardrobe in front of it. The dryer was supposed to be moved back downstairs several days previous to the fire, but this hadn't happened and apparently Mum had started using it again where it was. While sticking the moisture exit hose into a bucket worked well enough to keep the thing running, the heat-escape vents were jammed up against the long bedroom curtains – conveniently fashioned from a combustible man-made fibre. Mum's laundry must have had the dryer put in a good shift the evening of the blaze and it was the curtains that went up first – thankfully spotted early by Mrs Windsor in Gillam House. I had only been alerted when the flames bested the tumble dryer itself, causing the boom, before moving on to the next job of razing Mum's tallboy to the ground.

The only good to come of it was that Dad had another insurance claim to get stuck into, though he never seemed to derive the same satisfaction from a legitimate one.

While we're dealing with Notable Explosions I Recall From My Youth, I must once more park the chronological narrative and bring you the tale of Paul Fennel's hand grenade. Paul was one of the crowd of us estate kids who made the local open spaces, which had lain undeveloped since the Second World War – literally bomb sites – our meeting places and playgrounds. There was one of these overgrown, rubble-strewn areas immediately adjacent to our flats in the shadow of the railway arches. It was here that *Going to Sea in a Sieve* began with that game of dare in a burning car.[2] One day – and I can't claim to have been present at the time – some of the lads were thrashing around amid the longer grass, digging for centipedes and beetles to put into matchboxes, when, as I understood it, they unearthed a hand grenade. Quite what it was it was doing there nobody can explain, but it was very real and loads of us went round to Paul's house to ask to see it. He was only too happy to oblige, taking us up to his bedroom where he would retrieve it from the box he kept it in under his bed. Without fail, every kid would pretend to pull the pin from it, although this would have been difficult because the device was far from pristine. How long it had been half-buried on the bombsite was anybody's guess, but on the several occasions I saw it up close it was a sorry-looking decrepit old lump of metal, that's for sure.

After secretly curating the grenade for a few weeks, Paul was eventually found out by his mum, Ivy, who came across it while she was Hoovering under his bed. Furious that her child had a bomb in his bedroom, she demanded he come upstairs and explain himself immediately. Paul babbled that it wasn't real and he was only looking after it for someone, but Ivy said that was no excuse, she didn't want it in the house and he should either give it back to whoever he got it from or just get rid of it. Paul took the missile and said she would never see it again. What he meant by that of course was that he would find a better hiding place for it.

After stashing it behind a couple of big flower pots in his back garden for a few days, Paul snuck it back in again and hid it behind a row of books in his bedside cabinet. He then placed several toy knights in armour in front of the hardbacks – he and I shared a common hobby in collecting plastic medieval soldiers – and left it

[2] Several people have pointed out that I never did get round to explaining what eventually happened in that bombsite game of chicken. Well, here's your spoiler alert: I did not die.

there, confident that his prized possession might be handily accessed for a fondle before bed each night while completely bamboozling any house-proud mums who went snooping about. Mrs Fennel found it again approximately forty-eight hours later.

This time she decided to deal with the matter herself. Doubtless muttering, 'The sneaky little sod,' she made her way down to the front door, up the short front path outside and bunged it in the metal dustbin by her gate. 'There – gone!' she would have said.

The next day was a Saturday and like many men on the estate, Paul's dad used the day off to set about some tasks in the garden. For a start, the grass had to be cut and plants thinned out and dead-headed. This he did and after hours of such toil he gathered all the garden waste he'd amassed and squashed it down into the same metal bin by the front gate that held our Paul's hand grenade.

Now then. I have never concocted a compost heap myself, but I have been invited many times to shove my hand into the base of one to marvel at the nuclear heat they miraculously manage to generate all on their own. Inside Mr & Mrs Fennel's tin bin, the bacteria and chemical process involved started heating the container up almost immediately.

It was about 2 a.m. on the following Thursday that everyone on the estate got woken up by the explosion. Rather impressively, one window as far away as Silwood Street was shattered as the great KABOOM! echoed off the arches and bounced off all the blocks. Everyone came out of their homes and stood about speculating as to what it might be. Detonators up on the railways tracks, often used in daylight hours to warn of work in progress, was the favourite theory. Some thought that Cyprus Alex's hot-dog van – an unsavoury, jerry-built affair that featured some poorly realized cartoon characters painted on the side along with its menu: 'Hot Doks' and 'Hamburgas' – must have exploded at last.

A couple of the neighbours joked that it sounded like a bomb going off, although nobody believed one actually had. Over in Westlake Road where Paul lived, the evidence was harder to deny. The dustbin itself had vanished, leaving a little hole in the earth. All the front garden fencing for yards either side had been knocked down flat and barely a window remained intact in Paul's house and the two or three either side. Alarm bells rang in the one or two arch-based businesses that bothered with such things. Needless to say, when we learned the facts, we kids thought it was just about the greatest thing that had ever happened on the estate. Even sweeter, Paul's parents were given all the blame for their lack of liaison re household bomb disposal.

I suppose a more superstitious type than I might have seen the detonation at my parents' house on the night I gathered my records as a sinister omen for my new job. The portents grew even more ominous when I got the vinyl back to my home in Scawen Road. The plan was to put the LPs in the cellar that ran under the entire length of the house, a long space but not deeply excavated enough to allow a person to stand upright. For much of the twentieth century it had apparently been little more than a coal hole and I'd enjoyed exploring it by torchlight when we had first taken possession. Propped up against a back wall I discovered several large framed Victorian prints of a young girl sitting beside a Husky and then posing on a swing. A small sturdy box of keepsakes was packed with rosary beads, costume jewellery and many cards of condolence marking decades of bereavement. There were also some photographs on glass plates, a couple of which showed a wedding taking place in what was recognizably the back garden of the house.

We had started to use the subterranean space for storing various tea chests of our own things – 'just for now', as they say; probably as the original owners had with all these forgotten bits and pieces a hundred years before. Having prepared a large area for the arrival of my record collection, it was hard work carrying load after load from Dad's car boot, along the hallway, down the narrow stairway that led into the cellar and then having to complete the last bit of the journey almost completely doubled over in order to stay clear of the supporting beams that criss-crossed the basement ceiling. I didn't manage every circuit successfully and after about the tenth time I had shouted out, 'Fuckin' hell, I've hit my head AGAIN!' Wendy gently asked whether I was planning on visiting my vinyl on a regular basis, because if so, a dangerous, pitch-black, four-foot-high crawl space was probably not the ideal storage venue. I reminded her that she did not want them – and there were thousands of them – in any of the otherwise tastefully decorated rooms in the house. So below decks they went, setting me up nicely for what remains the only time I have ever been knocked spark out in my entire life.

On the Friday night before I was due to start the first radio show of my career I had just finished sorting out all the records I thought I would need when I found myself humming 'Who's Gonna Love Me (When You're Gone)' by a soul group called the Imperials. I couldn't shake it from my mind and, it having been a minor hit in 1978, I decided I would have to remind everyone of it when I made my debut the following morning. The thing that made me smile most about the record was its spoken introduction where the singer has just discovered his wife is leaving him:

Where you going, baby? No – you can't take the car! Take the kids! Take all these bills on the table over here! We've been together too long for you to walk out on me now . . .

It then leads into a gorgeous breezy melody of the kind I favoured 100 per cent over the relentless punk stuff I was ostensibly immersed in at the time of its release. I HAD to find it. Down into the cellar I went. Directly before this latest descent, I had the following shouted conversation with Wendy, who was upstairs in one of the bedrooms:

'Wend!'

'What?'

'Where's the torch?'

'What torch?'

'The torch I use for the cellar!' Then tetchily: 'How many torches have we got?'

'All right, calm down. You had it, don't ask me.'

'Well, somebody's moved it! It was here.'

'Where?'

'At the top of the cellar stairs – on the gas meter. Has one of the kids had it?'

'Dan – how could the kids reach up to the gas meter? You had it, don't blame them.'

I remembered at this point what I'd done. The last time I'd gone down there I had been trying to locate a bell – the kind they have on hotel reception desks. The reason for this will become apparent later. Anyway, I'd started my search in an area where I had an adequate pool of light coming down from the cellar door and so I had put the torch on the floor while I went through a box of things. Lo and behold, I found the bell in question pretty quickly, but I had obviously neglected to pick up my torch again as I scuttled back to street level. I couldn't possibly allow Wendy to know this.

'Well, it's not here now!' I thundered. 'Someone's had it and now I really need it. I've got work in the morning, you know!'

Point made and, as far as I was concerned, argument won, I began to make my descent into the darkness. When I arrived at the box where the bell had been stored I looked around the floor for the errant illuminator. It was nowhere. Many months later I discovered that when I'd hurriedly stuffed all the things that weren't the hotel bell back into the container, like an idiot, I'd scooped up the torch and packed that away along with the rest. As I sat on the cellar floor that night, though, I was absolutely flummoxed.

For a moment it occurred to me that perhaps I should just abandon the quest and go without the Imperials' single. I dismissed this ridiculous idea almost immediately. Raising myself into the required stooping right angle, I now started groping ahead to where my records were. The plan was to locate the tea chest in which all my singles were stacked and carry individual armfuls back to base camp at the bottom of the stairs. There in the half-light I would sort through until the Golden Sound was found. One difficulty here was that the singles were not with the LPs but in an area I hadn't visited since depositing them down into this inky underworld. Bent double, one arm waving in front of me like a wizard conjuring up a toad, I inched onwards into total darkness.

Now let us go back in time from that moment as I shuffled about in the Stygian gloom to a few months previously – the Christmas holidays, in fact; my favourite time of the year. Though I always long to prolong the festivities, on Twelfth Night, following the big day, I refuse to allow the decorations to remain up a second longer than tradition allows. Wendy and her sister Carol had taken the children off to the pictures and I said the house would be decoration-free when they returned. This was quite a boast because I am only truly terrified of three things in life: lightning, wasps and balloons that suddenly go bang. I would literally rather put my head in a lion's mouth than sit beside someone who refuses to concede when a balloon is fully inflated. However, when Sonny and Bonnie were small they liked to see these treacherous gasbags on display, signifying as it did for them that a celebration of some sort was in the offing. This particular year I feel we had rather overdone it with the amount of ghastly, distended orbs hanging about the place; when I set about gingerly removing the drawing pins that anchored them to various points, I found there must have been north of twenty. Against all odds, I bravely managed to pop three of this number, but the agonizing and nervous sweats involved in doing even that trio had meant the process took over twenty minutes, by which time I was on the verge of passing out. You couldn't just bin them because I worked out that our council wheelie would only take about six fully inflated balloons, and that was probably enough to cause the fixture to float up and away across Deptford like a refuse-tip UFO. So I decided to postpone the day of reckoning by gathering them up and chucking them to the back of the cellar where there was nothing else of interest and where they could just deflate of their own accord over the coming weeks. Because that's what balloons do eventually, isn't it? They start to sag and then gently collapse as the air within escapes via minuscule flaws in the once secure knot. Don't you believe it!

Let us now return to me, all those months later, slowly making my way, step by step, step by step, bent double and blind across the pitch-dark cellar landscape. When I had previously stated that nothing of interest was stored at the far end of the space I meant it. A tea chest full of classic 45s came under that heading in the brief lunatic period when I thought I had put vinyl collecting to one side with all other childish fascinations. Indeed, I had already *thrown away* one bulging suitcase of singles a year previously, and when I come to tell you what eventually happened to them I promise you will consider it a flight of fancy worthy of Jules Verne.

Anyway, determined to reinstate my remaining legion of seven-inchers to their rightful throne, I crept toward them in the darkness. As the enforced crouch grew ever more uncomfortable, I almost called out, 'Patience, my beauties, I am coming, I am coming! Daddy swears you will never be forgotten like this again!'

The very last thought on my mind was those seventeen unseen rubber landmines that, far from becoming baggy with age, were as taut and fulsome as the moment Spud had tied off their straining ends. I suppose through sheer dumb luck I must have managed to avoid treading on the first four or five of them, but such oblivious good fortune was never going to last.

I'm not sure how long I lay unconscious on the cold stone floor, but Wend says that even though she was upstairs with the telly on she definitely remembers hearing a loud thud and a moan at about five minutes to eight. She came downstairs again just after eight and gave a short scream as she encountered me emerging from the cellar, dazed, covered in coal dust, bleeding from the forehead and with the bedraggled remnants of some party streamers and a burst balloon hanging limply around my shoulders. Assisting me to a kitchen chair she anxiously kept asking me what had happened. This concern melted into a poorly muffled hysteria when I, still reeling, tried to piece things together.

'I'm not sure,' I said, my head starting to throb. 'I was making my way across the cellar and I think I trod on a balloon from Christmas. I must have shot upright and hit me head on a beam. I've been spark out.'

To her credit, Wendy did make a pretty good job of not laughing the house down. Instead she cleaned the angry graze on my noggin and got me a cold flannel to help the swelling go down. It was only later, as I lay on the settee wondering if my concussion was going to clear sufficiently for my debut show the next morning that I heard her on the phone upstairs, ringing each of her six sisters in turn and relating what had happened to me between huge whoops of helpless laughter.

In nine years of television I hadn't so much as broken a fingernail by way of industrial injury and here, even before I'd said a single word as a DJ, I had twice faced a premature death.

Maybe someone or something was trying to tell me I wasn't cut out for this.

Black Sheep

In the early seventies an obscure American record label called Increase released a short series of LPs called Cruisin'. Each record took a particular year from the early days of rock'n'roll and featured a single radio show by a well-known disc jockey from the period, complete with station jingles and nostalgic commercials. There had been a steady sale of these evocative time-capsules when I worked in One Stop Records, mainly because they were not available from the usual music outlets and had to be imported from the USA. I loved these LPs and one in particular, *Cruisin' 1963*, that featured a hyper-manic DJ called B. Mitchell Read. From the moment his performance started he spoke at breakneck speed, yet wittily and entirely in character, featuring a lunatic array of bells, hooters and table thumps to punctuate his tumbling monologues. It was exactly the kind of crazed bravura I always believed radio ought to sound like, a full-tilt audio whirlwind where the host strains every nerve to match the pounding sounds slapped on to turntables seemingly at random. This was my only guide and desire as my debut approached and, thanks to my utter ignorance at how radio shows really do get put together, I genuinely believed it was simply a matter of hauling in a box of your favourite records and making up the hoopla, in the moment, as you went along. It was just you and the audience, and once that red light went on you had better have something to say to surprise them or why the hell were you there getting paid instead of one of their number? From the snatches I had heard of the current radio scene, it seemed that too many of the show anchors were content to appear rather than work. Thus, as I sat at 6.27 a.m. watching the minutes tick down to my very first appearance as a 'jock', though

I had no idea what I was going to say I had a very good idea of how I was going to say it. I saw no point easing listeners into their day – which seemed to be the accepted norm – so, taking in the deathly quiet of the GLR building, I thought I may as well swim against the tide. Or better yet, ride a powerboat against it. I think even Chris Evans, himself then still full of untapped anarchy, was shocked at the firework display I leapt into once he gave me the nod to indicate we were now on the air. Picking up one of the various hand bells I had brought with me, I began ringing it for all I was worth. Then, over the intro to the opening record, Fleetwood Mac's 'Don't Stop', I began shouting:

'Get up! Get up, you deadbeats! You weasels! Get up! New sheriff in town! Stop slumbering, crumbs! None but hollow-eyed creep VAMPIRES should sleep now. Hark! Hark! The dogs do bark! I'll come to your house and rattle your beds! I'll chase you up trees! Nothing matters any more! Everything you know is wrong! Throw away your lives and follow the noise! Bell-ringer radio! It's Campanology FM!'

I closed the mic again, the song began its vocals, and both Chris and I crumbled in fits of laughter.

'What the FUCK was that?' he said.

'I don't know,' I managed to splutter, 'but I'm having a go.'

I suddenly felt more alive at work than I had in years. Quite where I was summoning up all this poppycock from I chose not to examine, but it felt wonderful.

As the Fleetwood Mac track faded – that had been Chris' choice and one that fit right in with the station's signature mature-rock sound – I challenged what audience there was even further by whacking into Donna Summer's 'This Time I Know It's for Real', a chart hit by the disco producers Stock Aitken Waterman and just about the antithesis of GLR's music policy. It was, however, in my view, a terrific radio song full stop, and ought not go unheard just because it might unsettle the weak-minded. As it detonated on to the air, I rang two bells at once.

'Are you listening, Capital Radio?' I bellowed, taking the unusual step of taunting by name the giant market leader in London radio at the time. 'You worms, Capital! The game's up, blood suckers! New sheriff in town! You have sores on your faces and I will hunt you to the ends of the earth! You Nazis! You fascists! The abyss yawns before you! Make way! Make way!'

We were six minutes into the show and the phone lines, usually a moribund parade that occasionally flickered into life when someone wished to comment on the new cycle lanes in Enfield, were suddenly jammed, lights blinking like epileptic semaphore lamps. Without exception, everyone hated it. They wished to complain and make me go away, and Chris was completely tied up doing his best to placate and soothe one caller after another. I, meanwhile, careered on, honking hooters while banging that recently unearthed hotel reception bell, going from the Mothers of Invention to Cajun two-steps to Barbra Streisand's 'Don't Rain on My Parade', during which I left the microphone open and sang along lustily, urging the audience to do the same. It was not even seven o'clock yet.

The programme sounded absolutely out of control, and though I was totally aware this cacophony would alienate most of the tiny market share the station traditionally played to, I hoped that at least a rump of the listeners would find this explosion bold and funny and fresh. Whatever the harvest, I was determined the show was not going to be ignored.

A few days later Trevor and Matthew took me out to a coffee shop to sack me. Chris was asked along too and what he witnessed there he says influenced his outlook in dealing with authority for the next twenty years. That may not necessarily have been a good thing.

I knew exactly why the two bosses had asked me for a chat and because we otherwise all seemed to get along well, I wasn't going to let it spoil our friendship or sour the cappuccinos before us.

Matthew began the formalities. 'Danny. I think you need to learn how our station is structured and what we're trying to achieve with our audience—'

Interrupting, I cut to the chase:

'Matthew, I totally understand and this must be awkward for everyone. But what you heard really is the only show I have in me. I know it's nuts and I know I called Capital Radio Nazis and said

Radio 2 was full of long-dead mummies, but I thought it was funny, I really did. Now I am completely happy to walk away from this. You have no option but to chuck it out, I'm sure, but that's the show and I just don't have the machinery to tone it down. So fire me now and let's talk about old bands we all like.'

This rather took the wind out of whatever Matthew and Trevor had prepared by way of advice or discipline. There was a pause. Chris' eyes went around everyone at the table about five times. Then Trevor took it up.

'Well, hang on a minute. There's got to be a way of, you know, making that show work, you know, for our station.'

I told them that I had absolutely no concept of how that could possibly happen and, to be fair, they both laughed at this obvious impasse.

'Look,' continued Matthew, 'perhaps we could just ease up on bollocking the audience and calling other stations vampires.' And he chuckled at even having to say such a ridiculous sentence.

'And the Donna Summer records,' chimed in Trevor. After a moment he did concede, 'You know, the more we talked about it, the more we actually rather liked it. It was just a bit . . .'

'Unexpected,' finished his colleague.

I asked them outright: 'Had you decided to give me the sack?'

'Oh, completely,' said Trev. 'I was ready to pull the plug after about five minutes.'

So we finished our coffees and our toasted sandwiches and they said they would be listening with keen interest again at the weekend. About ten weeks later, some sort of interim listening figures were released and there, as the station's usual level of audience flatline came out from the stagnant overnight programming, a tiny peak of interest appeared at 6.30 a.m. Nothing that signified anything sensational – but something nonetheless. And it hadn't been there before.

One Sunday during those initial weeks of Sturm und Drang, Chris and I had, as usual, repaired to the pub across the road after the show. As we nursed the cold drinks, talking about anything other than work, a woman came across to our table and very politely asked me to confirm who I was.

'I thought it was you,' she said nervously. 'We used to watch you every Friday in our house. Are they ever going to bring that show back?'

I suggested that the possibility was a remote one.

'Sorry to be a pain,' our pleasant interloper continued, 'but could I have your autograph?'

I was of course happy to do this. I had signed hundreds of bits of paper during the *Six O'Clock Show* run, but since its termination the requests had somewhat dwindled. And when I say 'somewhat dwindled' I mean I now got asked at about the same frequency as long-dead members of the shadow cabinet.

I scrawled upon the back of the woman's proffered envelope and she withdrew, seemingly satisfied. When I looked back at Chris he was wearing an expression as if I had just caused the table we were sitting at to levitate up to the ceiling.

'Fuck-ing hell!' he gasped. 'What the fuck happened there?'

His eyes were wide behind his Buddy Holly glasses and his mouth literally open in astonishment. Chris hadn't been in London when I was the capital's favourite child star, and though he knew I had been on some regional show, he had never considered until that point that I might have any kind of public profile. He looked thoroughly, mightily impressed.

'What the fuck does THAT feel like?' he said, lifting his bottle of beer to clink with mine. A sort of heavenly choir looked to have started playing trombones inside his head. His mouth flooded with the ambrosia of ambition. I could see there and then that he wanted some of that. He howled a long laugh of excitement and, pushing his baseball cap further back on his head, he sat and stared at me.

'You're famous, buddy!' he chirped, as if our fun had somehow just ratcheted up a few notches. I made no effort to adjust his statement into the proper tense.

Jump forward a decade from this otherwise unremarkable encounter and you would be hard pressed to avoid images of Chris Evans, now Britain's number one TV talent, splashed over tabloid front pages as he exits some of the smartest venues in the capital as well as many of its murkiest dives. Look a little closer at these pictures and there, lagging in the gloom behind him, is what at first glance appears to be a fat old tramp looking for a handout. That'll be me. In the captions and articles that accompanied these shots documenting Chris' daily adventures, this unfortunate itinerant is rarely given a name but often contemptuously dismissed as 'One of Chris Evan's growing entourage of new "friends" hanging on to his famous shirt-tail . . .'

And that, my friends, is as good a guide to the giddy roulette wheel of show business as I can offer you.

Back home in Scawen Road life continued to bounce along beautifully despite me earning slightly less than the postman who continued to bring Mervyn's charming if increasingly puzzled letters from the bank. We had completed our family picture by buying a mongrel from Battersea Dog's Home. We called him Twizzle. Bonnie and Sonny loved Twizzle and Twizzle loved them. But that was about as far as Twizzle was ever going to open his heart; aside from those two, plus Wendy, he disliked every other human being in the world and at every opportunity tried to expel them from his orbit. A lithe, chocolate-brown sort of greyhound/Labrador/Staffordshire compendium – we never did discover what had gone into his construction – Twiz was not so much a dog as a missile. As soon as he was fully grown he developed a remarkable habit of launching himself at the front door whenever anyone came within two yards of it – and when I say launched, I mean not only snarling and barking with front paws outstretched but often flying through the air, broadside-on, at the letter box as if he had been fired from a cannon. When he made contact with the door a noise like a sonic boom would rattle through the whole house. We soon got used to this but visitors – who always had to be entertained shut inside rooms lest Twizzle wandered in – would drop their teacups and pieces of cake as the sudden racket startled them. Observing the terrified flight of some hawker who had opted to leg it rather than shove another pizza menu into our home, they would say, 'Are you sure it's all right to have that dog in your house? I mean, it is a dog, isn't it? Sounds more like you've got Mike Tyson locked in the passage.'

I hadn't set out to buy an intimidating canine; there were no outward signs as to his temperament and throughout his life everyone who saw him – mainly through windows or in photographs – could not believe that the medium-sized, ordinary-looking animal they saw sleeping in his wicker basket was the terror from number 46.

Twizzle and I eventually got along famously, but only after he had staged a failed putsch to gain control of the household. I was stretched out on the sofa one Thursday night watching *Top of the Pops*, a bowl of popcorn balanced on my chest, when into the room came Twiz. He was walking ominously slower than usual and after completing a couple of strange circuits of the carpet he came and sat about two feet away from where I was sprawled. I knew he was staring hard at me but I wouldn't look round at him because I sensed something was up and knew that anything I did to acknowledge this would signal the next step in whatever he was planning. So for quite a few moments there was something of a stand-off; Twiz defying me to look at him and me taking an artificially keen interest in the gentle funk and hopeless miming of Level 42. Twizzle then started to growl very low. This growl said, 'You know I'm here, you bastard. Let's do this.' I continued to let this go on even through a filmed contribution from the group Poison, whose strangulated stadium rock I would normally have given the juiciest of raspberries. While this horrible power ballad droned on, I surreptitiously grasped the edge of one of the sofa's cushions with the aim of springing a counter-offensive before he had a chance to launch the main thrust of his attack.

Cushion in position, I decided to give Twiz the benefit of the doubt and snapped my head around to confront his gaze. His eyes were cold, dead and narrowed. Ignoring this, I confronted his mood outright.

'What exactly do you want, you moody old git?'

This was what he'd been waiting for. Leaping toward the sofa he thudded his two front legs down hard on my chest and, thinking I was now pinned, bared his teeth, snarling, from about six inches away. I knew this was a coup and, like any ruling authority faced with the same threat, recognized I had to crush it immediately. Letting go of the cushion, I balled up my fist and let him have it right in the ear.

Instead of going full-on with the knuckles I had landed the blow with my thumb wrapped across my curled fingers. This lessened the impact while letting him know I still had plenty in reserve. Twizzle jumped down and ran over to the fireplace, where he shook his head several times. When he turned again I saw his eyes were back to normal and his demeanour the usual loose-limbed playful mutt he was 95 per cent of the time.

I never had any more trouble with Twiz after that – at least, not in terms of the power struggle. He was to have plenty of other adventures with us though. One day we came home and on unlocking the front door were alarmed to find he wasn't doing his normal 'Welcome back!' dance in the hall. Indeed, he wasn't anywhere to be seen, although we could hear a noise from the front room like a ceiling fan having a fight with a series of shower curtains. This description wasn't too far from the actuality: on dashing in to find out the cause, we discovered Twizzle had become completely entangled in the white plastic blinds in the lounge windows. He was hanging in mid-air, his head looking toward us through the slats, one paw poking out further down and both back legs wrapped up in the string you raised and lowered the things with. I got the blame for this, having left the front-room door open when we went out.

'You know he'll try and get anyone who knocks,' said Wendy huffily as she set about the difficult task of freeing our imprisoned pet as he wriggled and swayed high up in the window. 'He must have gone to jump through these blinds and got all mixed up. Struggling made it worse for him – he could have hung himself!'

In fact it would be another two years before he succeeded in hanging himself, in what I count as one of the greatest metaphysical events of recent times.

Twizzle was not quite the undisputed leader of the lunatic animal fraternity in our neighbourhood. There was one other challenger for this crown, a more traditionally built mad dog called, of course, Rambo. This solidly built pitbull terrier lived in a junkyard close to the back of our house. The people who operated the business also owned the alley that led up to it and this long thin lane separated the row of back gardens in our street from those in adjacent Trundley's Road. It was in this narrow thoroughfare, littered with old fridges, car parts and pallet boards, that Rambo was allowed to roam, noisily taunting all his pampered domesticated peers who bordered the park in comfort.

Although Rambo's home turf was directly behind our high garden fence, it was further sealed off and hidden from view by a long row of strategically planted trees, so even though you couldn't escape Rambo's incessant barking, he could only ever be glimpsed if you took the trouble to walk around to the gates of his scrap-metal kingdom.

Twizzle had never actually seen Rambo, but he certainly knew he was there. Alone among all the dogs in the area he would argue long and loud with his unseen bête noire, standing right at the far reaches of his own turf to the rear of our place, while on the other side of the thin tree line Rambo replied in kind. It was a tremendous racket and two or three times a day either Wendy or myself would have to physically bundle Twiz back indoors as he fought to continue his squabble to the last breath. One day, Twizzle – who, temper notwithstanding, was a supremely intelligent dog – spotted a way to break the verbal deadlock and have this thing out once and for all. Though he had many times thrown himself at the back fence in an effort to break clean through it, the old railway sleepers that shored up the bulwark showed no signs of giving way just yet. So Twiz, weighing the thing up and looking at the problem from all angles, came to the conclusion that he would have to go over the barrier, through a small gap in the trees that he judged sufficient to see him through. This would be no mean feat for a medium-sized dog, and would require he add several inches to his previous personal best: the wall around the allotments in Blackhorse Road (a feat prompted by the sudden appearance of a squirrel).

I have no idea whether Twizzle made any early abortive attempts at clearing the obstacle standing between him and his rendezvous with Rambo, because all I saw was the successful one. Walking out into the garden to cut some mint for a jug of Pimm's I was preparing,

I was just in time to see his rampant old rear end, elevated some eight feet in the air, disappearing into the thicket above the fence. Screaming his name, I bolted back through the house. The reason for this was the only access to the yard beyond was to go almost fully around the block to the large metal gate at the end of the lane that led to the scrap piles. Tearing along our street, shrieking 'Twizzle!' to the utter bafflement of any non-locals passing by, I felt utterly sickened as I mentally prepared myself for the awful violence I would have to deal with when arriving at the point of battle. I had no doubt whatsoever that a dreadful bloody fight would be in progress, because both dogs had been fantastically vocal that day, right up to the moment I had set out on my mint-hunting expedition.

As I raced towards the yard, I was relieved to see the gate was already open. Fearing the worst, I rounded the corner into the alley.

I was stopped in my tracks almost immediately. There was Rambo, standing in the sun regarding the passage of a passing beetle, but not a sign of my dog. Far from appearing as if he'd been wreaking bloody carnage, the pitbull seemed remarkably calm and content. Had he eaten Twiz whole? I knew that in Looney Tunes cartoons – from whose lore I have drawn the majority of my life lessons – anytime Butch the bulldog swallowed Sylvester the cat, the act would be signified by a few inches of Sylvester's tail hanging from the corner of his mouth. I saw no such evidence around Rambo's jaws. In fact, the entire scene was one of utter beatific peace, broken only by the gentle hiss of CFC gasses escaping from abandoned fridge freezers.

'Do you want something, mate?' came a gruff call from outside the hut in the scrap yard.

'My dog,' I called back, my thoughts a little fractured by the unexpected twist. 'He flew over the fence and now I can't see him.'

'What – this fence?' the latter-day Steptoe asked, advancing on me. 'No dog has come over that fence, mate. Rambo would have murdered it, I promise ya . . .'

What on earth had happened? Two further scenarios entered my reasoning. One: Twizzle had landed, hit the ground running and, seeing the size of his opponent, had carried on running straight out the gate. Two: He hadn't landed, having somehow sailed across the alley, clear through an open window on the other side.

I had just begun to say, 'Well, I definitely saw him leave our air-space . . .' when I heard a slight rustling and there, several yards ahead, I glimpsed patches of chocolate brown amid the dappled green branches of a tree. It was Twizzle, dangling downwards, stuck fast and helpless, trapped by the neck and back legs just as he had been in the living-room blinds. The surface of the alley in which we were gathered was about three feet lower than the level of the gardens and what may have looked like the base of a tree's boughs from our side was revealed as merely the middle of its limbs on the other. Twizzle had partially made it through what appeared to be a gap before becoming hopelessly snagged as he began his rapid descent. Rambo must have been elsewhere when Twiz arrived in the branches. I suspect, not gifted with a brilliant brain, he figured any Twizzle-like smells he caught a whiff of were completely normal. Twizzle, on the other hand, being a clever hound, had recognized he was temporarily at a disadvantage and decided to blend in with his surroundings until the cavalry arrived.

'Mate,' I said with extreme caution to the oncoming junk man, 'mate. Grab your dog. Don't make a fuss – just take him away.' I measured my words as if each one were a stick of wet dynamite.

'Why should I?' he answered aggressively and I sighed, reflecting that there is a certain type of bloke who can feel disrespected by a baby's gurgle.

'Mate, please,' I urged him while trying to remain motionless.

'He's harmless – he won't hurt ya!' continued the tattooed sal-vager, still not grasping my urgency.

'Mate, I'll give you a tenner if you just get your dog by the collar,' I now implored.

'Come here, Rambo!' he yelled, and grabbed the studded band at the animal's bulging neck as if his life depended on it.

I walked past the dumbfounded duo and stood beneath the tree where Twizzle was imprisoned. He rolled his eyes toward me and licked a nervous lip. People who have never owned dogs don't know how canines can register embarrassment every bit as clearly as humans, but they can, and here was an excellent example of it. Underneath his sleek brown fur, Twizzle's face was as red as a beetroot – as any face would be if it found itself wedged halfway up a tree in broad daylight.

As I reached up to bend back some of the limbs that pinned him, Twizzle suddenly began to thrash about. This in turn alerted Rambo that, far from this being just another idyllic day at the junkyard, he was in the middle of some sort of air raid. Pulling clear of his owner's iron grip, the pitbull began leaping at Twiz, who was still trapped but strategically occupying the high ground.

The next ten seconds exactly resembled one of those huge dust clouds that Andy Capp used to disappear behind whenever he had a punch-up at the pub. By the time the man managed to wrestle Rambo away again and I had stopped frantically attempting to push Twiz back through the hole out of which he had recently arrived, people were leaning out of upstairs windows all around to see what that ungodly row had been. Dragging his enraged beast to the workman's hut for safety, the scrap man advised me in no uncertain terms that I should 'keep my fucking dog in the house' in future. As I at last managed to extricate Twizzle from the tree, I resolved that while that might be impossible I would definitely get one of the brothers-in-law to heighten the fence that divided the bitter foes. This was done a few days later while Twizzle looked on with great interest. What we didn't know was that his brilliant mind was already working on Plan B.

Like all great strategies, its genius lay in its total simplicity. Now that the option of going *over* the fence had been ruled out, Twizzle saw that the only alternative open to him was to go *under*. Waiting for overcast days when he could be sure that neither Wendy or I would be spending much time outdoors, Twizzle, I see now, created his tunnel in a series of shifts disguised by whining at the back door to nip out for a wee. Perhaps tunnel is too elaborate a word, but he did burrow quite a cavity at the base of the fence and soon was able to squeeze his head and shoulders under it. It was his impetuousness upon discovering that he could do this that led to his downfall. Had he taken away six inches more earth from the floor of his excavation he might have been able to pop up in Rambo's alley as if sprung from a trap, but the sheer excitement of suddenly being able to see the enemy got the better of him and Twiz started attracting attention as soon as his muddy nose broke through on the far side. Like a maniac, lost in a crazed red mist, he now attempted to take on this monster of an adversary with just his head sticking up through the earth.

This time I was only alerted to the fact that the persistent old bastard had once again invaded sovereign soil by the awful sound of a vicious fight in progress. Running to the garden to confirm my worst fears, I was startled to see that a good deal of my dog was, in fact, still in our garden. His sturdy back quarters were facing toward me, the legs beneath making repeated attempts to gain fresh purchase, causing his whole rump to rise wildly in the air. What was happening on the other side I shuddered to think. Grabbing him by the haunches, I yanked him back through the hole. The bout had not gone well. Despite some impressive bobbing and weaving, accompanied by a rapid offensive from his own, not insubstantial, jaws, Rambo had clearly landed quite a few telling blows. The revulsion I felt as I looked at Twizzle's bloodied cheeks was only offset by the fact his wide eyes and happy panting told me that I had just interrupted the most fun he'd had in ages. I got the feeling that, had I applied grease to his cuts and sent him back through the opening for round two, he couldn't have appreciated it more. In taking on the reigning Deptford champ without the use of his arms and legs, Twiz called to mind the insane black knight in *Monty Python and the Holy Grail* who refuses to stop fighting even when all his limbs have been hacked off. His actions had been horrifying, disgusting and downright wrong, and yet it was impossible not to feel a scintilla of admiration for a creature so recklessly determined to follow his dream. It was a goal that, on his next attempt at settling scores with the enemy without, would see him attain an almost God-like status whenever I sit with other dog owners who like to tell tales of unique canine characters they have known.

Following the episode in the tree we had raised our fence higher. After the episode with the tunnel we had laid paving stones along the back. We tried to anticipate where Twizzle would move next and saw that we had a weakness either side with the relatively low fences that separated us from our aged neighbours, Ethel Jones and Maud Birch. These two wonderful old ladies were our very good friends. Both in their late seventies, they had lived in Scawen Road since they were little girls. Maud used to tell us what a high reputation the street had when she was younger:

'Before we moved here, we lived up by the high street,' she would tell us as we sat by the fire in her kitchen. 'And if my mother ever took us into the park or we had to walk along the road here, we had to wear our best clothes and spotless gloves. It always was a beautiful square. Then in the war a mine got dropped on the far side one night and blew down a lot of the houses and the whitewash factory that stood over the back. That's why the Grinstead Road side is just open ground these days.'

Maud's memories of the area took up many a Sunday afternoon after I would take her in the extra dinner that Wendy always prepared. One tale concerned the chilling moment the terrifying reality of the Blitz first intruded on the lives of those who lived in the street.

'It was a late afternoon,' Maude began in the clear but hoarse tones this fiercely house-proud widow delivered all her tales. 'My Bob was home on leave for some reason, but he'd gone to the big pub that used to be over on Evelyn Street – it kept a monkey, that pub, and that was a big attraction then. Any rate, the sirens had gone but at that point we hadn't really had any what you might call big raids and so we'd got to ignore them a bit. All us women were in Deptford Park, which had become an allotment and had big barrage balloons tethered in it – you can't imagine such a thing now. So we decided to stay, because nine times out of ten nothing happened. But this time some planes did come over and they started dropping these bombs – but not like you see on telly, more like thin cylinders that burst into flames but didn't blow up or anything. So we all ran indoors, but it didn't last long and when we come out there were little fires going everywhere. So we all got out these stirrup pimps that they'd issued that you were supposed to use on any blazes before they got too bad. Some of the trees were on fire and a few of the roofs near Hicks

Street too, but the main damage seemed to be over at the warehouses and docks across by the river.

'So there we all were – having a bit of a laugh about it, if truth be told, because we'd all heard it said that these bombs could bring your house down when really it was just starting these fires, so we was all a bit relieved. Then back comes my Bob and his mates and said we all better get down the shelters quick. He looked really pale, I remember that. Well, we all said he should get a bucket and give us a hand, but then he told us what it was all about. These fires were just the markers, he said, there to point out the targets for the heavy bombers coming behind. It was getting dark then and as we looked about we could see all the places where these flames were starting to get a hold. "Everybody in!" he said. "This thing ain't even started yet."

'Well, we all gathered our stuff and started for the shelters. Nobody was saying a word any more. And that night was the first night of the Blitz. We'd never known anything like it. The pub he had been in came down like a pack of cards. All the blokes who'd stayed inside got killed. Even the poor little monkey. Nobody knew what to expect, see . . .'

As the logs in her fireplace spat and crackled, Maud would fall silent and sit staring off into the distance. I stayed quiet too. There was nothing anyone from my generation could add to that.

Ethel Jones on the other side was of a similar age to Maud, but the peculiar thing was that the two women did not get on at all. When forced to acknowledge each other – we always invited them both to the parties we seemed to continually host – they would only ever say a clipped 'Mrs Birch' and 'Miss Jones' when holding their stilted conversations across their teacups. Neither of them had any children; Ethel, because she had stayed at home with her mother until late in life, and Maude because, as she once gloriously told Wendy and I with a grimace, 'My Bob was never very good in that department.'

Fortunately, keeping these two frosty old gals from actually being neighbours was our house and, germane to Twizzle's story, our garden. Because we were friends with E&M, the fences between us were not very high and topped with a simple trellis that allowed us to see and chat to each other on sunny days. It was through the obvious weakness this amiable arrangement offered that we now believed Twizzle would launch his next invasion of Rambo's turf.

Ethel's side was clear favourite, given that her back wall adjoined the junk yard at a height Twiz could easily clear with three paws tied behind his back. So, after explaining the situation to the old ladies, we decided to bolster defences on either side by a few feet, though not so high that our yard would start to resemble some sort of canine Stalag.

Now comes just about the most extraordinary tale any dog owner has ever recounted to a cynical public. In the short interim between the hole-digging and the new barriers going up, we took to restricting Twizzle so that he only had the freedom of a short passageway that ran outside our back door and along the length of the rear of the premises. This was a space about twenty feet long by four feet wide, with another fence along Ethel's boundary we judged high enough to thwart even a runner in the Grand National. At the end of this passage was the garden itself. A tall narrow gate fashioned from curlicue wrought iron marked where the alleyway ended and our garden began. This gate, topped as it was by a small brickwork arc, coupled with the fence, firmly denied Twiz access to his Eden beyond. He was, at last, penned in.

It took him about an hour to figure out that, while he couldn't jump over this latest enclosure, he was able to look over it. With a mixture of wonder, admiration and outright hysteria, I discovered him hanging over the top of the fence, its upper edge wedged beneath what I suppose we must call his armpits, surveying the world from his suspended perch. From the other side it must have looked as if he was ten feet tall and leaning over for a natter. The only drawback for Twiz was that, once in place, he couldn't get down again and so at regular intervals I would have to go out to the passageway, stand on a box and unhook him.

Fed up with him grumpily growling at me as I did him this favour, I told him what I thought of this ingratitude.

'Don't you fucking growl at me, you mad sod – I'll leave you up there all night next time.'

On about the third day of this series of suspensions, Ethel knocked. Ethel, unlike the Amazonian Maud, was a classic little old lady who spoke in the wavering tones her appearance suggested.

'I'm sorry to bother you, Danny,' she began, looking embarrassed, 'but Twizzle has started hanging over the fence looking into my front room.'

I told her I knew and apologized, saying it was only a temporary situation until other enclosures were in place.

'It gave me a terrific shock when I first saw him. I thought it was a man. The trouble is, neither of my cats will go out now. They see him looming up there and run back indoors.'

She laughed as she said this, but I could see it was a worry for her. Also, when Ethel said 'neither of my cats' that was something of an understatement. Wendy and I were never sure exactly how many cats Ethel had, but if ever she left her back door open in summer the waves of ammonia emanating from unseen cat trays deforested hedgerows for several miles around. If just two cats were responsible for that, they must have had bladders like nuclear reactors.

Promising Ethel it wouldn't happen again, I closed the door and vowed to keep Twizzle indoors for the remainder of the work.

After bringing Wendy up to speed with the latest arrangements, I went out to work on a voice-over for a TV ad – a further sign that my radio presence was getting noticed. This commercial was for Weetabix breakfast cereal and I was very flattered to be asked to perform the lines for one of the five wheat-cake-based cartoon characters that comprised the gang fronting the campaign. Previously my character had been played by Bob Hoskins, whose gruff, 'If you know what's good for you!' contribution finished each commercial. Bob, understandably, felt he had taken the role as far as he could and had decided to step down before his performance began to deteriorate. As I travelled up to Soho to make my debut as the tough, streetwise, no-nonsense Weetabix, I was hopeful that I could bring something fresh to the role. Tragically, the waiting nation was never to know what might have been.

As soon as I arrived at the studios, I was told by a concerned-looking receptionist that I must phone home immediately. Nobody likes to be told this and as I dialled the number I desperately hoped it would be something as trivial as me going out with both sets of keys in my bag. When I got through, it was clear I wasn't to be so fortunate.

Straight away I could tell there was anguish bordering on panic in Wendy's voice.

'Oh, Dan . . . it's Twizzle . . .' Wendy was now sobbing.

Though looking discreetly away as I stood at her desk, the receptionist must have noted how silent I had fallen as I listened to Wendy's terrible news with just the occasional 'Oh no . . . oh no . . .' by way of reply. But even she looked around when she heard me say, 'But how could he hang himself?' followed by a low, 'Christ almighty . . .'

Saying I was coming directly home, I placed the phone back on the cradle and with a rushed, 'I've got to go . . .' ran out into the street again.

There were no cabs to be had and in a daze I ran to Piccadilly tube station and rode the Bakerloo line to Waterloo. There I jumped in a taxi from the rank. In those days a fare to SE8 was not greeted with a cheery 'Right away, guvnor!' and so in order to shortcut all the huffing and puffing I just yelled, 'I'll pay you double the meter if you get me to Deptford without stopping,' as I leapt into the back.

Even then the journey took over half an hour. Chucking the cash at the cabbie through the partition window, I strode up our front path ready to burst into tears at this awful turn of events. As I twisted the key in the lock I hesitated just for a moment, took a deep breath, then threw open the door.

The first thing I saw was Twizzle at the foot of the stairs, doing his 'Welcome Home' dance.

I looked at his wild circling and energetic shakes for several seconds before putting my hand on his snout to make sure this wasn't some phantom vision. It wasn't. Or if it was this was one of the new hyper-realistic phantom visions that came with genuine whiskers and a wet nose.

Trying to take it all in, I now became aware of Wendy talking to someone in the scullery. Making my way there I found Wendy sitting at the table with John and Adrienne, our good friends from two doors down and our first call in a crisis.

For a moment nobody spoke. Then they all laughed as Adrienne said, 'You're too late, you've missed it all.'

I'll be honest with you. I didn't laugh along with them. And if I'd missed anything, my first thought was that it was the chance to bring the world my own take on a cartoon skinhead Weetabix that came with repeat fees. What kind of ghastly practical joke was this?

'I just saw Twizzle in the passage,' I managed to eventually mumble. 'You said he was dead.'

'He *was* dead,' said Wend, uttering perhaps the most peculiar three words of our entire marriage. Then she topped that with: 'But he came back to life.'

I shall make my précis of how Twizzle was apparently rejected by St Peter – possibly even by Beelzebub himself – as coherent as I can.

Though thankfully infrequent, there arrives into the life of any grown-up householder moments when minor events combine to form a perfect storm. Let's say you have enough to do already and things are not going well. On top of this you have workmen in. Another lot arrive to estimate a future job. A friend pops by. The phone goes. And there's someone at the door. You begin to feel like you have somehow become mixed up in a strained sixties stage farce, and will even say, 'I am going to scream in a minute,' to invisible cameras you believe must be placed around your home.

It was during one of these extreme fits of domestic turbulence that Wendy found she could no longer keep shuttling our dog from room to room in case he took a snap at someone or made a bid for freedom. So in desperation she took him out into his alleyway enclosure and, putting him on his lead, tied the other end to a drainpipe and said she would be back in ten minutes. He was now prevented from charging into the garden, launching himself at strangers, or popping up like a pantomime villain over Ethel's skyline. The job of enlarging our garden perimeter was nearing completion at this point, although one section, on Maud's side, remained completely open. It may have been this tempting portal that caught Twizzle's eye and set in motion the unbelievable events that followed.

The drainpipe to which his lead was attached was about two feet from the wrought-iron gate. Walking back until the lead extended to its fullest, Twiz must have noted that he had a five-foot run-up before any proposed launch and after doing the maths reckoned that, while he would never clear the gate itself, if he made himself thin enough once in flight he might just get through a large gap in the curlicue pattern at the top of the fixture. It was, as always, worth a shot. Because he was a brilliant dog he got his calculations absolutely spot on and flew through the opening like a dart. Unfortunately, because he never thought things through, he had failed to factor in what might happen beyond this. Arriving airborne on the garden side of the gate the silver chain by which he was tethered suddenly came to the end of its reach and yanked hard at the collar around his neck. Twizzle, as yet some five feet from terra firma, was left helplessly suspended against the ironwork. When Wendy came out into the yard to allow him back into the house, it was this horrifying sight that greeted her. Her first action was to go to pull the gate open and support Twiz from the other side, but we'd had it fitted with a padlock just recently to stop burglars coming in via the junkyard at the rear. Wendy knew the key to the lock was on the big bunch in her bag upstairs (probably) but there was no time to confirm that now.

She put her hands through the gate and tried to release the metal clip that affixed lead to collar, but working from behind was difficult and, once she did locate it, Twizzle's dead weight made it impossible for her to get her thumb under the required catch to spring it. Next she scraped and tore at the knot fastening the leash to the drainpipe, but again the tension created by his drop simply refused to let it yield. All the time she was screaming for help.

Hearing the commotion, Adrienne, along with her partner John, tore up the road to our house with Wendy rushing through to let them in. While Adrienne called the vet, John set about trying to release the catch at Twizzle's neck though, unbelievably, in what appeared to be the very last act of his life Twiz momentarily recovered just enough strength to groggily try and bite John's fingers as he worked beneath his head. Then he slumped unconscious once more. John then decided to break the chain lead that held poor Twizzle aloft. After about thirty agonizing seconds he succeeded, causing Twiz to fall heavily on to the paving stones out in the garden. He was totally lifeless, so much so in fact, that when Wendy brought the key to unlock the padlock that secured the gate, Twizzle's prone body prevented it from opening and he had to be shoved aside so that the door could be inched open.

Our dog was not breathing at all and blood was issuing from his nose. About ten minutes later the vet arrived and did what he could, but it was hopeless. Looking at Wendy's ashen face and red eyes he apologized for not being a miracle worker and asked, practically but rather tactlessly I feel, if he could use one of the empty rubble sacks nearby to transport Twizzle to his car. Wendy objected to this but the vet said he had another emergency to attend to and couldn't roll up to that with a dead dog on the passenger seat – that might shake a client's confidence. To this day my wife doesn't know why she okayed this action, possibly through shock, but it was once our late-lamented lunatic had been decanted into this plastic shroud that something inexplicable happened. They heard growling. They had barely a second to comprehend the sound when Twizzle started to writhe and thrash around inside the bag like one of the Three Stooges with a wasp's nest in his pants. The vet leapt back and Wendy fell clean over. From the top of the sack rose Twizzle's head, his tongue licking away at the dried blood on his snout.

Wendy asked the vet with some urgency what was happening. The vet, she said, looked utterly panic stricken.

'I promise you he was dead, I promise you he was gone . . .' he kept repeating.

Registering the outraged look forming on Twizzle's face as he eyed up the vet, Wendy advised that *he* might do well to be gone now.

About twenty minutes later I arrived home, having, as Adrienne so correctly pointed out, missed it all.

Twizzle suffered no ill effects whatsoever after having been officially pronounced dead. Nobody could explain it and we don't blame anyone if they find the whole story to be totally far-fetched. I now believe he had merely popped over an ethereal fence to the other side, as he had done with so many earthly barriers. Taking a brief look around, he probably noticed all the 'No Chasing, No Fighting, No Barking' signs they undoubtedly have in Heaven, then, having weighed things up, decided to slide back to where all the action was.

One last note about Twiz. I wrote earlier that he liked very few humans outside our house. Well, it'll come as no great shock to learn that the one person he absolutely adored above all others and would roll over to be tickled by any time of the day or night was Spud. And Spud LOVED Twizzle.

In old age, both of them, now calmer and at peace with the world, would sit for hours on park benches or walking slowly on the beach down at Dymchurch. My old man was never prone to outbursts of emotion, but the day Twizzle died – and I had to hold the old warrior while a vet gave the injection – when I told Dad he just sat down on the pavement swallowing hard, his eyes refusing to blink lest it release a welling pool of tears.

'The poor old bastard,' he said quietly a few times, followed by, 'Do you reckon they had to do it?'

I told him they did . . . and this time he really was gone.

A tough old nut to the end, Twizzle had lived to be almost twenty years old.

Nights On Broadway

Chris Evans gave up overseeing my GLR show in order to make his own programmes at the station. These went fantastically well and by 1989 this local network had a weekend line-up that achieved a creative peak many radio devotees coo about even now. I would do the early shows and on Saturday I'd hand over to Chris for his boisterous, often bawdy, reliably brilliant zoo format, while on Sunday I gave way to one of the few broadcasting geniuses I have witnessed first-hand.

This was Chris Morris, now a filmmaker, but then just about the most jaw-dropping ideas machine British radio has ever nurtured. While I was making up shows on the hoof, now comprising a growing element of bizarre audience participation, Chris M's shows were meticulously planned in advance right down to the last daring cuts between live mic, prepared tape, original music, insane scripted links and varied regular characters all played by the host. He'd arrive a full hour before my show ended, and I'd watch dumbfounded as Chris would convert the studio to his needs, erecting extra mic stands, installing keyboards and loading up reel-to-reels. Quiet and intense away from the programme, once it started he would become a whirl of animation, spinning this way and that in his chair, arms waving, firing off several machines simultaneously, all the time reading from the pages of notes fanned out in front of him. That his entire output from that era has never been archived and made available to future generations to marvel at truly staggers me. Then again, nobody in radio today would give Chris Morris the absolute licence afforded him back then.

Like most of the over-staffed, management-choked flat-pack media, radio does not want to hear from mavericks who can just 'do it'. Self-contained talent is the enemy of those who require their jobs to be bolstered by an Everest of fatuous titles and who think creativity is a formula. Worse, they believe the more people in business suits who work on the formula in a series of deathless meeting rooms, the better the end product will be. Or perhaps they don't, not really. In my experience, most of the dreary phalanx of managers and their ilk who clog up the simple show business world of 'being any good' are well aware their supposed 'skills' are completely worthless. It is an unspoken truth among their nervous ranks, and it forces them to create ever more blustering levels of unproductive desk-bound subservients whose only function is to mask the overpowering smell of horse shit. Anyone who seems to somehow be able to make programmes without their utterly unqualified interference is judged to be 'trouble' and gets suffocated under a welter of wordy PR and another round of empty self-serving meetings. It is not how fresh and original you are any more, it is how compliant, how malleable, how much you will tow the timid company line. To really seal your place on the vacuous inverted media pyramid these days, it is absolutely essential that you never draw attention to how many people in the room are 24-carat fucking imposters.[3]

On my own programme at GLR I had backed off the bumptiousness, driven the play-list to new levels of disparity – typically playing Ry Cooder's 'Down in Hollywood' followed by Charlie Chester's 'The Old Bazaar in Cairo' – and had hit upon something that nobody else seemed to be doing, and that was to create a phone-in show that few people could actually phone in to. This inversion of the accepted format of throwing out topical or generic subjects that anyone might have a view on or example of, created an audience who listened to the show just to see if anybody had, for instance, eaten their dinner out of a hat. It remains my only piece of advice to

---

[3] And if that paragraph is your sort of thing – just wait till we arrive at volume three!

any hopeful broadcaster – eschew whatever tired first-thought news agenda is suggested to you by the pusillanimous committees above and challenge your audience to raise its game to that of the show.

Overwhelmingly, the sort of gargoyles who rise to power in media have a mortal fear of the frivolous and insist on stiflingly close supervision of programmes whose workaday dreary solemnity creates the illusion that they are serious thinkers when in fact they haven't a single original thought in their banal, limited brains. Their greatest terror is that they will get into an elevator with whatever bubble-blower is just above them in the corporate pile, who will then turn to them and say:

'Hmmph! Caught a bit of your station the other day. Instead of discussing what's in the newspapers, house prices and the danger mad dogs pose to us all, chap seemed to be asking can shoes be haunted, notable things you've had stuck to you and did anyone's aunt ever dance with Emperor Hirohito. What sort of operation are you running over there? Hmmph!'

However at GLR back then, possibly because the wages were so low they really didn't dare flex any managerial muscle, everyone was allowed to create whatever radio world and persona they chose, free from editorial interference. I realize now how lucky we all were.

In the middle of my first six months on the radio I received an offer that could not have been further from the frenzied yet cerebral rock'n'roll brew I was bubbling up each weekend. I was asked to star in a pantomime – actually star, with my name above the title and everything. I had not been involved in any stage work since the age of seven when I'd given my highly regarded Mad Hatter in Rotherhithe Junior School's Christmas adaptation of *Alice in Wonderland*. This had been a terrific hit and while nobody actually said it, I think I had found some things in Hatter that many of my peers overlooked. So now I was being asked once more to parade beneath the proscenium, eh? Well, well, well. I wondered if I still 'had it'.

The production was to be staged at the Broadway Theatre, Barking, and the offer was to play Idle Jack in *Dick Whittington and His Cat*. Quite why they had chosen me for the part, I had no idea, though subsequent events would provide a few clues. The run was to be for just three weeks, twice daily, and I was engaged for the sum total of £4,500. In the event, they may as well have promised me a sack of rubies and a solid gold car because *Dick Whittington and His Cat* remains the one job in my life that I was 'knocked' for. That is, neither I, nor anyone else in the cast, saw a single penny for our efforts. It was, in short, a scam. Hooray!

If anyone had told me that I would one day use the hoary old turn of phrase 'it wasn't the money, it was the memories' about a job where I was required at one point to wear nothing but a grass skirt, I'm sure I would have thrashed them about the private parts with a rolled-up newspaper. Yet I'm afraid I have to because, coin-free though my labours on stage in East London were to be, I had a truly wonderful time during my brief diversion into panto. The producer/ director of it – and as it turned out the secret arch-villain – was a man called Paddy Dailey. In the seventies heyday of British comedy double acts there were four major turns. In order of importance, the list ran:

1. Morecambe & Wise
2. Mike & Bernie Winters
3. Hope & Keen
4. Dailey & Wayne

Only the first two are remembered much these days, and even Mike & Bernie's star is now fading fast. Absolutely no one remembers Dailey & Wayne. Yet they had generated quite a bit of celebrity heat for a while, until Bill Wayne's early death left Paddy high and dry. I certainly hadn't thought about them in decades until I sat with Paddy in a café noting the appalled look on his face as I told him I had no experience at all in live theatre, had never been to a pantomime and had no idea what the expressions he kept dropping in regarding bits of stage business could possibly mean.

'But you know what I'm saying when I say we could do "Syphons" in Act Two, right?' he begged, as though even a pre-school toddler would know this most basic routine for a duo.

I told him that I had as much idea about 'syphons' as I'd had about his previous mentions of 'counting out' and 'the walk around'.

'Christ. Listen, I'll come round to yours on Thursday and I'll learn you how they go. It'll be a crash course, but you can record it and play it back when I've gone. If you can't, then I hope you know how to entertain people by trick cycling or something!'

I told him I couldn't ride a bike either.

The day Paddy came round and began rehearsing me in all the ancient bits of business I would need to amuse a junior audience was one of the most satisfying of my working life. Every spin, slap, verbal misunderstanding, 'cheeky' response and slapstick pay-off he taught me felt like being allowed into a welcoming secret society. He even brought with him two soda syphons so that I might master the correct way to give and receive the series of water-jets required to build to the big moment when he finally got it straight in the kisser. I couldn't wait to lay this gold on the toddlers.

The only time I rebelled against tradition was at the initial read-through. Also in the cast was *Blue Peter*'s Michael Sundin, sitcom actresses Sarah Dangerfield and Sally Hughes and, a particular thrill for me, Michael Robbins, best known as 'Arthur' from *On the Buses*. As we flicked through the pages of Paddy Dailey's adapted script, all the seasoned pros seemed a little detached from its content while I gave all my corn such bursting enthusiasm that 'Arthur' said at one point, 'Save something for the night, eh, boy?' Looking back I can understand that playing down the bill to a local TV reporter at the Barking Broadway Theatre over Christmas had probably not been the dream they envisaged at stage school.

The moment I clashed with the piece's author came very early on.

My entrance was about five minutes into the show. The Ship's Captain (Paddy Dailey) is talking on the quayside to Alderman Fitzwarren (Michael Robbins) and his daughter Alice (Sally Hughes) about the tremendous difficulty he's been having recruiting new hands for his upcoming trip to South America. Just as he says, 'There doesn't seem to be one likely lad in the whole of this town!' the band strike up 'Consider Yourself' from Lionel Bart's *Oliver* and I (Idle Jack) stride on from stage right to deliver a powerful rendition of this borrowed standard. At its conclusion, the Ship's Captain grabs my arm and the following dialogue ensues:

SC: You there! You look like a lively prospect! How would you like to go on an adventure?

IJ: Oh, I'd like that very much, sir!

SC: Well, before I take you aboard, I need to ask you a few questions to confirm your suitability, OK?

IJ: Fire away, Captain.

SC: Now question number one: name me a bird that can't fly.

IJ: A penguin.

SC: A penguin? Why can't that fly?

IJ: Because it's a chocolate biscuit!

Well, I ask you? Do you see my objection? That feeble bit of word-play was to be my first joke of the night, my calling card in hoping to win over the restless hordes of under-tens waiting to see if an interloper from television had the chops to carry an entire production. I could imagine them hearing this pancake of a whizz-bang and, looking up in disappointment at their parents, pinching their little noses with thumb and forefinger as much as to say, 'Oh-oh. Told you we should have gone to *Cinderella*. This hambone is really laying an egg.'

So I objected. Once the reading was through, I asked Paddy if he had a moment.

'Paddy, it's this opening gag of mine,' I said, hoping not to completely crush his faith in his own abilities.

'What gag? Chocolate biscuit?' he replied sensing rebellion.

'Yes, I'm not entirely sure about it. I mean, it's strong, of course, but is it strong enough?' I thought I'd let him down gently.

'It'll be fine,' assured Paddy and he went to walk away. I stopped him.

'See, I know you probably only know me as the bloke from the *Six O'Clock Show* but . . .'

'And the other one,' he interrupted. 'I've put that on your billing too.'

'The other one?' I muttered, suddenly derailed.

'Yes, the *Bottom Line*. The thing you did on ITV. I've included that on the posters as well.'

I screamed inwardly. Did this man not want to sell *any* tickets?

'Well, anyway, Paddy,' I continued, thoroughly rattled now, 'see, I have done a bit of writing myself and I wondered, you know, if I could change it to something . . . a bit cleverer.'

'Clever?' Now he looked affronted. 'You don't think they'll like the Penguin joke?'

'I just think they might be expecting something a bit more up to date. Can I mess around with it and come up with a few alternatives?' I stopped short of providing him with some of my celebrated triumphs with photo captions at the *NME*.

'Whatever you want, Dan,' he suddenly conceded. 'Just do it my way in the first show, please. If that doesn't work – change it to what you think will.'

Great. I set to work on several different exchanges that I fancied would get the crowd checking their programmes to see if this was a new work by Neil Simon.

On the opening night I decided that I would be big about the distressing old groaner that opened my dialogue and give it the best shot I could. At least then Paddy wouldn't be able to say I buried it on purpose. On I went. 'Consider Yourself' went over well enough, but all the time I was telling the packed house in song that it was clear, we're going to get along, I was thinking how all this promised bonhomie would soon vanish once they heard my deathly jest about flightless birds. Song over, I embarked on my first ever stab at comic cross-talk, a stab I knew I was attempting with a very blunt blade. The big moment arrived:

SC: Now, question number one. Name me a bird that can't fly.

IJ: A penguin.

SC: A penguin? Why can't that fly?

IJ: Because it's a chocolate biscuit.

Now then. The loudest noise I had ever heard in my life until that moment had been the opening bars of a Deep Purple concert in 1972. But what exploded after I completed the second syllable of the word 'biscuit' made those chords seem like the sigh of a far-off dormouse across a fresh-mown field. The joke not only got a Krakatoa of an initial laugh but as the kids savoured the full nuance and invention of the line it seemed it would simply never end. Paddy and I looked at each other smiling as the guffaws bellowing down from the balcony met the uprising howls from the stalls and rushed over the stage like a whirlwind. Just before the noise began to abate, he leaned in to me and, barely moving his lips, mumbled,

'Anything else you wanna fucking change?'

In wonder and with due deference I shook my head almost imperceptibly. Nurses administered oxygen to many of the toddlers who remained helpless. Once order was restored, Paddy winked at me knowingly and we moved on.

Not all the off-colour stage whispers during the run went so skilfully unheard. The actor playing our Dame was called Terri Gardener. He had once been part of a very successful drag double act and had appeared in many lavish post-war pantos as well as several feature films. Terri was every bit as bawdy in life as the blowsy old washerwomen and cooks he specialized in onstage and one night as I stood in the wings waiting for the ingénue, Alice Fitzwarren, to finish the frankly soupy ballad she was required to stop the action with, he came up behind me in the dark and held me round the waist.

'I know you think that's my rolling pin you can feel against your arse, darling, but it's not . . .' he growled in my ear.

I laughed, but Paddy, standing just beside us, hissed, 'Terri, come on now, no time for that.'

Our Dame, who had a voice identical to the camp coarse rasp of his more famous friend Danny La Rue, momentarily forgot himself and, raising his tone to address Alderman Fitzwarren, remarked,

'There's time enough for a wank!'

Horrified at his own volume, Terri put his hand over his mouth straight away and we all checked to see if the wee tots and their parents in rows A to F had picked up on this unusual embellishment to the story of London's first mayor. Remarkably, they didn't seem to have done, although Alice Fitzwarren, sitting beside her wishing well, mid-song, shot a startled look to her left, clearly alarmed that Dick Whittington might have decided to take their romance to an unexpected new level.

After the performance Terri was given a written warning about his gaffe. Removing his make-up he chuckled with me.

'I got into terrible trouble once, doing that,' he said. 'I was at the Dominion in Tottenham Court Road doing *Sleeping Beauty* with my partner. In them days, for the finale they used to use real horses, enormous drays, to bring on the coach. Nothing like this . . .' He looked despairingly at the modest surroundings and waved toward our stage with its simple painted backdrops. 'This was proper no-expense-spared stuff in the fifties and the finale was the big setpiece of the show. So there we all were, stood stock-still, the costumes, the head-dresses, arms up, tits and teeth, everyone awaiting the big finish, which is the arrival of the prince and princess in their golden carriage. All the music is swelling up and on comes the horses. Well, I looked at one of them and I could see it wasn't only the music that was swelling up. It was *aroused*. How they could have let it come out on to the stage like that I do not know. I looked at this enormous thing hanging beneath this dray horse then turned to my partner who was next to me and said, 'Oh my God – if only I could take the weight!' Well, I didn't think anyone could hear me above the orchestra, but they did apparently and quite a lot of people complained. I didn't get fired, but I didn't half get a bollocking, that's for sure.'

As the run continued I found myself loving the job more and more. I'd even been given permission to leave the stage when the children of the chorus performed their five-minute dance routine. Previously I'd been asked to stay to one side of their synchronized shuffle and perform a few spontaneous steps of my own. 'Just skip and laugh,' Paddy had said, 'as though you want to join in but they won't let you.' Too wet behind the ears to question this awful prospect I had, in the first few performances done just that, but at best I looked spare and at worst like I couldn't bear to surrender the spotlight for one second for fear these youngsters would upstage me. I had prepared nothing, hoping, as with the radio, I would just discover inspiration when it was needed. But the first time the band began to play their gentle theme and the children all held hands to begin their sweet presentation, there I was doing a series of meaningless high kicks and rapid arm flaps completely at odds with their delicate gyrations. I even ran around them in a circle a couple of times completely distracting everyone from whatever mood the youngsters were trying to put across. The audience must have thought I'd lost my mind, and as I pointlessly raced about I thought the only way I might win them back would be to tell them the penguin joke again. The nadir came on the third day when, trying to limit my movements so I wouldn't appear such a manic limelight hog, I hit upon the idea of whistling along to the song while lightly jumping from foot to foot.

It is important to understand here that I do have a special skill with whistling. I'm very limited in the usual way of doing it, but I learned as a boy that I had a real gift for blowing into my cupped hands and creating a loud noise not unlike an owl hooting. Quite a lot of people can do this to make a single satisfying note, but I discovered that if, while my hands were forming the necessary hollow to produce the tone, I moved my little finger up and down, it altered the pitch. If ever you run into me, ask for a demonstration – it really is quite impressive for somebody who otherwise can barely master a kazoo. What I'd overlooked when deciding on the spot to accompany the kids like this was just how loud a sound it is. As soon as I'd piped up the first couple of blasts I saw the bandleader shoot me a look like I'd thrown up into the saxophones. Suddenly nobody was looking at the dance school toddlers, they were all agog at this deafening Pan figure kicking up his knees for no discernible reason.

Sensing the rising panic in the hall, I carried on with the awful trumpeting but made my way, absurdly skipping sideways, toward the wings where once out of shot I immediately quit the distressing display. The abject horror in my eyes as I pleaded with Paddy to drop me from the segment must have touched him deeply because a new line was added to the show where instead of Fairy Bowbells saying, 'I'll show you all where my magic house is. Idle Jack you stay and look after the children!' she now said, 'I'll show you all where my magic house is. The children will be fine. Idle Jack, why don't you come with us?'

It was music to my ears.

While the panto went from strength to strength each night the first person to suspect we in the cast were all being taken for a ride was Michael Robbins. I had presumed the theatre was like the other entertainment mediums I moved in and that you would get paid weeks, often months, later. That was not how the older professionals in the show saw it.

'I don't like it, darlin',' said 'Arthur', agitatedly pacing his dressing room, his gruff voice softened by the showbizzy use of endearments. 'We are supposed to get our money at the end of each seven days and I'm getting a shitty feeling about this.'

Ever the sunbeam, I did what I could to offer reasons why Paddy was being evasive. I simply couldn't imagine a scenario where Michael's gloomy anxieties would be borne out. On the day of the final performance it became clearer. Alerted that it was tradition in the theatre for the star turn to buy little gifts for everyone when the run ended – at least I think it is, they may have simply decided, 'Yonder comes a sucker' – I sank the stiletto of overdraft deeper into Mervyn's ribs by splashing out wildly along Barking High Street. I knew Paddy Dailey liked a particular brand of whisky and so bought him a rare blend of it in a presentation case. However, between the final matinee and last show he was nowhere to be found. Michael Robbins sat in front of his illuminated make-up table and with a face etched in resigned amusement gave me his 'I told you so' speech.

'He's a bastard. He's got debts all over the shop. Even the dancing kids and the little firm who painted the scenery haven't seen a penny. None of us will. I'm going to march up to the box office myself in a minute and just grab what I can. If you've got any sense, son, you'll beat me to it.'

A meal had been arranged for everyone in a nearby restaurant after the closing bows and I said I would confront him there. 'Arthur' gave a derisive snort.

'He won't be anywhere near that Chinese, mate. Once that curtain comes down you will not see his arse for dust. We're going on now because we've got to go on, but during the fight with King Rat at the end tonight I plan to let a few of my punches go astray.'

During that final show the increasing distraction that Paddy had been displaying over the last week came to a head and he refused any attempts at conversation as he stood with various cast member in the wings. Their threats and swearing at him were all delivered in stage

Meeting my absolute hero Anthony Newley while dressed as my own five-year-old son.

This is weird. Made up to look like an old man and pictured begging money from my old man. I wildly overestimated how much hair I would have at that age.

Breakfast at the caravan. People often take pictures of food now but this was the first-ever one and started the craze.

My father-in-law Jim possibly recalling the night a molten lampshade scarred him for life.

n Spain with Rodney, who stumped up my VAT cheque. The surgical wadding in my ear is part of a terrific story that I just realized is not in this book.

Our wedding in 1988. I just realized that is not in this book either. Which will go over big I'm sure.

Wendy and Sonny with Jonathan Ross, Jane and Honey at Universal Studios in 1992. I take Jonathan on holiday with us in case I get awards that need presenting.

Thumb chums. Sonny in our front room with Paul Gascoigne. Paul is on the right.

(right) At the beginning of Donald Duck films he looks like this, like he can't believe his luck. It is my default expression whenever I'm asked to pose. 'Don't do your DD face,' begs Wendy. I always do. (Craig Easton)

(below) Atop a mountain in Spain on yet another holiday. I convinced my thinning hair to gather on the western slopes of my skull to fool the camera.

In New York at 5am with the Saw Doctors who I'd met in a bar. We were broadcasting live, loud and very drunk back to Radio 1.

Burying pianos on beaches for Radio 1. Stunned, I have just realized I will be needing this shirt for the cover of *Going to Sea in a Sieve*.

My Spitting Image. As I got balder the puppet strangely began to grow more hair. (See Oscar Wilde, *The Importance of Being Gormless*.) (Spitting Image Productions Ltd)

(left) Saturation Point in 1993. Within thirty minutes of this portrait I was utterly bald and as fat as a house.

(below) The Zapruder footage of the Kennedy assassination has been reproduced more than this photo. The story behind it is, arguably, more shocking. (Fiona Hanson/PA Archive/Press Association Images)

whispers and their twisted faces of hatred dissolved into appropriate expressions of joy and wonderment the second they stepped into the lights. It was a very strange evening. Still not fully believing that I would never be paid, I went to the dressing room and grabbed my gift for him during a spell when we would both be offstage for a few minutes. He was facing directly on to the performance and would not turn around to look at me, even though I was repeatedly tapping his shoulder. In the end I had to reach around and put the wooden box in front of his face.

'Paddy,' I whispered as loud as I dare. 'Have that, mate. Thanks for everything.'

He took it, looked at it, and placed it down by the lighting desk to our left. He still didn't look round.

'You are coming to the restaurant after, eh?' I asked.

At last he moved his head to look over his shoulder. With tight thin lips curled into a wretched smile, he nodded. Tears were flooding his sorrowful eyes. Even though the money was pretty vital to me, I genuinely wasn't angry with him – how could I be? I knew too many people who had been 'at it' in various ways and could almost hear the old man's voice saying, 'Ne'mend about dinner, he's holding the pot. Ask him how you can get in the swim too.'

Receiving his cue, Paddy marched onstage once more as the boisterous Captain, barking orders at, by now, a genuinely mutinous crew. He didn't make it to the Chinese.

Later it transpired that he and his wife had ploughed quite a lot of money into various failed ventures. A dancing school – the same one that provided the kids who'd had to put up with my carthorse capers – was the latest of these. Whether Paddy had staged this pantomime hoping for it to result in a huge flop à la *The Producers* or, more likely, had seen it as some quick cash, I cannot say. I met him once more, about three months later, and in the most coincidental of circumstances. Obviously, after the end of the *Six O'Clock Show* there was very little reason for me to be in the LWT building, but one evening I was, probably to meet either Paul Ross or Jeff Pope for a reflective glass of Tio Pepe. As I rounded one of the snaking corridors on the second floor, I ran smack into Paddy Dailey. I remember he was wearing a soft hat that he removed upon greeting me as if I was his social superior. I was unnerved by that and also by the pitiable speech he immediately launched into of how he had never been in this position before, his reputation in the business was ruined and how he was determined to pay back every last penny he owed me. The tears were welling up in his eyes again and he chewed his bottom lip with wretched emotion. All I had said up to that point was, 'Paddy! What are you doing here?' Once he'd stopped his torrent of words I asked him again and it turned out the story of the Great Barking Pantomime Scandal had been taken up by the local paper after several members of the show's cast had contacted them. This item in turn had been spotted by a new *Bottom Line*-style consumer programme on LWT and, having tracked Paddy down, they had now insisted he come to the studio to explain himself in front of the cameras. I don't think he believed me when I said I knew absolutely nothing about this. In fact, as he continued to babble, I remember thinking that it was a sign of how persona non grata I had become that nobody had asked me to contribute to the spot. . I wouldn't have done it – 'serious' shows rarely pay – but at least it would have constituted a job offer. What good would it have done anyway? Poor old Paddy was obviously anguished, his life in show business all but over, and there was plainly zero chance of us all getting paid anyway. And so it proved. All I got from Dick Whittington and his Cat was a bout of virulent flu that kicked in the day after it finished and kept me from appearing on the radio that weekend – so no money there either.

Would I do it again, given the chance? Absolutely. I still have my glowing review from *The Stage* newspaper that singled me out as 'a natural performer' and 'a real surprise package'. This was only slightly tarnished when, after I had read it out to Terri Gardener backstage, he said, 'Yes, very nice, sweetheart, and I'm very happy for you, but let me tell you an expression we have in this game. The three most useless things in the world are a nun's minge, the Pope's cock and a write-up in *The Stage*.'

You can't buy experience like that with vulgar cash.

*

Rubbing along on the GLR job, coupled with some bits and pieces of writing and the odd voice-over, I managed to bumble through about eight months of not doing very much before receiving three big job offers in the space of eight days. The first was from producers at the fledgling BBC Radio 5, who were concocting a quiz show called *Sports Call* for the new national network. They were fans of the GLR programme and asked me if I'd like to host their venture. The two key words here are 'national' and 'host', which, to be utterly vulgar about it, can be freely translated in the broadcasting game as 'ker' and 'ching'.

The second proposal was never to come to fruition and remains the Great Lost Project of my career. It was a television game show called *Hoodwink* that was in the planning stages up at Scottish TV. I had had dealings with the station's controller, Sandy Ross, previously when Jeff Pope, my chum from the *Six O'Clock Show*, and I had written a script called *P.E.* based on the sports master in Ken Loach's peerless film *Kes*. Brian Glover, who played the character in the movie, had been a regular contributor to *SOCS* and, intrigued by what Jeff and I outlined, had even agreed to reprise the role for television. P.E. stood for both the character's duties and his name, Preston Eppleside, and Brian particularly liked the idea that twenty years on from *Please Sir!* – the huge hit comedy wherein a modern young master is placed in a school full of teaching dinosaurs – we were going to turn that premise on its head by having his reactionary old ways adrift in the fast-changing modern education system. It was a funny, spiky little script and remained in the scheduling process right up until it was announced that the time slot it was pitching for was being given over to an extra edition of *Coronation Street* each week.

When Sandy later commissioned the *Hoodwink* show he said he immediately thought of me. This is not quite the unfettered compliment it may sound, because I was not to be the main star of the programme. No, this was to be the honour of a character called the Professor whose job it would be to determine and dole out the prize money at the end of each episode. The twist here was that the Professor was a chimpanzee. I knew that only a lunatic would attempt to steal the show from a monkey each week and so I was quite happy to play, and I think the phrase is apt, his 'second banana'.

The way the show worked was that a group of individuals would work their way through a series of rounds whose machinations today I no longer recall because, like everyone else, I just wanted to get on to the chimp part of the proceedings. The winner of the preliminaries got the chance to come face to face with the Professor. At this showdown they would stare at each other across a table with five levers at the centre. The Professor, who of course was wearing a velvet jacket, cravat and tasselled smoking hat, had been trained to pull one of these levers at random upon hearing the word 'Go!' So, a question would be asked and the corresponding right answer would only be revealed once the correct lever was activated. The contestant's job was to locate this lever before the monkey did. If the chimpanzee got the answer first, he would then get up on the table, reach into a large jar full of ten-pound notes, grab a handful and fling them in the air. Any money that remained in the jar after five questions had been asked would then be given to the contestant to take home. Now do you see why I call this the Great Lost Project Of My Career?

Hoodwink first ran into trouble because the two chimps who were hired to perform as the Professor were held up abroad when shooting on the film *Gorillas in the Mist* overran. These chimps had actually been working inside gorilla suits on the movie because gorillas themselves aren't good actors. I know this book tests your credibility at times, and never more so than now, but I promise you this is absolutely true. This extension of their time with Sigourney Weaver, plus the necessary quarantine period these busy pros would have to face on re-entering the UK, meant that *Hoodwink* had to be put in mothballs for a bit. This greatly inconvenienced Scottish TV, whose Glasgow studios had already been refurbished with specially enlarged and adapted dressing rooms for the prestigious primates, complete with one of those tyres on a rope that monkeys seem to insist upon. Again, not a word of this is fantasy. I was told that people working in the building couldn't help but be curious as to who all these special modifications were for, with backstage betting initially favouring both Sheena Easton and Robin Day.

It was during this lull in production that animal rights groups got wind of the project and, believing it to be underway, began circulating stories of untold cruelty on the set. In fact, the hairy stars of the programme were still, at that point, sitting in their air-conditioned trailers in Africa, sipping mango smoothies and poring over that week's *Variety*. Once one of the major Scottish newspapers got behind the brouhaha, the jig was up. It was a sad and rueful Sandy Ross who rang me to say *Hoodwink* was now on permanent hold, where it remains to this day.

The third call I received in that eight-day period was from London Weekend Television. *Friday Now!* had tanked so badly that viewers were rushing out to buy special bargepoles so that they wouldn't have to touch the toxic old stinker with them. The bosses at LWT had come up with an idea how to fix this. They had decided to bring back the *Six O'Clock Show*. Realizing that, if they simply announced this, it might expose all the previous trumpeting about the fast-paced modern age and its cutting-edge vitality as overheated hogwash, they had come up with a new name commensurate with the show's place in the buzzing zeitgeist. And so the *Six O'Clock Show* was now to be rebranded *Six O'Clock LIVE!* (which it always had been).

Could I pop up to Waterloo and see them?

When the next letter arrived from Mervyn at Barclays, I opened it with aplomb and even replied by return of post, informing him that the loud noise he would have heard the previous evening was in fact an enormous blast from the funnel of my ship coming in. What's more, this ship had now connected at the dockside with a long sleek gravy train equipped with delicious biscuit wheels.

This was, as it turned out, not the usual hopeful bravado. Within eighteen months I would be so in demand that not only would brother-in-law Rod have got his money back in full but I would be in a position to tell my chums at LWT that this time around I would be the one saying goodbye to them. I was now entering the period alluded to in the previous volume where, over the next five years, the British public would quite rightly become sick of the fucking sight of me. But, like Scarlett O'Hara tearing at the Tara turf, by God, I was determined to make sure that my days of wearing one shoe in a Norfolk bank were over.

Unfaithful Servant

T he upward trajectory of my career between 1990 and 1994 was swift and expansive, but whether that in itself is enough to make interesting biography I'm not so sure. Finding you are immensely hireable and the media's flavour of the month, albeit for forty-eight months in a row, is both enriching and pleasurable, but unless it is what you have striven for all your working life you don't feel any real sense of triumphant vindication. As outlined above, I had been swinging down the lane with my hat on the side of my head since about the age of two, so promenading about in my thirties in a series of faintly ridiculous vehicles for television and radio, while obviously a wonderful way to make a living, lacks sustained dramatic interest. You can find yourself falling into the 'And then I made . . .' mode, which quite rightly has the punters rushing en masse to bung your life's story on eBay for a Buy It Now price of £0.01 plus free postage. On the other hand if I omit the parade of productions completely, or pass it off in a brief literary montage sequence, the casual student of my career may assume I remained in a darkened room during those years, teeth clenched and shivering from the effects of a powerful drug habit. So allow me to pepper these next few chapters with what I hope are some of the more interesting moments that arose from becoming nationally famous.

Before we get down to individual cases, let me state that I knew much of the work was of what I insist we agree to call here 'variable quality' – although inevitably some of the more bug-eyed and slithering of the newspaper critics at the time described it in alternative language. Having been one of their number at the *NME*, where particularly in the singles reviews I had penned some pretty raw stuff, getting a few laughs at the expense someone's act, I knew I couldn't have the brass neck to be outraged when someone decided my latest offering had the whiff of four-day-old fish. Dad took a different view. Whenever he read something that didn't quite say my work should be enshrined at the Museum of Performing Arts for future generations to have something to aspire to, he would drop the paper to his lap and say, 'Have you read this?' Then, before I could ease his rage by making light of the harsh remarks, he would ask, 'Do you want me to go up there after 'em?' I must say, there were occasions it would have been terrific fun to know my old man had arrived at the *Daily Mail* or *Daily Telegraph* or some such organ and, not even bothering to announce himself at reception, barged straight in and smacked someone right under the earhole.

'You wouldn't get away with talking like that about someone in the docks, I tell you that,' he advised me more than once. 'They would have gone straight in the drink. The trouble with your game is there's not enough right-handers dished out.'

I once arranged to meet Dad in a pub called the Rose of Kent in Deptford. I was a little late getting there and as the pub came in sight I saw a man, dressed in brown and running at top speed, holding on to the chocolate-coloured trilby on his head and looking as though he was in fear of his life. As he passed me, I heard the voice of my father, some fifty yards hence and standing outside the pub, shouting, 'Danny! Trip that ponce up! Trip him up!' I didn't do as requested but instead turned to watch the chap run at full pelt into one of those twirling cab office signs that brought him crashing to the ground. As he sprawled on the pavement I heard Spud shout, 'Serves you right, you dirty bastard! You fucking coward!'

On sitting down in the Rose of Kent, and after Spud had plonked a pint of lager-and-lime down in front of me, I felt I ought to ask what had happened. You never asked Dad about these things immediately and always had to go through a little verbal dance even when you did.

'What was that all about when I arrived?' I said, taking the first glorious sip of the L&L, a classic drink that has sadly been sidelined of late. Slices of fruit in the neck of the bottle are one thing. Lime cordial is quite another. Anyway, I was getting no answer, so as required, I went at it again:

'That bloke looked terrified. Had he nicked someone's purse?'

'Dunno,' stonewalled Dad, arms tightly folded to signal non-communication. 'He was a nuisance, that's all.'

'So was he just running from you?'

'I wasn't chasing him,' he snapped indignantly. 'He was running – but only because he didn't have the spunk to have a straightener.'

'Well, what had he done, Dad?'

'Nothing. Talk about something else.'

The correct procedure at this point was to say nothing. Usually, after about twenty seconds of silence, the dam would burst of its own accord. On the count of twenty, it did:

'He come right unstuck!' Spud suddenly announced with a broad chuckle. 'I don't think we'll fucking see him in here again – or over the park!'

A few of the old boys up at the bar joined in the laughter as he said this. As it transpired, they were partly responsible for the contretemps too. Apparently the bloke was a council park keeper who had been working for the last few days in Deptford Park. Walking into the Rose for the first time, he had fallen into conversation with the regulars. One of them told him he should keep an eye out for me because I lived on the park and was often in there with my children or dog. Not much of an incentive to go to work, I'll grant you, but I like to think, as my star rose, the locals thought of me as a novelty. For reasons only known to himself, the bloke, totally misreading the tone, launched into a first-rate trumped-up story about me. OK, let's start with what led up to all this. I forewarn you, it is pretty small beer.

Two days previously I had been over the park with Sonny, then about seven, and a couple of his primary school friends playing football on one of the vacant pitches. We were just kicking about among ourselves, but it does get to be a bit of a drag when you have to keep chasing after the ball when it goes behind the goal toward either the flower beds or where other kids are playing.

'Wait a minute, kids, I'll be straight back,' I said.

Legging it over to the 'parky's hut' – the small cabin where council employees made tea and compared rakes, etc – I put my head around the door and addressed the only man there.

'Mate,' I began breezily, 'don't suppose there's any chance I could have a net to put up at one of the goals, could I? I'll give you a tenner.'

The man seemed sympathetic but explained that the nets were locked away and if someone saw one of them out he would get into all sorts of trouble. He then told me that if I contacted Lewisham Council I could arrange to have them erected on another day if the pitch wasn't booked.

'Ah, no worries,' I replied. 'It's only a few seven-year-olds knocking about, nothing formal. Just on the off chance, that's all.' And away I went, reflecting that I had been unfortunate to come up against one so rigidly 'unapproachable'. And that was the end of the incident.

For some reason our brown-uniformed chum decided to parlay this pallid exchange into something far more self-aggrandizing. Propping up the bar in the Rose, he responded to the news that I lived nearby roughly like this:

'Yeah, I know. Don't talk to me about him. He came into our workplace the other day, giving it plenty. "You!" he shouted at me. "Put up some nets so my son and me can play football!" When I said I wouldn't, he said, "Do you know who I am?" then started screaming and shouting and reckoning he was going to get me the sack. In the end I squared up to him and chucked him out. These telly people think they can do what they want. Right snobby fucker, he was.'

The old boys said that this didn't sound like me, the Rose of Kent being pretty much my regular then, but apparently the transient park keeper wouldn't be swayed from the 'facts' as he presented them. A few minutes later, enter Spud. Greeting his chums at the bar he orders a Guinness and then one of the regulars says to the parky, 'Here, tell him what you just told us about that Danny Baker.'

The man did so, with, I am assured, extra lashings of big-shot entitlement from me. Dad, who did not lack for theatre in his make-up, read the situation early. Simmering nicely, he let the man finish. There followed a pause.

'Is that right?' he said with a controlled smile. 'You done? Because I'm his father.'

He allowed just enough time to enjoy the bloke's look of absolute panic, then the chase was on. I like to think they went round and round the pool table to the accompaniment of a silent-film piano, but apparently the man just bolted for the door, knocking over several drinks in the process. I chanced upon him just as his already impressive sprint had found another gear, leading him direct to his cab office collision.

Another occasion when Dad took the direct approach to a perceived critic of mine – this time erroneously – has almost passed into show business legend. It was during my 1992–94 stint as a talk-show host on BBC1 – another case of an employer making a job offer based on a miscalculation of my abilities. Because I had garnered a reputation as a good talk-show guest, they assumed I'd make a good talk-show host. It's one thing to be able to talk up a storm – listening is a different skill altogether, and it's one of the things I really look forward to having a go at once I have retired.

On the night in question Spud was in the green room during the chat show, called *Danny Baker After All*. He rarely sat in the audience because, as he so rightly put it, 'There's so much ballsing about, it drives you mad.' He had been to many of my programmes and, as was his wont, invariably formed a tight bond with both the catering and bar staff who serviced the guest celebrities. He knew most of them but even when a new bow tie was serving behind the little bar backstage he would make a beeline for him to conspire and discover what the 'strengths' of such a job might be. Ignoring whatever big names might be in the room, Dad would stand with what I suppose we must call his fellow workers. Nine times out of ten, he'd be exchanging phone numbers with them before the night was out.

'He's a good bloke, that Chris in there, ain't he?' he would say later in the BBC car taking us both home. I would reply that I knew who he was talking about but didn't really know him. 'Oh yes, he's one of the chaps, all right. He's going to get hold of some vodka for us.'

I would beg him not to enter into these negotiations while he was my honoured guest on the property, but it never made any difference.

On another occasion it might be, 'That Pam, taking the food around. Her old man was in the docks. I'm trying to place him.' Spud believed he must know every single docker there ever was. 'She said at Christmas she can put her hands on all sorts. Big hams, the lot . . .'

Making a weak joke about the actor connotations in what he said, I could see I was wasting my time. Dad had found a new contact and in his mind he was already selling the stuff on. A casual chat with one of the cleaners in the corridor might lead to everyone in his circle being good for mop-heads and Mr Sheen for the next nine months.

Green rooms rarely offer hard spirits unless, for instance, Bruce Willis' people request it in advance, but very soon into my tenure as show host the hospitality staff began providing a bottle of Hine or Rémy Martin brandy on the off chance Spud was going to be in. The night I featured Harry Enfield as a guest on *After All . . .* Spud was in his element holding court and, as usual, not taking a blind bit of notice of the outgoing show. Whenever I mentioned something that had happened on the programme on the way home he'd invariably say, 'Must have missed that bit – still, I'm taping it tomorrow so I'll watch it back.' In defence of such an indifferent attitude very few shows aside from *Match of the Day* and *The World at War* interested him, and, as anyone who has ever attended a recording knows, they do drag on and on and on. The night Harry Enfield was in I asked him if he was working on any new characters for the forthcoming series of his successful sketch show. Harry, a quiet and genial man away from his work, answered that there was one explosive role he was currently enjoying performing very much. It was a character who would at first rationally mull over a subject before quickly getting into a rage about it, and then he'd talk as if he was confronting whoever was responsible. The catchphrase for this character was some variation on the bellowed phrase, 'And if it was me, I'd say to Carole Vorderman. Oi! Vorderman – NO!' Then he'd go on to outline a series of rabid reasons for his objections. As we sat opposite each other in the studio, Harry decided to use me as an illustration for how the thing worked. Starting in his usual voice, Harry led me into it:

'So for instance if he was discussing what we're doing right now, he would begin, "Watched that Danny Baker show last night. Yeah, quite liked it. Although, to be fair, he's not a patch on Michael Parkinson. And some of his jokes were a bit personal. I mean, if I was a celebrity and I found myself the butt of one of his tortuous bits of logic and wordplay, I don't think I could accept the jest in the manner intended. I mean, why should I [voice rising now] have to become a laughing stock just so he can help himself to the licence fee I pay with my hard-earned wages? It makes me sick to think I'm financing my own public lynching! I'm a private citizen, not Shirley bloody Bassey! And if he dared try any of his puerile babble while a guest in my house, I'd say, Oi! Baker. NO!! You may think your-self the heir to the late-night talk show crown, but . . ."' and here Harry started to enjoy the audience's reaction perhaps a little too much "'. . . to me you'll always be a loud-mouthed, talentless, balding cockney cunt!"'

Yes, he actually said that. Thus making the tremendously funny bit unusable. The studio audience, realizing they had been treated to something that would probably not be aired, exploded into shocked applause. The green room crowd had been appreciative too. All, sadly, bar one key individual. Spud had been in conversation with his chums behind the bar and had only turned to look at the TV relaying the show as Harry's voice began to get shouty. Therefore he missed the reason for the 'rant' and got it into his head that Harry Enfield had gone nuts and was itching for a fight. Dad decided to give him one. Swiftly leaving the green room he made toward the studio doors and waited for Harry Enfield to emerge at the end of his segment. About three minutes later out he came and Spud, possibly – though not necessarily – inflamed by a few brandies, launched at him. Pushing Harry up against the wall, he put a hand hard on his chest and went into a real-life version of the character Harry had just been lampooning.

'You fuckin' little ponce!' began Dad. 'You speak to a boy of mine like that, I oughta throw you down these fucking stairs!'

By now security were running over to the scene. Harry managed to say that the exchange had been a joke. Spud wasn't having that. 'A joke? What? What you said? How's that a joke? His mother could have been sitting in that audience! I heard ya! See, he's never been a fighter, but I fucking am! Go on, say that to me!'

Hauled away by several members of the Corps of Commissioners – a platoon Dad had once been part of for about twenty minutes after leaving the docks – he freed himself and made straight for Wood Lane tube and a seething early journey home.

Oblivious to these goings on, when I came off air I walked breezily into the green room rubbing my hands together and beaming that that had all gone rather well. Noting a somewhat muted atmosphere, my first thought was that my initial upbeat review must have been the raving illusions of a deluded ego. Double-checking, I saw that even my old man had abandoned this one. The show's producer, Bea Ballard, took me to one side and filled me in about what had befallen poor Harry even as the applause was ringing in his ears. Good man that he is, Harry Enfield then handed me a bottle of beer with a wry smile. Twenty years later, on the rare occasions that we meet, his initial is greeting remains: 'Hello, Danny. Your dad's not with you, is he?'

When I look back on the early nineties it is quite beyond me, and I suspect most of the country, how I came to be so in demand. This is no disingenuous attempt to court a counter-argument. It happens to certain performers every now and then, and usually not as a result of clamouring from the public. I certainly don't recall any great swell in requests for autographs, public appearances or being asked to place my healing hands upon poorly babies, yet the cry continued to be raised within the industry, 'Get Baker! It has to be him!' So ubiquitous did I become during the period that *Spitting Image* featured a sketch where multiple puppets of me popped up on various programmes simultaneously, including the news and the epilogue. It is some testament to how well I can spend a pound note that during this heyday hurricane I didn't move house, buy a second home, or even a top-of-the-range car, or set up a production company, invest in any schemes or shares, fork out for a holiday home, or develop a spectacular drug habit to assist in hoovering up the bank balance. And yet I managed to knock the entire lot out on living well and having a good time, just as we had during the days of Mervyn's marvellous letters – albeit now on a much larger canvas.

I remember one holiday – and always being close with the in-laws, there would often be a gaggle of us – where I had the idea that it would be wonderful to gallop about New York for a bit, having plenty of everything, then eventually take a sleeper train way down south to Miami, from whence we would drive to Key West. It was the sleeper train that excited me most. I knew that these were fantastically romantic transports, the Iron Horses upon which America was made, smoke billowing from the stack, whistling as they thundered over wilderness bridges, cow-catchers up front and cabooses to the rear. They had fringed lamps in all carriages, Mae West holding court in the restaurant car, Marilyn Monroe drinking from a hip flask in a top bunk. As soon as we pulled out of Grand Central Station I realized I had perhaps been getting a tad carried away. In fact, our first-class three-day Amtrack Express to Florida bore a striking resemblance to the 11.05 Virgin Rail from London Euston to Manchester Piccadilly. Far from a cosy communal hotel, we were all in poky plastic-walled rabbit hutches where you pulled an impossibly narrow bed from out of the wall and the toilet door flew open at every shake, filling your rattling cubicle with the acrid smell of whatever blue chemical sloshed about in the small stainless-steel fixture within. As for the restaurant car, suffice to say it made Nandos in Walsall look like Maxim's, Paris. The corridors were full of stoned students and through the fuzzy windows, rather than the herds of stampeding buffaloes I'd promised, were spectacular views of Philadelphia's finest tyre factories and breakers' yards. We finally abandoned my fantasy on the rails in Savannah, Georgia, and chartered a private plane to get us down to the Keys as quickly as possible. So, yes, I can spend a few quid all right, but I am fantastically proud of that. It is a very working-class trait. I've said it before, I'll say it again, and may the record show these attitudes are affected by neither circumstance nor budget. Living 'within your means' is a filthy lie that only allows someone else to steal your pleasure during these few dozen summers below the sun. Eschew the middle-class habits of frugality, caution and making do, the cheap camping holidays and the parental lessons about the value of money. Knock the fucking stuff out. Buy the best prams, the best clothes, the best times for your children – and buy new ones for every child. When friends come round – and they should come round often – don't budget and see if you have any half-open bottles of long-corked wines to finish first or any 'value packs' of anything. Offer more than they could possibly eat, drink or laugh about. Buy the best. Live the best. Sort things out tomorrow. And Knock. The. Fucking. Stuff. Out. As another of Spud's maxims ran: 'The only reason all these silver spoons have got a few quid is because they never fucking spend any of it – and where's the pleasure in that?'

Does This Kind Of Life Look Interesting To You?

S o now let me recall some of the vehicles – others may prefer the term 'get-away cars' – that provided the war chest for such trips as the Great American Railroad Disaster. The projects themselves may not be memorable, but I'll attempt to furnish at least one incident from their existence to justify inclusion and offer clues as to how such a celebrity feeding frenzy gets underway.

The football phone-in show *606* lay the foundations for pretty much everything else that was to come for me. Radio 5 in those days, long before its rebrand as Radio 5 Live, was a peculiar network with no clear idea of what it was supposed to be. The show *Sports Call*, which aired at lunchtime of a Saturday, had proved to be a big success, with the basic quiz element consisting of five individual rounds that anyone could phone in to, offering very good prizes for the winners. These were the days when most radio shows gave stuff away, ranging from VHS videos to holidays abroad. A few years down the line when a couple of stations were found to be handing out the odd CD to close personal friends a tremendous media outcry ensued, but it really didn't amount to much and I don't believe listeners were ever that bothered by whether there were six copies of *Die Hard 2* up for grabs on the other side of George Benson's 'Love Times Love' or only five because the host had tucked one away into his backpack. With a certain degree of mischievousness, even today I love to say on air:

'Remember when we used to be able to give you tickets to shows, box sets and solid-gold cars as prizes? You know, before we got caught with our fingers in the till? Then a couple of you out there blew the whistle and now look – NOBODY gets anything! Well, I hope you're happy, Mother Teresa.'

Anyway, *Sports Call* – a totally legit racket, by the way – was doing very well and the ad-libbing I was engaging in with contestants between the questions appeared to surprise the station controllers. They had a plan to extend their afternoon sports coverage with a phone in programme – amazingly still a novel idea in the era just before the dawn of the Premier League. Currently their sport stopped at six on Saturdays to make way for the *European Chart Show* – such was the ragbag of an agenda Radio 5 had back then. After I had finished *Sports Call* one week, the station manager, Jim Black, asked me if I could spare a moment to hear him outline their plan. Two things I remember from that conversation. The first was his greatest worry seemed to be that I would find it inconvenient to finish *Sports Call* at one, go home and then come back at six to do another show. I said most Saturdays I would be watching Millwall play, but if they didn't mind sending a fast car to fetch me, that would be fine. The second thing was they were having great trouble coming up with a name for the show.

Various titles were mooted but, apparently, a decision had yet to be reached when the time came to send the schedules to *Radio Times* for printing. All that was provided was the time the programme was due to begin. Thus on Saturday evening, Radio 5's line-up read:

6.00: News

6.05: Weather

6.06: Sports Phone-In

Devotees of the show today may note the word 'sports' there instead of 'football', and indeed the idea was that every game, contest and outdoors hobby would get a look-in. On the very first show I took calls about chess, cross-country and fencing. However, I made it plain that the last thing I was interested in was commonplace opinions or descriptions of someone's pastime. I wanted the rare, the maverick, the strange. For example, only an ocean-going crackpot would want to foist some old fossil harping on about his success at the local chess club on a fevered audience fresh out of a football cauldron. So any calls had to be about giant chess – a variation you used to see often outside pubs and in the grounds of stately homes. To put heat under the subject I concocted a story about how, a few years previously, a queen piece from a giant chess set had taken flight during a gale and after crossing many counties had landed on a sow called Victoria, who had recently had a litter of piglets. Victoria had tragically been killed in the incident, a plaque erected to mark her passing, and authorities became alerted to the dangers of these unstable, outsized medieval bludgeons. Now, I contested, you simply never see these once-popular big boards and their huge black-and-white armies anywhere. What's more, nobody aside from the pig had ever been injured by a chess piece, large or small.

The upshot of all that balderdash was a surge in people wishing to prove me wrong – particularly on the last boast. One caller held us all mesmerized as he told a story of chancing across a giant chessboard while on a mountainside in the Himalayas where he was challenged to a game by a group of monks. While holding a colossal bishop and lost in his pondering of where best to place it, he stepped backwards over a ravine and broke his leg. He was rescued and then tended to by the monks, who chanted by his bedside round the clock. The shattered leg, he insisted, healed in just three days. Now I don't know whether that tale contains even a grain of truth, but it was brilliantly told and certainly beats some old bore droning on about whether Manchester United should play 4-3-3 or 4-5-1. Also I will never forget that our Himalayan correspondent was, as he told his metaphysical story, on his way back from watching Port Vale get beaten by Shrewsbury, which, for me, added further poetry to his claim.

The point was the show was highlighting the hitherto ignored chasm between football itself and football supporting. Overwhelmingly, football supporters do not talk obsessively about the sport in the manner journalists and pundits do, and in the way advertisers insist. Fans are not submissive, nor are they of a type; a bore is a bore, no matter what your interest. Most supporters I know, sat next to a stranger on a long journey who attempts to open intercourse with, 'So do you think the England manager got it right playing Coggins wide on the left?' would willingly hurl themselves through the nearest window rather than endure such numbing small talk. However, if you start proceedings with, 'I know someone who used a dead lion as a goalpost – bet you can't beat that!' then the motorway miles will melt away at high speed. To me, the giant chess game with the monks had far more in common with the kind of conversations carried out on football coaches than any of the dry analysis.

That is not to say the show did not provide catharsis and even assistance to the outraged and the furious. If funny calls were in the majority, sedition was a very close second. It was never my intention to make *606* a debating forum; it was a broadside, a clarion call and I would often help organize supporters to fight back against the bullying corporate encroachment already paving the way for the suffocating brand of the Premier League. I barred anyone involved with or representing any club from coming on air. These people seemed to get enough opportunities to skew the argument everywhere else in the media, so I declared *606* would be the supporters' voice and nothing but. One of these impromptu on-air salvos would result in a visit from some plain-clothes policemen who suggested strongly that I lay off one very famous team and its chairman, but that would be in 1998, when I'd returned to the show after a lengthy break, so let us return to that in due course.

On the very first *606*, our flag was well and truly speared into the battleground by one response in particular. My ban on club staff had not yet been announced and under the delicious umbrella question, 'Just How Crooked Are Referees?' we in the studio were both astounded and impressed when we received a call from Andy Townsend, then playing for Chelsea. Andy, in a way that would probably find him suspended from the game today, was driving home from that day's match and began to heatedly outline the significant shortcomings behind the whistle at his fixture. When I asked him was this unusual, he roared with laughter and gave a few more examples of open bias he had known. Thanking him for his honesty, the show then moved on to the pros and cons of being trapped underneath those gargantuan flags that supporters pass around stadiums. The next day, though, it was Andy's remarks that made the Sunday back pages and *606* was instantly declared to be the only place to go for all football fans when in transit each weekend. Other sports were soon phased out, but the bizarre, unique and enraged content continued to grow and flow in all directions.

One other note before we move on. It's long forgotten now, but *606* used to feature music – an ingredient that may have seemed superfluous, but one that I tried to make vital. Between calls I would play ever more insistent records from all genres that I felt might make the show seem like it could influence the wheels of the audience's trains, coaches and cars to turn a little faster. Once more I had been given complete freedom on air and the show blindsided a hierarchy not overly paying attention. By the time they became aware of what was going on it was too late to rein it in and the show was a hit. It was a tremendous thrill and a privilege, being able to spit on my hands and run up the black flag like that every week, but such a renegade style was soon to be extinguished as the industry lurched towards today's model where, inexplicably, the further you are away from the microphone the more control you wield over what is ultimately said into it.

Radio 5, cock-a-hoop at having a show that people were talking about, then approached me to see if I would be interested in taking over their daily breakfast show, a moribund magazine affair called *Morning Edition*. In that one sentence you can see how this overexposure thing achieves lift-off, can't you?

This programme too went with some zip for a couple of years and even delivered a couple of lifelong friends in Danny Kelly and Mark Kermode. As newspaper reviewer and film critic respectively, I inherited both the chaps from the previous format and while I was always going to get along with Danny, given that he had joined the *NME* just after I left and his upbringing in North London almost entirely mirrored that of my own across the river, Mark and I were sort of slung into a spin dryer and blended. Until we later spoke about it I had no idea that 'guest' spots on the show were supposed to be self-contained and not designed to be interrupted. The first time Mark came in with, quite correctly, his written script and a bunch of audio clips from the films under review, he said something in his introduction about how he hated John Hughes' films and frankly don't we all? I couldn't let this pass and as he attempted to press on with his five-minute spot I pointed out that to suggest such a thing about the director of *Home Alone* he must be some kind of notorious ratbag with extra lashings of pickled sourpuss. Appearing stunned, he looked up from his script and after an initial 'What?' set about me with a vim and wit every bit a match for my own. I like to think that, in that moment, Mark was freed from his previous role as robotic reader of fixed dialogue to the magnificent jousting free-form broadcaster he is today.

My favourite tale from the *Morning Edition* years happened in my absence, though it was then joyfully related to me by those who were present. Once the show started doing well, a meeting was called by a senior management figure at Radio 5 to see if anything could be done to make things better. I was naturally asked to attend, but explained that my daughter's (imaginary) pet racoon had been a bit down lately and I was at home blowing bubbles through its cage in an attempt to perk it up. Early on in the meeting, the executive turned to the show's producers, Nick Morgan and Oliver Jones, and said,

'Is Danny happy with the show and the station, do you know? I mean, can we do anything to help him?'

Knowing me well, the pair of them were tempted to reply, 'Yes, never call another pointless meeting like this again.' Instead they elected to go with more diplomatic answers. The superior, however, seemed convinced that they had become disconnected from the station's star turn and so pressed them further, leading to what I consider to be one of the greatest reported exchanges in show business history.

'Well, what are Danny's interests? Are there any guests we could get on the show he would really spark off?'

Now it just so happened that Frank Sinatra was in town to play one of his final concerts. Oliver, who has on many occasions been reminded that his sardonic wit is prone to being misunderstood, piped up,

'Well, Sinatra is playing the Albert Hall. Danny likes him. Perhaps he'll come on.'

This drew a laugh around the table. Except from the exec. He continued to look at Ollie.

'Well? Has anyone made the call?' he said in all seriousness.

'No!' the producer guffawed. Then, noting the furrowed brow of his superior, he attempted to explain the problem. 'No. It's Frank Sinatra. Frank. Sinatra. We're Radio 5's new breakfast show. Frank Sinatra doesn't even receive the Queen!'

The suit at the top of the table was having none of this.

'I want someone to find out where he's staying and ring him up. Ask if he'll come on and do something for us.'

'Do *what* exactly?' asked Oliver, aghast.

The suit was not to be swayed.

'I don't know, perhaps he could come in at six to look over the morning papers.'

That was his idea. In all seriousness he believed there was a world in which I could say, live on air,

'Well, the time here on *Morning Edition* this Tuesday is just coming up to eight minutes past six and now we're going to look at some of the stories dominating today's newspapers. Casting an eye over the headlines for us, I'm joined by singer Frank Sinatra. Frank, what's caught your eye this morning?'

Presumably the same member of management would not have turned a hair if I had followed this with,

'Let's see what's happening on the roads now with our eye in the sky, Marlon Brando.'

As my radio profile grew I began to get my first experiences of what Jerry Seinfeld once described as 'show business people's obsession with giving each other jack-off bowling trophies', though he did qualify that by later saying, 'Believe me, I would not be talking like this had I not already won most of them.' The first award I was nominated for was at the New York International Radio Festival in 1991 and, like the two others that swiftly followed, it involved an element of fiasco.

I had just arrived in Florida for a holiday when I received a call from GLR's Trevor Dann, extremely excited that something on the station had caught the attention of a prestigious international jury.

He explained that the actual ceremony would be in Manhattan three weeks hence and it would really give my chances of winning the gold a boost if I was in attendance. Naturally happy at the news, I told Trevor that, sadly, I would be with the family in the Sunshine State at that time and leaving the kids to fly up to New York for a business jolly just wasn't on. Trevor asked me to reconsider my decision, underlining that the honour was something very important to a local station like GLR. With equal stress I replied that my wife not hitting me over the head with a tyre iron was just as important and this would doubtless be the outcome should I say I was going away for a few days.

The truth was I didn't want to go. When I'm on holiday I never call home, go online or seek out information about what might be happening back in the UK. If I so much as see anyone reading a British newspaper I genuinely feel like setting fire to it, so the idea of sitting with my boss – chum though he was – at a radio convention carried all the allure of a weekend's unpaid overtime in a window-less room.

In the end a desperate Trev put a compromise to me that only a heartless weasel would have nixed. The ceremony was at 8 p.m., GLR would get me a seat on a 4 p.m. flight out of Orlando that would arrive in New York around 6.30. This would take me straight to the do, and while I would miss one night of my holiday I could catch the 5.30 a.m. plane next morning to be back with the family for breakfast. This was deemed doable and the connections and hotel were duly arranged.

Shortly after signing off on this deal I began to have mixed feelings. On the one hand I had sold out a family principle and suddenly found myself to be one of those wretches who receives work calls while away with the kids. On the other . . . I was a big noise in New York! Oh yes. You will forgive me if in the days after being alerted to this my 'bombs' into the hotel pool were a little more flamboyant in their execution. That said, when the Friday of the awards arrived I mooched about Disney World with a melancholy air. As our little boat chugged around It's a Small World After All, I sensed the hundreds of animatronic dolls the attraction features were not singing the famous ear-worm the ride is notorious for but instead leering out at me with disapproval, changing the chorus to, 'You're a Poor Dad After All'.

I left it to the very last moment to head to the airport. Amazingly, I had not thought to pack either a dress or lounge suit for walking around the sweltering theme parks, and what's more I was damned if I was going to hire one. The temperature that day in Florida was around a thousand degrees, so I set off for the plane in loose Hawaiian shirt, garish Bermuda shorts and pool shoes. In my bag I had packed a plain white shirt, a clean pair of jeans and a pair of black crepe-soled brothel creepers. This was as formal as I wished to be and, while not wishing to appear markedly disrespectful, I felt if a rocking radio festival couldn't cope with that look then its awards weren't worth the pewter they were struck from.

The first hiccup in the carefully wrought schedule was that, of course, the plane was delayed by thirty minutes. Even with a good run into mid-town, I would be cutting it very fine. Trevor had flown out from London and I was scheduled to meet him in the reception of the Hilton hotel at 7.30. Now I would be turning up as the drum roll that announced our gala got under way. I started to tense up. WHY had I agreed to this preposterous intrusion? Answer: because it was in New York. Had I been at home and the honours bash had been held in Huddersfield, would I have gone? Not a chance.

The second rock in the road was that I had forgotten to pack my normal glasses and, as day turned to night, all I had were the wrap-round prescription Ray-Bans that I had dashed out wearing. Every time I wanted to see a gate number or find the toilets, I had to bung on shades. Given that I was now dripping with sweat, agitatedly checking the arrivals board and muttering furiously to myself, I must have looked like a helpless cokehead awaiting his latest important parcel from Colombia.

It was not a great flight. One of Florida's infamous weather events meant we dropped, rattled, shuddered and lurched for the entire first hour. With bitter irony I realized that these were exactly the sorts of sensations I had been queuing up to an hour to experience in Universal Studios. Having made up a little time on the journey, the pilot announced that we were now beginning our descent into New York. This was my cue to make it to the toilets to get changed into my show clothes. From what we had heard about the weather en route, I began to wish I had also packed a jacket, but I'd decided against it because, like British newspapers, once I'm under the sun the sight of functional city garments make me feel positively greasy.

Once inside the cubicle I wearily removed my Hawaiian top and watched myself in the mirror replace the pictures of palms and dancing girls with the traitorous white shirt of surrender. With every button I fastened it seemed like I was walling up Wendy and the kids on the other side of the world. Now down came the psychedelic Bermuda shorts, still fragrant with the chlorine from our pool, and I reached into the bag to fish out my heavy Levi's, last worn on the outward journey. After all these weeks away, I fancied they would envelope my legs like a mummy's bandages. Stepping into them, I hauled the denim up with a sigh. Something was wrong. I tried again. For some reason they would not come past my knees. For several seconds I remained doubled over, jeans about my ankles, holding them by the waistband. My eyes cast themselves upward in thought. I saw myself back in the Florida hotel room, working myself up into an angry state about departing, reaching into the cupboard and . . . oh fuck. These must be Wendy's jeans. I put it another way to myself. 'You have no trousers to wear to a glittering ceremony at the Hilton Hotel.'

Then came the reverberating bong that precedes an announcement. 'Ladies and gentlemen, we are making our final descent into New York La Guardia Airport, please return to your seats and make sure all baggage and meal trays are stowed safely away, with seat belts securely fastened. Cabin crew doors to manual.' Oh for God's sake!

By the time I legged it out to the rank of yellow cabs it was 6.55 – so basically an hour to make it to my meet with Trevor. I would need every second of that, but knew I just had to buy a pair of trousers, *any* pair of trousers, somewhere along the way. Bundling into the back of the cab I blurted out the address – three times, Americans resolutely believe I speak in some sort of queer Bulgarian dialect

– before saying, as clearly as I could, 'Could you stop at a gents cloth-iers on the way?'

My driver, a turbaned chap listening to his ethnic radio station of choice, said 'Eh?'

'A men's shop. I need to buy some jeans?' I enunciated slowly.

'Eh?' he said again.

'Trousers. Do you know of anywhere I can buy trousers on the way?'

There was silence.

'Trousers,' I stated hopefully, following this up with another, more plaintive, 'Trousers?'

The man left another pause before replying.

'Eh?' he said, this time with a hint of anger.

I struggled with how I could make it any plainer. Then I suddenly realized where I had been going wrong. It was in the key word. This meant little in the US.

'Pants!' I now blurted. 'I've come away without any pants. I need to buy a pair of pants.'

'Pants?' said my man at the wheel, followed by, 'Pants?'

'Yes, pants. I have no pants. And need some. Do you know of any pants stores we pass?' It is a measure of how desperate I was that I didn't even laugh at the drivel I was now breaking down into single syllables.

Once more there was silence.

'Eh?' he eventually said.

The traffic was not kind to us and as we sat in the Friday rush I craned my neck this way and that, searching for anything that might look like a gent's outfitters or working man's store. I racked my brain for somewhere I might have seen on any of my previous visits, but all I could recall were the copious XXX adult-store neons that overran midtown back then. At exactly eight o'clock the cab arrived outside the Hilton and I ran up the few steps into the lobby wearing a white shirt, psychedelic shorts, yellow socks and brothel creepers. Trevor, replete with black bow tie, was so relieved to see me he hid his reac-tion to the full horror of my appearance and just led the way for-ward. Inside, the ceremony had already begun and as we made our way to our table I sensed many of the dinner-suited and designer-frocked gathering were thinking, 'How pathetic. This guy can't leave his whacky persona outside for one evening. What a goon, get over yourself, buddy.'

Settling down, I hid as much of my legs underneath the tablecloth as I could and smiled silent greetings to the other ten strangers circled around in the half-light. About five minutes later, the opening speech from the stage finished. Trevor and I applauded and then one of the most disheartening things I have ever witnessed swung into full effect. The lights went up and a pair of co-hosts, each behind a lectern, started rattling off names of medal winners at a speed identical to that of Texan auctioneers selling off cattle. Soon a line had formed to one side of the stage, very much like the queue for the buffet at a wedding reception, and people just jogged up and were handed a trophy before coming down the other side to be photographed with it against a cheap golden backdrop emblazoned with the event's logo. After about twenty minutes of this we heard my name called. After a short wait in the line, up I went. I don't think I was on stage long enough for anyone to notice what I was wearing. If at the end of an hour there was anybody in the room who wasn't holding an award, I certainly didn't see them. Trevor and I looked at each other.

'Well, not quite the Oscars . . .' he said with raised eyebrows.

I ventured that the 'event' seemed to have more in common with those time-share gatherings you read about where your attendance guarantees a Parker pen or miniature carriage clock. Naturally we agreed not to breathe a word of the perfunctory free-for-all we had been part of and simply wire London that we would be returning home with a gold.

A far more prestigious honour is the Sony Radio Academy Award. This bash is held annually in London, and in 1992 I was nominated for Radio Personality of the Year for *Morning Edition*. Once again the news was a big deal for the station and once again I had to tell them I would not be around when the big night came because, you will not be staggered to learn, I was going to be in Disney World. This may strike some as unadventurous, but all I can say is that, while we did go on other holidays, the kids adored their stays in the Magic Kingdom and that was enough. The station asked me if it was possible to delay the trip, but after the New York debacle I was doubly determined not to give way. We went that year with Jonathan and Jane Ross and their family, and on about the third day my heart sank when I came back to the hotel room to find the red 'message' light flashing on the phone. Nobody likes that.

It was a call from my agent saying that, though this was highly irregular, Radio 5 had been told in advance that I was going to get the gold and they were offering to fly me home to collect it. The network was struggling a bit and this boost to their profile would be a real shot in the arm. Well, while happy to be a hit once more, I had to reply that there was zero chance I was going to leave Donald Duck and Snow White behind in order to traipse up Park Lane and drink warm white wine with Ed 'Stewpot' Stewart.

The following day the red light was flashing again. This time it was to flag up that the station felt if I wasn't present at the do, they might gift the award to someone who was. As you can imagine, I reacted to this with some force. Either a bloke *was* their radio personality of the year or he wasn't. To give it to someone simply because they didn't have much on that day seemed, in my amateur opinion, to smack of flightiness. Such an award might be perceived to lack depth.

And there the matter rested. For another twenty-four hours. The solution next presented remains just about the most fantastical thing any person could hear while knocking about what the deadbeats still insist is this vale of tears.

'Would it be possible,' my agent enquired, 'if they could get the award out to Florida in time, for you to accept it over a satellite link from Disney World?' And if I had no objections, would I ask Jonathan Ross to present it to me?

I mulled this over for a few sumptuous seconds then said I would consent to this, provided they didn't keep me away from my French toast and coffee too long. Then I sauntered along to Jonathan's room and knocked on the door.

'Old mate,' I said as he opened it, 'I am SO sorry about this, but would you present me with a glittering trophy next Tuesday? I've won most handsome man or something, and you know what children these organizers are – they insist on me getting the thing. They will probably require you to say a few words about how magnificent I am, so I'd get right to work on that if I were you. Oh, and it's all being beamed back live to London, so put a tie on, eh?'

And that's what happened. At 10 a.m. on the little beach that borders the Seven Seas Lagoon, a US camera crew linked to a satellite truck, along with Mickey Mouse, Donald Duck, Goofy, Jonathan Ross and myself, all waved at everyone back at the Dorchester, they all applauded, and I thanked them for this wonderful honour that Jonathan had just passed over to me with gritted teeth. I was, it seemed, making a habit of picking up prizes while wearing swim shorts.

About two months later I was more properly dressed when presented with a further Radio Personality of the Year by the Television & Radio Industries Club at yet another hotel bash where Sir David Frost was dishing out the faux-bronze statuettes. As he handed me mine, I noticed it was wobbling a bit on its wooden base and I made a joke about this from the stage. A week later it fell off the shelf on which I'd placed it and broke in half on contact with the floor tiles. It would be well into the next decade before anyone bunged another award my way, although, without doubt, it was these three rapid industry plaudits that launched the staggering bonanza and spectacular over-exposure I was to experience over the next two years.

Don't Think Twice, It's All Right

In case anybody is getting the idea that life was suddenly all jet planes, hot media projects and wild celebrations where starry new friends exchanged specious awards, I should point out that I spent a good deal of time during the early nineties on the decidedly modest Piper's Caravan Site, Dymchurch, Kent. This was where my dad had acquired a very basic caravan under circumstances that were never fully explained. The only clue to its true registration was in the instruction that, while there, should any strangers ever call by asking for either 'George' or 'Roy' then they should be pointed toward Fred, my father, who, of course, was better known as Spud. This unfixed attitude toward his own name was not a new thing and reached its apogee for me one day when, as he was driving me to some appointment or other, Dad said he just had to shoot into an arch to talk to a bloke who had a bit of work for him. The job in question was to help clear everything out from the former newsreel cinema on Waterloo Station in preparation for a more modern incoming business. These miniature theatres, seating a hundred patrons at most, were quite common up until the seventies and could be found on several London mainline terminuses as well as dotted about the capital, where they squeezed into any spaces between bigger buildings. For a small entrance fee customers would watch a sixty-minute programme consisting of an edition of Pathé News, a breezy short documentary in the series *Look at Life*, plus a string of Warner Brothers or Tom & Jerry cartoons. When I was a youngster my old man would often say on slow days indoors, 'Fancy the cartoon cinema for an hour, boy?' and off we'd go on the bus to the very one he was now being hired to gut, or the one in Piccadilly.

As an alternative to the spectacle of Bugs Bunny and Sylvester the Cat, Dad sometimes took us to a destination that, for some extraordinary reason, seems never to have been attended by anyone else of my generation that I've come across: the courtrooms of the Old Bailey. On days when he'd take my brother and I up to town for a trip to the zoo or Trafalgar Square, we'd toddle off afterwards for a lunchtime sausage sandwich and a cup of tea, and he would say, 'I know where we can go next . . .' Then we'd take the tube to St Paul's for an afternoon watching justice dispensed. All I remember of these unusual excursions was an almost church-like atmosphere as we climbed the steps up to the public gallery, where Dad would ask us to wait while he had a short discussion with the uniformed men who stood in the ante chamber that lead to the various courtrooms. Presumably to make sure we didn't hear explicit details in any of the sexual trials underway, I do recall him always asking, 'Is it all right for them?' although this may have been in reference to a thirteen-year-old and an eight-year-old being allowed in. He would also canvass as to which court currently had a 'good 'un' in. It is entirely likely that the odd two quid changed hands to get us access. Inching along the polished pine pews high above the action, I truly enjoyed the performances and the atmosphere, though I was seldom able to follow what was going on. Spud sometimes leaned over occasionally to ask if I was following the story and when I replied, 'Not really,' he would whisper in my ear, bringing me up to speed with the proceedings:

'That bloke there says he wasn't with that bloke over there when that woman says he was. I can't quite gather what the plot is, but I think her husband's disappeared and him in the yellow tie reckons she's in on it.'

After about an hour he would look at Michael and me and say, 'Had enough?' and we would all leave. On the way out, I can remember Dad having another chat with the police on duty, usually laughing about how the trial he had been watching was turning out.

Anyway, to get back to Spud's prospective job of eviscerating the little picture house on Waterloo Station: I followed him into an arch just off Southwark Park Road where he called out to a man stacking large wooden pallets against a far wall.

'Are you Barry?' said Dad.

'No. We ain't got a Barry here,' replied the worker, making sure his fag stayed lodged between his lips.

'How about Bob?' Spud offered, to see if that would stick.

'Nope,' said pallet man. 'Who you looking for?'

'Not sure. Harry Sarti sent me, about clearing the shit out of the Waterloo Station place.'

'Frank-ie! Someone to see ya,' yelled the bloke, and from a rickety lean-to 'office' to our right an enormous fat fellow in a sweatshirt emerged.

'Whass going on?' he asked.

'Harry Sarti said about the picture house,' Dad told him. 'Said I ought to ask for Barry. Might have been Bob.'

'Well, it don't matter, does it?' said the sweatshirt. 'I'm here now – so d'you fancy it?'

Dad said he did and the fat chap walked back into the office and fished out some keys on a ring.

'Give them to Harry and tell him he's got all of next week, but try and spin it out till at least Sunday. It should only take two days though, so don't go mad. How many of you doing it?'

Dad said just the two of them.

'All right,' responded Barry or Frankie or Bob. 'I can weigh you out middle of next week, if you want. He's told you how much, has he?'

Dad said he had and took the keys. As we turned to leave, the following exchange gave this already unusual conversation a new twist:

'What's your name, mate?' called the fat fellow.

Dad looked at him. 'What do you think it is?' was his bizarre reply.

'I dunno. Henry?' replied the bloke.

'That's it – Henry!' Dad shot back, and out we went.

Once we were in the car, I asked him why he was Henry at this place.

'Well, when it's all cash in hand, you just have to give a name, don't ya? Henry'll do. I was Mick when I worked at the car shop, Terry on the cleaning gang. They don't care, they just need a name.'

Many years later I was stopped by a man in the street who said he knew who I was from the telly and told me to tell my dad Charlie that Ronnie's mum had died. I still have no idea whether he had the right person or not.

Piper's Caravan Site sat some way back from the seafront on a winding lane that opened onto the Kentish marshes. It had no clubhouse, no available activities, no pool, just a small shop at the entrance and a couple of swings for the toddlers. Even in the mid-nineties it was a slow, serene location, mainly occupied by Londoners whose children had grown up and moved on. The sound of kettles being filled every so often punctuated the bleating of lambs or the welcome whistle of the Romney, Hythe & Dymchurch miniature steam railway chugging by, taking day-trippers to Dungeness lighthouse. The caravan we had there was of the old school, with no modern facilities bar a single tiny toilet that you were loath to use in company because of the inescapable noise even the smallest piddle would rouse. The van had gas lamps and only a cold tap above a minuscule sink. There were two narrow, cramped bedrooms to the rear, one fitted with rudimentary bunks; the living space consisted of a little dining table, a few shelves and a couple of bench seats that, when lifted, contained the bedding that allowed extra people to sleep over, providing they stayed on their sides.

It was, of course, the very primitiveness of the accommodation that made everyone so adore the time we spent there. The only drawback was when ablutions rolled around and you had to walk over to the low concrete bath-house to muck in at the sinks, showers and latrines with everyone else. This struck us all as a bit too close to life in the prison block and the trick became either to rise very early or very late to avoid the often noisome clamour.

One weekend Wendy, Bonnie, Sonny and I were down at the caravan and the weather on our last evening there was awful. It was a Sunday and the very next day I was due back in London for a lunchtime screen test with Leo Burnett, the American-based advertising agency who wanted me to become the face of their Daz washing powder campaign. This of course would turn out to be the job that most people would come to identify me with, and some still hope it will bring me up short if they 'cheekily' bring up the brand in conversation. Ironically, this is a manoeuvre that simply won't wash, but we'll get to my time as the nation's number one commercial salesman presently.

When the weather turns gloomy over the desolate marshes on the Kent–Sussex border it is easy to see why the creepy legend and ghoulish visage of the eighteenth-century smuggler Dr Syn continues to hold such potency in the region. As the huge ominous skies and forked lightning bear down on the dismal terrain, you can convince yourself that you see loose mares driven mad by the storm and distant gibbets creaking under the weight of recently executed felons. At least, these were just a few of the images I was conjuring up as I sat at the large window of the caravan with Bonnie, Sonny and their cousin Becky all sitting spellbound alongside. They were absolutely, deliciously terrified as they listened to the details of Syn's ghostly rides across the landscape, their imaginations racing as my wild descriptions competed against the driving rain on the caravan roof.

Now the truth is I am not entirely sure of the component parts of the Syn story and so there was every chance I was laying it on a bit thick and borrowing from sources as disparate as *Frankenstein*, *Great Expectations* and the *Abominable Dr Phibes*. Anyway, I held them absolutely rapt and had the pay-off good and ready. My plan was to tell the kids that I was just nipping to the toilet and that they were to keep a lookout and tell me if they saw anything that even remotely looked like a headless horseman racing across the marshes with fire coming from his eye sockets. At first they begged me not to go, but I said that it would be quite safe because Dr Syn had, under an ancient treaty, promised never to come on to Piper's Caravan Site because he had once loved Lady Marion Piper whose tragic early death had, in fact, sent him round the bend in the first place. This seemed reasonable to them and as I crept away they held on to each other, eyes front, peering out through the squall and across the bleak fields beyond.

Wendy's sister Carol was staying with us and the two women shot me silent looks as if to say, 'What are you up to?' and 'You know they won't sleep tonight now?'

I put a finger to my lips and opened the caravan door as if it were made of delicate high explosive. Once I judged it sufficiently ajar, I eased myself through the gap and stood on the sodden grass outside. Here's what I intended to do next: I was going to race around to the front of the 'van and suddenly leap out in front of the window the children were breathlessly looking through, shouting, 'Behold, Dr Syn!' with my arms spread wide. This would undoubtedly give them a big shock and the tension release that I felt they secretly all wanted. Taking a moment to gather myself and allow a stifled private giggle, off I ran. I figured the swifter I came around the vehicle's corner, the less time they would have to register it was me.

Now then. In my mind I had the lie of the land all mapped out. I had been around the exterior of our caravan countless time and from all angles. So familiar was I with the humble old retreat that I had ceased to think of it as any sort of mobile home and more of a tumbledown chalet. I believe it was this oversight that made me completely forget that these things are not permanent and can be towed anywhere. In order to be towed, of course, they have to have tow-bars fitted on them, and it was this heavy, two-foot long, solid metal extension to the premises that I made no allowance for as I rounded the corner at about ninety miles an hour.

Before I had chance to say my line and perform my star jump, I blindly hurtled into the tow-bar at full pelt, hitting one leg just below my knee and the other full across the shinbone. Later I was told that, from inside, all anyone remembers was hearing something like a sonic boom before I appeared to fly at high speed straight past the window and off to the other side. Carol says the caravan lifted up on to one wheel and almost toppled over, but I think that must be an exaggeration. What everyone agreed on was that, as I sailed past, I had an expression on my face that, while still bearing traces of the glee I had been trying to suppress but a nanosecond earlier, was now overwhelmingly giving way to one of utter horrified confusion.

I hit the ground with an almighty thud and the wet conditions caused me to slide along the grass until I came to a stop almost entirely underneath the caravan next door. The pain throbbing up from my legs was immense and I lay there among our neighbour's tanks of Calor Gas, deflated airbeds and long-forgotten tennis balls for about a minute before gingerly edging myself back out into the pouring rain. I could barely stand. With a wide unsteady gait that must have looked like I'd been caught short on my way to the communal khazis, I lurched back toward the scene of my calamity. Pushing open the door, I stood in the frame and at first the words failed to come as both Wendy and her sister put their hands to their mouths in shock. This was quickly replaced by the exact same failure to suppress hysteria that I'd noted when I knocked myself out in the cellar.

The kids were much more concerned. While Sonny and Becky burst into tears – possibly believing Dr Syn had just 'got' me – Bonnie ran across and hugged me around my thighs. This loving gesture actually managed to put extra pressure on the blood vessels in my legs and it was all I could do not to pass out completely.

'Oh my God, what happened?' Wendy eventually managed to blurt out in a voice that wobbled dangerously on the edge of convulsive laughter.

As with the balloon incident, the more I tried to recollect the accident in my scrambled mind, the funnier it struck the women present.

'I was trying to frighten the kids,' I stuttered hoarsely. 'I ran straight into the tow bar. I went flying.'

Wendy looked down at my shins and the merriment monetarily disappeared from her face. 'Oh my God, your legs!' she gasped.

Looking down I saw two raw contusions with pure white gatherings at their centre and blood starting to ooze in thin lines from the narrow gashes within. I don't think I have ever experienced more acute pain in my life and I stood rooted, trying to control the agony. A few seconds later, Bonnie, who had stopped her comforting, arrived back at my side. Knowing I liked a slice of pork and egg pie on occasion, she had quietly got me a slice from the fridge and put it on a saucer along with a fork. 'Here, Daddy, eat this . . .' she said. Dazed and not wanting to hurt her feelings, I even lifted it to my lips but in that moment simply couldn't remember how you ate things. 'I'll have it later,' I mumbled, but the truth is I don't think I have so much as looked at a slice since.

Eventually Wendy handed me a clean flannel, some disinfectant, some plasters and a towel and told me to hobble across to the men's showers to fix myself up. I agreed and turned slowly to make the trip to the cold concrete amenity block. As I took the first few steps away from the caravan I heard loud peals of helpless laughter coming from inside. Wendy subsequently told me that when the giggling dam burst, Bonnie flew into a real rage at her mum and aunt and for the first time in her life let fly at them. 'It's NOT funny, you . . . you . . . you pair of mares!' she screamed and flung herself on the bed sobbing.

When I came back with my wounds bound I had to sit her down and explain that, though it seemed so terrible it could not possibly be funny, it really, truthfully, actually was. Daddy, when you thought about it, was a bit of a twit. And she allowed herself a short guilty snort of laughter.

Approximately eighteen hours later I arrived stiff-legged and at snail's pace into the tiny studio the advertisers had set up for their screen tests. I had to do a few ad-lib links to camera and then several 'cold' interviews with paid extras about their home life and domestic chore routines. The gash in my left shin thumped like a bass drum throughout, but I suspect it was when I shared the story of how I came to be so injured that they really warmed to me and decided I was the man for the job.

There isn't much to say about the three years I appeared on the campaign, other than that, for the seventeen days a year I was required to knock on stranger's front doors, I earned an absolute fortune. The commercials themselves, and by extension their bumptious front man, were widely deemed to be the brashest, rottenest, most irritating things on television. Daz as a product, meanwhile, suddenly began overtaking all its competitors in the mysterious, yet apparently vital world of the forty-degree wash. It was almost as if these people knew what they were doing.

The thing that most astounds people who gingerly enquire what the hell it was like making such notorious bilge is that these thirty-second scenarios in which overwhelmed housewives invited me into their homes to look at their 'whites' were all completely genuine. The victims of the camera crew 'hits' upon their home were entirely unaware they were going to be on TV. What would happen was that a local supermarket would be staked out and anyone seen exiting with another brand of washing powder would be asked to try a 'new' product that came in a plain white box with no hint as to what it was. The only stipulation was that they had to be ready to receive a phone call two weeks hence to talk about the results. This phone call would in fact be up to twelve advertising people barrelling down on them, filming the whole nightmarish intrusion. Very few seemed to mind this, even when some of the homes we piled into looked as if they had not tidied up since a gas main exploded in their front rooms carrying off Granddad and the family cat. Every now and then of course somebody would open the door and say, 'What? No! Fuck off!' These never failed to cheer us all up, because it swiftly ticked another one off the list of our *seventeen* different locations in a day and also would undoubtedly get a good laugh when shown on the client's Christmas out-take video.

One notable Doorstep Challenge, as the commercials were known, had me feeling more guilty than I usually did when barging into someone's day. We were in Sheffield and I had knocked on this particular door four times without getting a response. The ad's producer told me that someone was definitely in because as usual she had phoned ahead about half-hour previously to make sure we weren't wasting our time. All the occupant knew from this was that they would be getting 'a call' sometime in the next two hours so please don't go out. I knocked again and from somewhere upstairs in the house I heard an agitated 'Who is it?' Followed by, 'Oh . . . um . . . hang on,' delivered in the unmistakable timbre of somebody who'd been interrupted while having it off. Sure enough, a few moments later a woman opened the door, clutching at the neck of a thin dressing gown, ruddy of face and with her wayward bed hair suggesting she had very recently been throwing her head about a good deal.

'Yes?' she panted at me.

I could hardly bare to tell her.

'Hello!' I said brightly, but with my eyes begging her forgiveness. 'It's the Daz Doorstep Challenge! Can we come in and see your whites?'

That she didn't kick me in the balls there and then bears testament to this saintly woman's good nature. Instead she uttered, 'What?' a few more times, to which I repeated my ghastly catchphrase in the name of dogged continuity. At the end of this repartee between us there was a couple of seconds wherein she looked at me uncomprehendingly before saying, 'Oh, for fuck's sake!' and slammed the door. As the crew marched back to the coach that ferried us all around, I think I stood there frozen for several minutes waiting for someone to throw a blanket over me. I believe it was then that I made the decision to leave the DDC band and return to private life. This I did at the end of that contract and I still have a letter from the Leo Burnett Agency thanking me for all the work and adding in a postscript that they were very impressed because they'd never known anyone walk away from as much money as their final offer to me contained. It had been £285,000 for one more year, but they perhaps overlooked the key fact that they'd paid me so much already that I just didn't need the gig any more.

Far and away the best perk Daz duty brought my way was coming face to face with Bob Dylan at last. I can imagine many of you have just sat forward in your seats. 'How on earth,' you are sputtering, coughing up that last swallow of tea, 'could all that deplorable baloney about sparkling sheets and shining results even at low temperatures possibly have come to the attention of possibly the greatest talent the modern world has known?' Well, allow me to fill you in on that one. First, though, perhaps you'll allow me a few moments of quiet triumph over all those who believed my Daz adverts were an irredeemable travesty that, as far as toxic waste goes, probably deserve to be buried deeper than all those spent plutonium rods that China never knows what to do with.

The story goes like this.

I didn't discover Bob Dylan's music until surprisingly late in life. Growing up, neither my brother nor my sister had any time for his tangled lyrical genius, preferring The Beach Boys and The Beatles respectively. This is all to the good, because I think exposure at too young an age to such prose might have made me prone to having a bash at the deep-dish stuff myself, possibly even moulding me into nascent student material, which, of course, would have been a disaster. It wasn't until around the age of thirty that I discovered there was a Bob-Dylan-shaped hole in my musical palate and, upon investigation, received a nasty shock when I realized I had frittered my life away until that point. Even then, I stopped short of going to see him in concert, mainly because I dreaded someone would ask me if it was my first time and I would have to lie like an actor, resorting to improbable guff like, 'Oh, far from it. I was at the Albert Hall in 1966, don't ya know. Yes, if you listen to the unedited bootlegs of it you will hear him dedicate "Visions of Johanna" to the little lad in the World Cup Willie T-shirt who knows all the words to the songs. That was me.'

However, my brother-in-law Brian – who some of you may possibly have seen as the mannequin King Harold with an arrow in his eye at the London Dungeon – was the real Dylan deal. Brian knew every song, every variation and hungrily sought out any obscure recordings of his hero as only Bob devotees can. So when Dylan came over to play something called the Phoenix Festival in 1995, Brian asked me if I still had any connections in the music industry who could sort him out anything special. As it happened I did, and decided to go with him to the concert site on an airfield near Stratford-upon-Avon. We had backstage passes too and one of the clearest memories I have of a pretty boozy day was seeing Brett Anderson from the group Suede looking a bit grey around the gills as he sat in a food tent. I surmised the reason for this was that his band had been declared as headliners some time back before Bob Dylan had been announced and contractually had to be top of the bill, no matter who was later added to the strength. I don't think they'd bargained it would be Bob Dylan. His name had added considerably to the demand for tickets and Brett's outfit, good though they are on their day, were now going to have to follow him. I didn't know Brett, but seeing his glum expression thought that if I acknowledged what I believed to be his malaise it might cheer him up.

'What ho, Suede!' I said as I passed him. 'Dropped a bit of a bollock there, going on after Dylan, eh!?'

Against all my hopes, this seemed to push him further into his shell and he never answered, simply sinking further down into his chair. Still, onwards and upwards.

About an hour before Dylan was due onstage an extraordinary and controversial edict went around the VIP area. Apparently, Bob didn't want to see anybody backstage when he arrived, so the whole place would have to be cleared of everyone but essential staff when he mounted the stairs to start his set. This included all other performers, roadies and technicians, plus the hundreds of hangers on, liggers and drug dealers usually found in this privileged paddock. I don't believe Dylan himself would have made such an imperial demand, but it's typical of the muscle-flexing nonsense management entourages – the scribble that surround top talent – arbitrarily insist on to show their importance. It's testament to the awe and respect Bob Dylan commands that some very big names of the UK music scene complied with this request, albeit accompanied by some grudging noisy protest. A row of heavy-set security men in black puffa jackets fanned out to gently shoo everyone to the fringes of the zone while a small marquee was erected and we all awaited the arrival of Dylan's motorcade. As this was happening, one of the bouncer-types spotted me slowly walking away.

'Hey, Danny Baker, y'soft bastard, for fuck's sake, eh?' he called after me in broad Glaswegian. 'Danny, where's ya Daz? I'll show ye me fuckin' whites, if ye like – put me on the telly, pal!' He seemed thrilled. Clearly, here was someone who didn't recognize a single rock star at the event but knew his TV faces. 'Danny – y'want to go round the front, up close?' he then asked me. Bidding Brian and myself to come towards him, he turned to his equally bulldog-like compadre: 'See who it is? It's the fuckin' Daz man!' To which his mate said, 'Aye, it is! Danny! Where's ye fuckin' doorstep challenge, ye wee cunt!' Aside from being a tad over-familiar, this made absolutely no sense as a question, but I sensed I was on to something good here and so swore something equally meaningless and insulting back at them. They roared with laughter. 'Danny, go with him,' said the first bouncer urgently, 'he'll sort ye right out . . .'

This we did and the perk we had garnered ourselves was a trip round to the photographers' pit right in front of the stage – also completely cleared of people – where several of the thick-necked security had already taken up their positions. As we entered the pen, our minder chum called over his shoulder, 'You stand wi' us, Danny. As long as you're no goin' ta attack the bastard, you're fine. You wait until I tell my mam I was with you – I might have ta get a photo after OK?'

I said it was.

Well, Bob Dylan came on the stage and was utterly superb. This was during his electric rabbi period where he and his band all wore bolero hats and long black coats while attacking his back catalogue with some verve. Several times he looked down into the pit and must have wondered who these two civilians were, sectioned off from the riff-raff and applauding like crazy. This would have been privilege enough, but as his set reached its climax with an encore of 'Rainy Day Women # 12 & 35' I made a fateful decision that changes the headline on this tale from How I Stared Directly into Bob Dylan's Eyes to How I Made a Complete Idiot of Myself in Front of Bob Dylan. During that dreadful extended chaotic final note that even the best of bands do to signify a song is ending, I nudged Brian and said, 'Come on, let's nip round the back again and watch him come offstage.' As we made to leave, our security pal asked us where we were going. 'Toilets!' I shouted. I don't know why I said that. It was a rotten deception after these blokes had gone out on a limb for us, but I was by now quite hyped up and, yes, on the outside of quite a few bottles of Budweiser, and I didn't want them to ask us to wait.

As Brian and I trotted around the rear of the stage, there was Bob Dylan and his band already descending toward the little marquee that had been erected for them to briefly relax and receive a few select guests within. Dylan, I remember, had removed his stage hat and had his head enveloped in a bright pink towel. As he disappeared into the tent, I felt we had missed our chance to get really close to the legend, possibly slapping his back or exchanging a few words during which he would realize that I wasn't a nutcase and invite both Brian and I to join them all under the canvas. Then two things swung the odds back in our favour. I saw the first Glaswegian bull-dog man was on sole duty at the marquee entrance, and beyond him inside was the unmistakable lofty, languid frame of the great Nick Lowe.

I knew Nick pretty well and was sure he would be pleased to see me. More importantly, he was already in conversation with Dylan and once at his side I was confident he would effect the necessary introductions. In short, I was in! Bustling over to the tent, I calmed the initial look of alarm on my puffa-jacketed pal's face by saying, 'It's OK – I know that bloke. He's asked me to pop by.' At this he even held back the canvas flap as I strode by. Nick Lowe had his back to me and was wearing a wonderful black-and-white cow-skin jacket that at that time was his trademark. Walking right up to him at a brisk pace, I grabbed him around the waist and said, 'Nick-eee! How ya doing?'

Nick turned around, surprised, almost spilling his drink. I beamed at him and made a gun-shape with my thumb and forefinger while clicking my tongue.

Only it wasn't Nick Lowe. I don't know who it was, but an individual less like Nick Lowe it would be difficult to describe even if you were asked to achieve this by a police sketch artist. So now there was me, some fellow who looked nothing like Nick Lowe, two other blokes and Bob Dylan all standing round suffering a ghastly silence. The man who wasn't Nick Lowe eventually broke the spell.

'Uh, buddy,' he stammered, 'could you, uh, just give us a few moments here?' Though he said this politely, his eyes were darting around, obviously hoping to locate security.

Saying nothing at all, I turned away just in time to see brother-in-law Brian, who had been several yards behind me, legging it out of the tent and possibly the county too. I exited right after him. My Scots friend grabbed my arm. 'Danny, what the fuck? You'll get me in all kinds of shit, what the fuck were you doin', f'Chrissake?'

I don't know what I replied. Indeed, I don't know what I said for the next few years. I bumbled through life in a sort of traumatized bubble, living in constant fear I would hear a Bob Dylan record and the whole disastrous episode would come flooding back. Today I am more sanguine about it and can even play 'Rainy Day Women' without sweating panic-stricken bullets. Whenever I run into Nick Lowe – the real one and not one of these weasels who go around pretending to be him right up until the last minute – I will always happily relate the story for any company with a light laugh. Against this, I think the fact that shortly after the Phoenix Festival our house switched to Ariel Liquid for all our washing machine needs, a decision that persists to this day, illustrates that perhaps further therapy is required.

I would place my wordless meeting with Bob Dylan slightly above my wordless meeting with Her Majesty the Queen. This too happened under serendipitous conditions when I nipped out to the local corner shop one evening to buy an *Evening Standard*. The convenience store was situated in Trundley's Road, Deptford, close to the yard where mad Rambo the dog marked his turf. Nobody has ever mistaken Trundley's Road for The Mall, so as I emerged from the shop with my newspaper I at first thought the outsize black vehicle stopped at the traffic lights was a funeral car that had come adrift from rest of the cortège. As I walked past the stationary limousine I looked inside and found myself exchanging an awkward glance with Elizabeth, Queen of Great Britain and Her Other Realms and Territories. She was wearing a pale lemon dress and hat, with her gloved hands in her lap. Like a character in a bad sitcom I literally stopped in my tracks and gawped at her while furrowing my brow. It was one of those reason-scrambling moments where normally you would find yourself being shaken awake by a railway employee telling you the train had now arrived in Folkestone, all change, please. The Queen continued to look in my direction and I remained frozen with my *Evening Standard* under my arm. There was no other traffic on this often quiet back street and not a single other pedestrian with whom I could share and confirm the improbable vision. The lights seemed to be taking for ever to turn to green, but eventually they did and the Queen sailed away. At a quickening pace I scooted back to tell Wendy what had just happened.

'Wend! I just saw the Queen! The Queen in Trundley's Road! She was just at the traffic lights!'

Wendy seemed mildly surprised but neither knocked out or incredulous. 'Oh, that's the Thames Barrier at Woolwich. She opened it today, she must have been on the way back from there.'

Something registered in my brain. Yes, I had heard about the new Thames Barrier but didn't know it was being opened that day and had no idea the Queen was officiating. Anyway, that wasn't the point.

'But she was in Trundley's Road! Outside the everything shop. In Trundley's Road. Where it goes into the bus lane. Trundley's Road. The Queen.'

'Well,' Wendy coolly reasoned as she swept by me with Bonnie on her hip, 'I expect they come around that way to avoid Evelyn Street at this time of night. That'll be solid.'

This was hardly the point. I could not understand why the huge event of chancing across the Queen when you pop out for a paper wasn't going over as big as I anticipated. In fact, whenever I got to tell the story later I always embellished it by saying that, as Her Majesty looked at me, I took a ten-pound note from my pocket and, pointing to her picture, said, 'Look, ma'am, I collect all your money!'

I wish I had done that instead of freezing, utterly pole-axed like an overawed serf. Which, of course, is exactly what I was. The *Evening Standard* when I eventually looked at it carried the story of the Thames Barrier opening, right there on its front page. Had I imagined the whole episode after subconsciously registering the newspaper splash? Even now I wrestle with that, but had I been tripping out surely the incident would not have been so mundane nor occurred in real time. No, there is no doubt that Her Majesty the Queen and I really did share a private moment over by Rambo's junkyard. The most reassuring part of the tale has to be that even the Queen of England doesn't just creep across red lights on quiet roads when there's no one around.

My Friend The Sun

The continuing success of both *Morning Edition* and *606* on the radio quickly spiralled into a welter of job offers from all points of the media compass. Financially, these culminated in the adverts for Daz and Mars Bars, so that during any commercial break it was possible to spot my happy old head popping up in consecutive shills, bellowing assured testimonials about forty-degree washes and promising chewy glucose goodness. I have to report that whatever goodwill the public may have towards a performer can soon be soured by such a brassy assault.

The Mars campaign was directly linked to my soaring profile as a sports voice to trust, and so I would find myself travelling with the England team on their official coach, all of us wolfing down the toffee-and-chocolate snacks while urging everyone watching to do the same. I can't quite remember the deathless copy I was required to deliver, but it was probably something along the lines of, 'These taste sensations are goodlylicious in anyone's language! Isn't that right, boys?!' To which all the England players would nod while trails of lightly whipped nougatine ran from the corners of their mouths. In fact, for the most part we used blocks of wood inside customized wrappers as real chocolate would have melted under the hot TV lights. People still raise an eyebrow when I tell them that Mars, like Birdseye, is a family name. At that time every single ad made for the company worldwide had to be personally signed off by Forest Mars himself, then ninety-three years old and living in New York. In terms of their budget, or 'spend' as I believe it is now called, the Mars commercials made Daz look like an old lunatic in sandwich boards walking the streets and ringing a bell. The high point for me came on the morning the 1992 Barcelona Olympics were due to start: I was one of the few people allowed into the final rehearsals of the opening ceremony, where I was filmed walking among the legion of dancers in crackpot costumes, chewing my lips off and holding up a disguised wooden block.

Another spin-off from *606* came about as a result of a throwaway remark during one of the early shows about there being far too many VHS videos on the market depicting the brilliance of footballers and not nearly enough looking at the game from the other end of the telescope. Why, I wondered out loud, was there no compendium of shocking misses, terrible action and wonderfully bonkers own goals? Within a few days a leading video distributor contacted me to see if I was serious about this. I said I was, and the resultant series of releases – *Own Goals & Gaffes* – sold through the fucking roof.

I had, however, featured in one video previously to this: Paul Gascoigne's *The Real Me*. It was thanks to this assignment that I first met Paul; neither of us could have anticipated that our friendship would become so close, nor that it would, for a brief while, dominate the tabloid agenda just a few years down the line.

The two of us had almost met in Italy during the 1990 World Cup. That year England had made it to the semi-finals, where they were to face Germany in Turin. I leave you to recall or imagine how berserk was the resultant mania back in Britain at the time. I was working on *Six O'Clock Live* and the story we were looking at was about the desperation of England fans to make it out to Italy in time for kick-off. All flights were full and by other means time would be tight. Somebody in production had the idea that there might be something in seeing if I could hitch-hike out to Italy in twenty-four hours, filming my own progress. This was long before the era of blogs or video diaries and the novelty, coupled with the ticking-clock element, was deemed to be worth the punt. As a further incentive, ITV Sport said that if I arrived before the game they would provide me with a ticket to the match. As a little film it all worked pretty well, although it required a little cheating to ensure that events attained the necessary level of drama.

Having arrived at Dover, I was filmed walking along the long line of lorries waiting to board the ferry, saying that the next leg of my trip would be trying to get to Paris. Beyond that, I was hoping to get a succession of private cars to inch me towards the Alps. Walking up to the lorry at the front, I tapped on the driver's window. As I did, I think my speech to camera went something along the lines:

'Now, fingers crossed one of these drivers will not only speak English but be willing to drop me somewhere near Paris where I can put out my thumb and begin the next leg of this adventure . . .'

The driver wound his window down.

Excuse me, where are you headed?' I asked him.

'Turin,' he said. 'Want a lift?'

This of course was a hopeless answer in terms of our proposed nail-biting epic. Just seeing me get in a trucker's cab and get out again at the stadium would hardly sustain dramatic interest. So we waved away driver number one and tried several others in the queue, but it was hopeless. Everyone, it seemed, was going my way and only too happy to drop me almost on the centre spot of the Stadio delle Alpi. This was not how we had excitedly imagined the story back in London. Once again tricky old real life had failed to acknowledge the fantasies of a feverish media. Eventually we did find a man who agreed to be filmed saying he was going in the direction of Paris and would get me as close as he could. In fact, he was going to Turin with a load of cherries, but we slipped him a tenner so that our epic thriller could at last begin with the required difficulty.

These days there would be an outcry that we had manipulated everything and we'd be forced to show the truth – me making small talk with an HGV driver from Poplar for seven hours. Allow me once more to direct you toward my earlier remarks about what full disclosure did for radio competitions and prizes. While we're here, I can tell you that when we all got 'caught' making stuff up, I introduced a phrase to our culture that has now been eagerly adopted by the political classes. During a particularly thin item about how the fans of Matt and Luke Goss, then Britain's leading pop sensations, Bros, had been upsetting the residents of the swanky new neighbourhood they had moved into, we found that nobody was upset in the least. This inconvenient detail rather put a crimp in our exclusive, so a friend of one of our researchers was filmed mouthing all the necessary disapproval. Even the producers on a programme as slight and knockabout as ours thought this was a bit much and so the item was shelved until some genuine crazy people could be tracked down. These were scraped together a few months later, happily for us while Bros were still hogging the notoriously fickle teen agenda. However, on the night of broadcast the original edit went out, featuring our researcher's chum. This caused many of those who lived near Matt and Luke to ask who on earth this posturing oaf was, spouting all the fury. A few local papers then went to town on this, and once the *London Standard* hopped aboard the growing imbroglio LWT found it had landed itself a reputation as television's leading deceit sewer, where supine stooges queued up to badmouth national treasures for the price of a hot meal.

At the height of the furore, I was stopped outside the studios by a journalist who asked how on earth we had thought we could get away with such horse feathers. I told him what had happened and, as a sort of sign-off, concluded, 'It should never have gone out at all – but it was a cock-up, not a conspiracy.' This diffused the scandal somewhat and today whenever I hear those last six words uttered, usually against the backdrop of Westminster, I roar out the chorus of 'Drop the Boy' in fitting tribute.

Back at the 1990 World Cup, the footage of my travels to Turin was adequately massaged to make it appear I got there in the nick of time and settled into my seat to watch England lose on penalties in a game they really should have won. This was the match of Gazza's tears and Gary Lineker's 'have a word with him' signal to the bench. Although there had been talk that I might talk with the team after the final whistle, the result and general mood in the stadium at the finish put paid to all that.

So I was not to meet Paul until a few months later, when I was asked to play the public's guide on *The Real Me*, a light documentary officially endorsed and starring the nation's darling himself. Our introduction came in the Tottenham Hotspurs' treatment centre, adjacent to their Middlesex training camp. We were left alone in one of the rooms and at first Paul busied himself with something, anything, rather than attempt eye contact. He then sat pretending to read a copy of the *Daily Mirror* while I spouted off stories. Every now and then he would look up, his face alive with pleasure, saying, 'Is that right? Fantastic! Tell me again . . .' Half an hour later the pair of us were exchanging rapid jokes and opinions about TV person-alities, the kind of kids we'd been to school with and the way the man who just came in to fix the sunbed spoke. It was an instant and joyful bonding and set the scene for some of the wildest times I have known in my life. There was hardly a week in the years immedi-ately after that first encounter when we didn't see each other; rarely a day passed without flurries of phone calls. Whenever we met up – though I have never been and never will be a larky sort – the infi-nite possibilities of each passing moment definitely became more heightened.

You could tell when he'd done something. He'd disappear for five or ten minutes and then return hopelessly casually, bristling with nonchalance, unable to prevent the corners of his mouth from turn-ing up and giving off a sort of silent alarm. Also it had been twenty minutes since the last 'thing'.

'Paul, I know you. You've done something. Please don't have done something.' I would plead with him, 'No, Paul, this is a great restau-rant – I come here a lot.'

'Ha'way man, you're paranoid. I just went for a tab . . .' And he'd fix you with dancing eyes, bursting to let you in on whatever booby-trap he'd just set beneath your social standing. This would rapidly evolve into a smile that would disappear clear around his jaw-line.

'What?!' he'd splutter. 'What?! Relax, y'old bastard. I swear, I just had a quick puff.'

And I'd receive a concentrated beam of inner hysteria, unbridled laughter in all but sound. Whatever it was this time, he was particu-larly proud of it and we'd all find out before long.

It could be anything. Paul was very fond of introducing stray cats and dogs to high-end locations. He could be found in the kitchens of unspeakably fashionable eateries, searching for 'real bread' in order to make an egg sandwich. And nudity was only ever a heartbeat away.

At Champneys health spa in Piccadilly – admittedly an unlikely rendezvous for the pair of us at that time – to the horror of both staff and clientele Paul arrived smoking an enormous Cuban cigar that thoroughly stunk up the entire reception area. On being told to extinguish it immediately, he physically jolted at his thoughtlessness, profusely and genuinely apologizing. Then, in the absence of any ashtrays, he placed the burning tip into the desk fan, sending not only a thousand shards of stogie into the atmosphere but extending the hearty smell of it to hitherto untouched portions of the club.

Going out with Paul Gascoigne was like taking to the town with a case full of wet dynamite. Like promenading with a hybrid of Hunter Thompson and Norman Wisdom. Like nothing mattered.

Everybody at some point in their lives deserves to know someone like Paul Gascoigne, someone so reckless and magnificent they have seemingly been raised by lightning. For several years I knew him intimately, and I cannot think when I've laughed more or felt more alive.

Few people can, as the saying goes, 'stop the mighty roar of London's traffic' simply by appearing on its streets. I know Madonna can't because I've seen Madonna shopping in London's West End and the sight of her pootling along Bond Street barely caused a pizza-bike to backfire. But Paul Gascoigne could.

Shortly before the above described cigar faux-pas I had watched him crossing the road in Piccadilly and every car, every bus, every taxi came to a halt and started sounding its horn. People leaned from windows hollering jokes and hellos that all became lost in the swell of the rising din. The tourists knew him, the policemen knew him, the newspaper sellers knew him. The social anarchy that followed his every move in the mid-nineties was totally genuine. He had no 'people' to organize and manufacture his celebrity, no agenda other than to simply get through each tumultuous day that his gift and nature had bequeathed him.

On an early visit to Paul's family home in Newcastle I was shown his trophy room. Though not a large space it was completely shelved and every shelf was full of cups, medals and prizes. The startling part was that only about a third of these were for football. Virtually every other mainstream sport was represented here, from cricket to snooker, and there were very few silver awards or runner-up certificates. Like Dustin Hoffman in *Rain Man* with his uncanny mathematical abilities, Paul could 'do' sport as easily as draw breath – and plainly had been able to do so since taking his first baby steps.

I later found out that his genius for games was so acute that it became difficult for him to find competition willing to play against him, even among his supposed soccer equals. Thus, at the England training camp, if Paul was playing snooker he was only allowed to hold the cue with one hand. If he played table tennis he would have to put the bat aside and just play with his hands. He could only get a game of darts on the condition that he threw his arrows with the point facing toward his nose. Not only that, he would simultaneously smoke, talk and keep an eye on the horse racing while doing all these things.

One Wednesday morning on the pitch at St James' Park – where we were filming *The Real Me* video – I challenged, possibly threatened, him to a penalty shootout. I mean, you would, wouldn't you? Anyone can win at penalties. Immediately, Paul began compiling a list of handicaps that he would take on.

'Right, you can take ten – I'll just have six. I mustn't have a run-up. I can only kick the ball by putting my right foot around behind my left foot. And I have to tell you in advance where I'm going to put it.'

Now look. I understand that I am not in Paul Gascoigne's class. I'm not even in the same school, city or universe. But there is a limit to the amount of patronizing tosh a chap can take. And he wasn't done.

'Even better. You can tell me where I have to put it. And on the last one, I have to run up backwards and heel it in with me eyes shut.'

It was then that it dawned on me these insane, self-imposed rules were neither a display of ego nor arrogant grandstanding. This was the only way he knew of giving tasks the edge necessary to engage his ferociously competitive drive. Like the chronic gambler who will agree to sit in on a poker game he knows to be crooked, Paul needed to stack the odds against himself in order to feel anything at all from the resultant victory.

Everyday life and action bored him. It always had. The constant need to assuage this gnawing inner ennui ran deep within him. By the nineties he was attaining the power, freedom and means to temporarily fend off the void by cranking up the heart-stopping risks on a daily basis. Even then he knew it was an addiction that would never be satisfied, no matter how spectacular its manifestations became. He knew it would eventually drive him insane. The brighter his star shone, the more its inevitable collapse into a black hole haunted him.

On many days, and with growing frequency, I could glimpse the fear of that impending sentence burning wildly behind his perpetually teary eyes. Gazza cried when he laughed and he cried when he hurt. He cried while telling stories and while miles away in thought. There is an argument that he was among the prime movers in making crying such a queasy modern British phenomena. Yet his were no tears for effect. He simply never wanted any feeling, any fleetingly distracting pulse of experience, to stop. The tears marked the moment. He was 'there' then. Soon the restless agonies would swallow him up again, denying him peace, denying him even a few hours' sleep.

For a while though, the 'cures' for his pain were both explosive and exhilarating.

I have a store of extraordinary stories about Paul, each one presenting a unique, astounding, sometimes hilarious, often portentous facet of a personality so huge it eventually obliterated normal everyday function.

But let me here simply reproduce one particular sack of monkeys that might help people glimpse what life in his orbit was truly like.

There is an infamous, much-reproduced photograph that shows Paul, Chris Evans and myself standing in the reception of the Grosvenor House Hotel, London, looking as if we had been drinking all day, out all night and had no intention of wrapping things up for at least another thirty-six hours.

It was actually taken at about midday and the build up to it, and the events that followed, pretty much sum up the circus that was Paul's life back then.

The first thing to say is that we are all stone-cold sober in that shot. Moreover, if you look at Paul, he is frozen to the spot in out-and-out terror. You'll discover why.

The plan – hastily arranged via a few phone calls earlier that morning – had been to go and spend the day at the races. Why, I have no recollection – none of us are gamblers. Paul was playing for Glasgow Rangers at the time and rarely made it down to London, so probably he was looking for something more to do with his furlough than just watch DVDs and down a few Budweisers.

Paul, Chris and I were three extremely close friends then, bonded by a love of basic proletarian low-life laced with liberating high jinks. We had no interest at all in the celebrity circuit and its fascination with exclusive media venues like the Groucho Club. Indeed, the fact that when we did have a drink we'd do it openly in ordinary pubs somehow set the tone for the whole 'Three Muska-Beers' tagline that has dogged the three of us to varying degrees ever since.

If we were photographed in a pub on a Monday and then again on a Thursday, it was presumed and indeed printed that we had been at it for the whole four days. To be fair, sometimes Chris actually had. (I have never in my life known anyone who could keep up an almighty pace like Chris Evans, but that truly is another story.)

Me? I could manage the occasional long day's carousing, but like most men, not the way I could in my teens and twenties. Besides, I had a terrific home life with young children and, though the idea that I was part of some new hell-raising elite could be flattering and amusing in equal part, it certainly did not fit with the lifestyle of a middle-aged dad making the school run most mornings. Also my wife is not exactly the long-suffering little woman who waits and weeps.

Then there's Gazza himself. Gazza never could and never will be able to drink alcohol. In those days this was true in every sense of that phrase, literal and physical. Not only would two beers have him swaying on his axis with the world doing a Watusi around him, but he never seemed to really like the stuff. Whenever possible, he did his best to avoid alcohol.

An early trick I observed, and a common one for men who feel intimidated by the capacity of those around them, was to surreptitiously pour booze away when he thought everyone else was distracted. I'd see him take a drink from the table and, while keeping his eyes directly on whoever was talking, slowly drop his arm down by his ankles. The glass would quickly emerge a couple of inches less full. He would then wink at me and silently motion that I should keep quiet. He would do this, of course, while regularly motioning the bar staff to keep them coming for everyone else. He loved nothing more than being part of – indeed, being *the cause of* – a good time. The fact that he was always slightly apart from and outside the euphoria might only be detected through longer exposure to his hosting technique.

In the early days, with just the three of us, Paul would actually seek 'permission' to either miss a round or have a soft drink. 'Lads, I'm lagging, I can't do it any more – do you mind if I have a Coke or something?' Yet if somebody else joined us he would say he was on the vodka and Cokes and, subsequently being bought one, dutifully drink it down in one huge gulp. Never wanting to disappoint, he would slip into the cartoon Gazza of red-top legend.

Later, he took to ordering bizarre and comical combinations as if to satisfy both sides of this ludicrous social pressure. If you hadn't seen him for a while it was intriguing to see which two disparate drinks he might have moved on to in the interim. Brandy and 7-Up. Malibu and blackcurrant. Pernod and Sunny Delight.

'Paul,' I would say, 'that is ridiculous, disgusting. There is no such drink.'

But he would be quite serious.

'Danny, it's brilliant – have one. It gets you blootered, but you can carry on drinking it.'

That desperate ambition to numb himself round the clock was still some way off at this stage.

Initially, with Chris and I, he didn't need to keep up any act. We were drinkers and he liked that. But the drinking wasn't *why* we all got on so well, and he liked that even more.

In Chris he'd met his restless equal in terms of keeping the 'craic' in constant motion. Chris, for his own, different reasons, lived his life then as a travelling circus of possibilities with an ever-changing backdrop of locations and faces, each pub becoming an essential base station as he mounted that day's sensory Everest. The point was simply to be out, to be doing something, and that dovetailed perfectly with Paul's dread of being alone.

Conversely, in me, or perhaps more pertinently my family, he saw a home. He loved our extended family with all the kids, the noise, the meals, the motion, the neighbours, the sense of permanence. On the many times when he came to stay and all that was planned was a big dinner and a night in, he would lie full-length on the sofa repeating over and over to himself – all who know Paul will attest he continuously carries on a personal mumbled monologue – 'This is it. Staying in. Stay in. Door's shut. Fook off, that's me in now. Done. Door's shut. Telly's on. Love it. In. *IN*.'

None of this is to say that there weren't times when Paul, Chris and I would get pleasantly lit up, but to my knowledge none of these excellent sessions were carried out within a flashbulb of a press pack.

So, back to that Tuesday morning with the phone ringing and the suggestion of a day at the races.

Peculiarly, the agreed rendezvous was a pub in Shepherd's Bush – a part of town that is only matched in its complete lack of promise by its total inconvenience for all three of us as a location. The meet was set at eleven-ish and upon convening it soon became clear that leaving the bustling metropolis and going to some racecourse to slog it through seven wallet-sapping races was something that only maniacs might consider progress, so what were the alternatives?

Now here I should perhaps re-cap how well-known a tabloid trio we actually were at this point. Yes, even me.

I had recently been noisily fired from *606* for suggesting on air that appalling refereeing, and one referee in particular, was a constant threat to law and order and should a mob one day decide to go to an official's house with lighted torches and demand a sacrifice, I could totally understand their ire. In fact, I might support it. The fallout from this glorious tirade made the front or back pages of most newspapers and even the nine o'clock TV news. I will deal more fully with the various times I have been fired and re-hired a little later in these recollections, but will have to speed past them for now or this particular chapter will end up about the thickness of a Harry Potter compendium.

Chris had of course raised his own profile just a little since teaching me how to play records on the radio and at the time of the Shepherd's Bush liaison was quite simply the best-known media personality in the whole of the UK.

And Paul was, well, Paul at the height of his pomp, one of the most famous people in the whole world and, as it turns out, *not even supposed to be in London that day at all.*

So given all that and our penchant for keeping a pretty low profile, it seems an unlikely course of action that we eventually decided upon.

We decided to pitch up at a nearby media award ceremony.

For those of you who don't live in London, award ceremonies are as common in the capital as branches of Starbucks or McDonald's. Most large buildings are hosting one of these events at any given time, sometimes several simultaneously on different floors.

This one was happening about twenty minutes away and was the Television & Radio Industries Club – or TRIC – bash, the same academy whose award had fallen from my mantelpiece a few years previously. If you are unaware of the TRIC Awards, that is perfectly understandable. Nobody has ever referred to the TRIC Awards as 'the traditional curtain-raiser to the Oscars'. It is a low key, un-televised, industry do that can sometimes be a little under-nourished in the high-profile recipient 'actually being there' department.

Chris' radio show had been nominated for two awards at this affair and his office had sent a message in reply to the invitation saying he would do his best to attend, diary permitting. This is agent-speak for 'no'.

However, as we huddled in that pallid pub, mulling the way forward, it did seem like something to pass the time before we decided what to do. My only objection was that, being grotesquely unshaven and wearing an enormous shapeless WW2 navy duffel coat, I was hardly likely to be mistaken for David Niven promenading around Cap Ferrat. Would the TRIC people mind? Chris said that, seeing as Paul and I weren't invited anyway, we shouldn't let such social niceties cloud our thinking.

And this is where the story really starts.

To get to the hotel on Park Lane from Shepherd's Bush is straightforward and takes about five minutes. Except that it doesn't, because the road is always so choked with traffic it takes about six months. And on this day it was going to take twice as long.

Stuck in the back of a stifling taxi, Paul, as usual, simply could not sit still. Head continually turning to spot some action, he was acting as though somebody had told him Michael Jackson had come back to life, was in London, and if you looked through the right cab window at exactly the right moment, you'd see him. Then there was the ever-running dialogue:

'Shall we get out? Is it far? Shall we get out? Shall we just leave it? I might walk – shall we walk? How 'bout we run through that park? Come on, let's run. Driver! Drive on the pavement, go on! Go through that sweet shop – I'll give you fifty quid. I'm getting out. Look at her in that Porsche. Look at that bloke's tie. I'm going to buy it off him and wear it roond me heed. I'm boiling. I'm gonna take me shoes off. How many legs has that dog got? Is it a dog or a rubbish bin? Look at him! Look at him! Jogging! Ha! Jogger! [Window down] Hey, mate! Git ya lig o'er! Run, Forest, run! Ya daft bastard! Come on, let's catch him up. Let's run with him. Driver – have ya got a cigar?'

Immediately behind us in the stationary parade was a double-decker London bus. Kneeling backwards on the taxi seat, Paul, via the rear window, began miming to its driver that there was something wrong with the bus's wheels. The driver wasn't buying it. So Gazza upped the ante and feigned horror because apparently the radiator now had flames coming from it. The driver shook his head, but, with a squint, suddenly realized who this antsy alarmist was and smiled broadly with both thumbs up.

This was when Gazza got out of the taxi.

Chris and I watched him walk up to the bus driver's roadside window and reach up to shake his hand. In an instant, most of the bus passengers became aware who was paying a visit. Cars in the jam began to sound their hooters in salute. Paul acknowledged all this but was carrying on a pretty intense dialogue about something with the driver. Whatever was under discussion was taking some thrashing out, but its purpose became clear when Gazza grinned triumphantly and then hauled himself up into the driver's cab alongside his new friend. The bus driver had to really budge up, but soon they were both in there . . . with Paul's hands firmly on the wheel.

In fits and starts Paul Gascoigne drove that bright-red double-decker London bus right along the Bayswater Road. Sometimes he came dangerously close to the rear of the cab Chris & I were sitting in, now helpless with awe and laughter.

When the bus eventually trundled up to Marble Arch junction we figured the fun was over and London Transport would get their bus back. Marble Arch is as dangerous a circuit as the capital has to offer. Vehicles are coming at you from all angles. It is not for sky-larking amateurs.

Arriving at the intersection, our taxi awaited its chance before quickly accelerating out into the mayhem. We turned to see what the bus was going to do and, Sweet Mother of Mercy, there it was – right behind us, picking up the pace and honking its horn. Paul, still at the wheel, was shouting something at us, pantomiming an irate motorist. As the bus careered across the junction, he even shook his fist.

Let me say this. Whenever I have told friends this story I inwardly wonder whether, like most men's tales, it has become polished and embellished over the years. But it hasn't. With Gazza stories, you don't need to. Paul Gascoigne really did drive a London bus full of people around Marble Arch in broad daylight. And *still* he wasn't done.

He brought the bus to a stop about fifty yards into Park Lane, where the traffic had once again solidified.

Jumping down from the driving seat, he pumped his sponsor's hand and then stood, arms spread wide, in front of the cheering passengers – none of whom I believe had any idea that he had actually been driving the thing and dicing with their very lives for the last ten minutes.

Jumping back into our cab, Paul's face was giving off sparks. It was clear the world had once again become his playground and that he hadn't felt so alive in ages. We all spoke at once but, within seconds, he was off once more, this time exiting through the other door.

What he had seen were a gang of council workmen digging up the pavement.

The group greeted him explosively and once again Paul quickly outlined to them his latest idea. After a brief consultation, on went a high-visibility vest and ear-protectors and one of the chaps hauled a huge pneumatic drill his way. Thundering the thing into life, Gazza began randomly digging up sections of London several feet from where work had commenced. I remember thinking that was as close to the philosophy and antics of Harpo Marx as real life ever comes. In a communal panic, the men eventually guided him toward the area that needed excavation and for a couple of minutes Paul concentrated intensely on his task.

He stopped. Chris and I, watching breathlessly from the sluggish cab, thought this might signal his return to us. It didn't. Gazza was merely negotiating a cigarette. One was provided, lit, placed between the lips and he was off drilling again. Gas mains would have to look out for themselves.

It was here, for the first time, that the driver of our taxi remarked upon the surreal events unfolding behind his back.

'Your mate,' he said drily, 'he's not all there, is he?' Then, narrowing his eyes toward the drilling, confessed, 'You know, that's the one thing I've always wanted to do – what he's doing now. Fair play to him.' Plainly the whole bus-driving episode was a bit down-market for a cabbie.

Deciding to walk the rest of the journey, we paid him off and crossed to the far pavement where Paul was hammering away. The watching workmen proffered both Chris and I some power tools too, but we politely declined.

'What shall we do now?' Paul asked, curtailing his shift. We reminded him of the awards show thing.

'How're we getting there?'

I told him that as it was barely half a mile along Park Lane, we were walking the rest of the way.

Paul's face registered that he felt this answer was a complete abdication of the better and more readily available options.

'Howay!' he announced and strode out into the traffic again. What had caught his eye this time was an enormous old-fashioned Rolls-Royce, of the type you will see decanting brides at weddings. We called after him but it was no good.

He strode up to the car and tapped on the darkened rear passenger window. It opened a little. A conversation ensued. Then the door open and Paul disappeared inside.

Amazingly the traffic immediately began to loosen up and so began a farcical period wherein Chris and I, now walking toward our destination, were continually parallel to the Rolls with Gazza at its window smiling and waving, heckling the pair of us as 'peasants', 'riff-raff' and much worse. The four people sitting inside with him found the gag as hilarious as Paul did. Only he could manage this sort of thing.

Thanks to some aggressively red traffic lights, we arrived at the hotel just ahead of the Rolls. What happened next we really should have predicted. Instead of it stopping and allowing its stowaway off, it simply glided on past us, heading towards distant Piccadilly, Gazza's hand regally twirling away in our direction.

Now what?

Chris and I sat down resignedly on a patch of grass and waited for our careering loose cannon to return. Or not.

Ten minutes later he was back, this time in a Toyota, driven, he informed us, by 'an Everton supporter called Tom'. He'd asked Tom to join us at the awards, but Tom had to get back up North.

And so, at last, in we went and . . . boom. A blitz of camera flashes, not unlike when a high-profile defendant arrives on the court steps, ricocheted around the foyer.

If you study that notorious photograph you can see that both Chris and Paul have simultaneously started to realize what a terrible idea this was. I am actually in mid-sentence, saying to one of the photographers, 'Snap away, matey, you've missed the scoop. You should have been with him the last half-hour . . .'

Now the fun had well and truly stopped. Paul had by far the most to lose by being seen lotus-eating the day away at some brash show-biz booze-up in the West End.

He was supposedly injured. He was supposedly in Scotland. He had promised, *promised*, his boss Walter Smith that he was going to stay put at the lodge by the lake that Rangers had rented for him, doing nothing more physically strenuous than channel-hopping.

As a table was made available and we shuffled our way toward it, Paul kept up a self-berating dialogue, albeit with several bursts of cathartic laughter. 'I'm finished, I'm finished,' he'd splutter. 'I'm dead!'

At one point he grabbed a waiter and told him that on no account must there be any alcohol visible on our table. This was done. But never underestimate a good Fleet Street photo editor. What there was on the table were several bottles of Highland Spring water. With a little cropping of the shots, the distinct tapering green-glass top of these bottles can look an awful lot like copious amounts of white wine just waiting to be quaffed. No further questions. Your witness . . .

Within five minutes of sitting down, and with every camera trained on our table, Chris made the obvious executive decision. 'We're going to have to run away,' he said. Rising as one, we made for the exit again before the ceremony had even got under way. For once, Gazza's magical feats of persuasion with car drivers had a practical edge. Trotting up to a waiting chauffeur whose client was obviously inside for the duration, he negotiated our getaway.

In the back of this commandeered Bentley – and by the way, don't ever try this spontaneous method of getting around town, it is exclusively a Gazza thing – Paul, as usual, looking out of the window and mentally miles way, let us all in on his continual inner dialogue.

'I'll ring Walter. Ring him. I'll say I had to come down to give you an award. Charity. You'd asked special. Presenting an award. Forgot to tell him. You'd asked me and I flew down on the spur of the moment. Just for the morning. Flew straight back . . .'

This he continued going over and over until he'd convinced himself the scenario sounded totally plausible.

'So do you want to get straight to the airport?' I asked eventually.

Paul snapped his head towards me and gave an astounded look as though he had no inkling of how a) I could have possibly heard him and b) how I could have arrived at such a preposterous idea.

'Do I, fook! I'm starving! Where's that hamburger place we went to with your kids that time?'

And so to Ed's Easy Diner on Old Compton Street, Soho. A glass building that might have been made with the paparazzi in mind. I think it was here, and I can't totally swear to it, that he took a swing at one photographer and chased another one up the street.

After an hour of this we decided to cut our losses and just go back to my house in Deptford. Chris opted to stay in Soho, where his own choices were still varied and appealing.

The rest of the day was blissfully and thankfully mundane with Paul – his shoes and shirt removed immediately upon arrival – chatting happily with my family and neighbours, doing magic tricks and gags for the kids and making a series of long calls to Walter Smith until he felt he really had it all smoothed out. He slept as he always preferred to – on the sofa. That way he could just keep watching TV all night with a few fitful bursts of oblivion rolling in until the sun came up. As soon as dawn broke, he'd stand on my doorstep smoking, having lively conversations with every early-morning riser who came by, offering them sweets and cadging further smokes. Once, before I was up, he rode for a few streets with the milkman, making deliveries alongside him.

The morning after the day described, the photographs of the 'Three Muska-Beers' were in every paper alongside tales of long thirsty sessions and all-night hullabaloo. Chris was seen leaving a bar at two a.m. and the clear insinuation was that he had left Gazza inside. That same morning Paul went with me when I took Sonny on the morning school run. Photographers outside my house took their shots and when these appeared later in print, Paul was invariably described as 'bleary-eyed'.

And he would see every snap, read every word. He was incapable of passing a tabloid newspaper without vigorously leafing through the pages to search out his coverage. Then, settling on it, he would devour the copy, reading aloud in a see-sawing mutter, as though he were being nagged, punctuating it with his own oaths, curses and threats. Invariably the rag would end up in a crushed heap several feet away.

Chris and I soon tired of pointing out the obvious cure for such self-torture: Just don't read them, mate.

'I have to,' he'd argue. 'All of it. I have to know what they are saying. The lads will slaughter me when I go training, so I've got to know what they'll be talking about.'

I had been aware of the crushing peer pressure that the squad mentality generates ever since former Chelsea player Pat Nevin told me why he always had to buy two copies of his beloved *NME* each week. 'The lads thought all the music I loved was a bit suspect,' he said. 'If they saw something with Echo & the Bunnymen on the cover they'd rip the piss out of me and throw it in the showers. So I got to buying two every Wednesday. One I'd hide and read later, and the other was for them to "find" and tear up.'

It may have been typical of Paul, so acutely aware of his 'otherness' that, like the spare *NME*, he created the mother of all redherrings in offering up his prankish ringmaster of a public persona for his cohorts. I promise you, the gurning thicko you saw wearing the false plastic boobs on the open-top bus was not Paul Gascoigne. That was 'Gazza'.

So what happened?

How did the warnings and prophecy become so shockingly ful-filled? What caused the cartoon tabloid Gazza to become the actual Paul Gascoigne?

Well, his period in Italy didn't help. Signing for Lazio was very serious. Grown-up. The big room. But they wanted Paul Gascoigne, footballer, full stop. This was entirely reasonable, because Lazio were splashing out a huge fee on the greatest property in the world. Somehow though they failed to notice that this house was on fire.

For Paul, just being a footballer was OK up to a point. When he was 'on', in the theatre, he was fine. But football as a culture bored the living bejesus out of him. He loved Italy and the Italians and learned the language within a couple of months. However, I noted that he would choose his fluency depending who was at the table, always wary of another pro chiding, 'Ooh, listen to you . . .'

When the injuries started piling up, so did the calls begging friends to come out and stay in the big empty house on the Tiber. Despite Jimmy 'Five Bellies' Gardener's Herculean sacrifices – and Jim had always been a totally loyal Jeeves to Paul's Bertie Wooster – sooner or later Paul would be alone in Rome, a physical isolation to accompany the emotional one. It was in Rome that Paul discovered wine, which he also began to learn like a language, and from wine came the numbing 'benefits' of getting sloshed alone.

Once back again in Britain, this time at Rangers, I think Paul had realized that his use for football and its use for him had reached a plateau. Sporting genius, his one great ally in staving off the every-day, was showing the first signs of starting to fade.

He remained a tremendous asset to any club, but whereas other pros might enjoy these later seasons of industry respect and entitle-ment, Paul could see nothing but the yawning abyss of decline. He started to talk more of the frightening and unmapped years beyond. When the world no longer saw Gazza, he felt, they would have to accept Paul Gascoigne instead, and he truly believed that that incar-nation of himself would not be acceptable to them. He would disap-point. Be found out.

That dreaded moment finally came, in Paul's mind, when, in one of the most notorious decisions ever stage-managed by an eclipsed star, the then England manager Glenn Hoddle inexplicably decided to leave Paul Gascoigne out of the England 1998 World Cup squad, a side that everybody else, including the rest of the players, knew he had every right to be part of. It was a shocking decision that utterly destroyed Paul's confidence and allowed his most destructive inner demons to gain the whip hand. Even though his greatest playing days were behind him at the time of France '98, there simply wasn't a team in the world who, had the scores been level with fifteen minutes to play, wouldn't have drawn breath had they seen Gazza warming up at pitchside ready to battle against them. Purely from a morale point of view, he should have been in the squad – the sight of Paul Gascoigne running on to a pitch sent an electric charge through crowds the world over. But Glenn Hoddle wanted to make his splash. In the event, it turned out to be just the latest in his long line of managerial belly flops – and one with catastrophic repercussions for the player.

From that point on, Paul's off-field stunts became more implosive, the self-loathing blossomed and his obsession with stopping the clock filled his every action.

Never quite having the faith in himself to buy into life when he was a global success, when ruin became an option he embraced it as if it were his destiny. He had been the greatest triumph in the world, now he would show how good he could be at failure too. Failure, ruin and despair – why not? It's something to do.

Initially, there was no shortage of volunteers willing to 'cure' the bad Paul 'Gazza' Gascoigne – the broken person Paul has always thought he must be – and Paul has been an attentive and, I suspect, lucrative patient. In those first years after retirement from the game, pyschobabble and clichéd self-discovery became his new Italian. Then, in more recent times, the need for rescue and redemption became all too physical, real and acute.

My phone number has never changed and yet he never calls, probably as part of the latest twelve-step programme or through a misguided embarrassment at what he later became. The last time we met up we went to a restaurant near my home and, while he didn't exactly wolf down his steak, he looked good and drank nothing but water. I drank wine and told him how sweet it tasted. His eyes twinkled because he knew how wrong and therefore appropriate a joke that was; an appalling jest that only very close friends can dare. The sort of joke nobody tells around him any more because he has supposedly become a tragedy, a walking cautionary tale. Except he hasn't quite, thank God.

That night Sonny, now old enough to hear and understand Paul's unexpurgated stories, came with us to witness his silly stunts and japes at those on surrounding tables. All the old traits were present and correct, and Son laughed, I noted, like nobody else – and I have to include myself here – has ever made him laugh. The kind of laughter when breath becomes exhausted and you make a genuine request for your tormentor to stop.

That is something that, in my life, only Paul Gascoigne can do.

More than anything in this world, I would wish Paul to get well and realize, once and for all, how widely loved, respected and important he is. Though these books may include many notable people who have punctuated our pop culture over the last forty years, nobody comes close to making the impression on me that Paul Gascoigne did.

I have never met anyone like him and certainly never expect to do so again.

Ain't It Grand To Be Blooming Well Dead

One of the few traits I haven't inherited from my parents is a belief in crackpot superstition, although some of the more widely held gags in this field I will go along with because they are bordering on tradition and often a lot of fun to perform anyway. So I'll walk around ladders, place unwanted mirrors carefully on to skips so as not to break them, throw salt about and open both front and back doors every New Year's Eve. The only exceptions to this are a couple that come directly from the old man and that I have never heard of being adhered to by anyone else. Therefore, so as not to let these loopy tics die out because of my sluggishness, I will never watch a light go out, and if I see an ambulance I will hold my collar until I chance across a four-legged animal. Dad lumbered me with these when I was about six. The first I remember was delivered to me as we walked along Rotherhithe New Road and one of the streetlights went out as we approached it. 'Fuck it,' Dad barked. 'You should never see a light go out. It means a death in the family.' He then carried on casually talking about something else while I, now completely freaked out, tried to process this dreadful new information. To this day I will look away when flicking off a table lamp, look back and watch it come on again, then look away once more for its final extinguishing. I even blow out candles with my eyes shut. As for the ambulance/four-legged animal thing – and here Spud had warned me that if I ignored the ritual it would mean 'something really rotten is going to happen' – I have to say I am a little more flexible. If I am driving and see the flashing blue lights of a hospital emergency, I do allow myself to simply trap my shirt collar under my chin. This counts, as far as I am concerned, although it does make you look like you are at the wheel with a broken neck. As a further concession, I include insects as part of my release from the deal because they do technically have four legs and a couple of others to spare. Nowhere in the rules does it say the freeing creature can't have more than a leg-quartet and I believe my loosening of the regulations is an overall sign that I am maturing. Against this, if I am walking my own dog and see an ambulance, he won't be allowed to count and I must source a fresh one.

Actually, let me begin this chapter again.

One of the many traits I've inherited from my parents is a dogged belief in crackpot superstition. The first time I became aware of these unseen forces that control all our lives was at about the age of five when, just before a trip to the park with Mum and Dad, Spud said he was going to nip into James Lane, the local turf accountants, to put on a few bets. This bookies was only a ninety-second walk from our flats but we had barely begun to make our way up Debnams Road when the old man suddenly exploded with rage. 'Oh, for fuck's sake Bill!' he stormed. 'What's the fucking matter with you? Silly bastard! If I lose money 'cos of this, I'll go off a-fucking-larming!' Going off alarming was Spud's favourite phrase to illustrate any kind of uproar or fuss. Looking to find out what had triggered this fury I saw our near neighbour old Bill Pitts mooching toward us. Dad and he were old friends, but they seemed to be having heated words.

'Fuck me, Fred, I have to go out mate,' I recall Bill pleading, to which Dad replied something about why, if this was so, could he not find alternative routes.

Sensing my concern, Mum leaned down to let me know what was going on.

'It's y'father,' she explained. 'He was going to put some money on a horse race, but now he can't because he saw Bill and he thinks it's bad luck to have a bet when you've just seen a boss-eyed man.'

Like any five-year-old, I accepted this bizarre data completely without comment and mentally placed it right up there with the shape of the earth and the ocular benefits of eating up all my carrots. There could be no doubt that Mr Pitts had jinxed Dad's intended wagering, for when it came to being cross-eyed, Bill was an undisputed leader in the field with a strabismus equal to, or arguably greater than, the great silent comedian Ben Turpin. Everybody called him Boss-eyed Bill Pitts, even Bill himself. When he would come to our door to 'order' whatever goods Dad had liberated from the docks that week, should the old man not be in, he would say, 'Tell yer dad to put me down for three of the ladies gloves he's getting. Tell him they're for Boss-eyed Bill, he'll know.' In fact, everybody knew.

'One home, one away,' was the most common way of describing his condition, although neither of Bill's eyes could technically be said to be 'at home', given that they both settled toward the inner recesses of their sockets. 'Fuck me, Bill,' people would say, 'can't you stop looking at your hooter for five minutes? It's not that fascinating.'

'Buckle-eyed' was the other term for it, and if Dad ever saw Bill on the street, providing he wasn't going to place a bet, he would shout a hearty, 'Aye-aye, Buckle! I'll be round the Duke of Suffolk later! If you see two of me I'll be the one in the middle!'

Before modern sensibilities lead you to start a campaign to get retrospective compensation for Boss-eyed Bill, I should point out that he had a popular wife, five kids and a temper that was a boon to glaziers who specialized in pub window replacement. Perhaps if he'd been living in the suburbs nobody would have mentioned how boss-eyed he was and even given him charitable status. Doubtless today there would be corrective surgery readily available or else he might better be known as Ocular Different William, but back then he was Boss-eyed Bill and just got on with being Boss-eyed Bill. It was only in taking walks near betting shops that he found his challenging way of looking at the world to have its drawbacks.

The point of all this concentration upon superstitions will soon be revealed, but before we move on I must record a story that goes beyond a belief in mere luck into a dimension beyond. In the late sixties there was a great revival in populist occult imagery, the most notable exponents of which were probably bands like Black Sabbath, Black Widow and the Crazy World of Arthur Brown. TV also fuelled this craving for the unsettling in strange, creepy series such as *Mystery & Imagination*, *The Liars*, and *Journey into the Unknown*, whose haunting whistled theme tune over scenes of an abandoned midnight fairground totally mesmerized me.

Children were given their chance to get in on the supernatural fad via Waddington's Ouija Boards, sold in all good toyshops. These wooden slabs emblazoned with the letters of the alphabet, numbers one to nine and the words 'Yes' and 'No' allowed all junior mystics to get in touch with the more garrulous sort of ghost, and newspapers of the time were full of stories about sessions that had begun by timidly asking 'Is anybody there' and ended up with people leaping possessed from high windows or sacrificing close friends at the centre of hastily drawn pentagrams. As a result, every kid wanted a piece of that action. Nobody I knew had a proper Ouija board but it was soon discovered you could achieve much the same results by writing all the necessary information on pieces of paper arranged in a semicircle with an upturned drinking glass through which to channel the spirit's message. I imagine a rumbled Waddington's wanted to suppress such infringement of copyright but soon everyone was at it. The problem now was that, when you're ten or eleven, waiting for longer than twenty seconds to engage with a chatty wraith tends to test one's patience, so most kids would give the sessions a bit of a helping hand by shoving the glass around the letters themselves while feigning shock and panic. You could always tell when one of your mates was manufacturing the mystery because whatever phantom they were pretending to be would have a penchant for words like 'bum', 'bastard' and 'tit', coupled with a curious eagerness to point out who around the table was, in fact, a secret homosexual. Thus 99 per cent of these initially sombre séances rapidly descended into farce.

Thus one day in Stephen Micalef's house, Mark Jeffries, Tommy Hodges, Peter King and I all promised, promised, *promised* that we wouldn't fake it and no matter how long it took we would wait until the glass began to move purely guided by an unseen force. After a few failed attempts at this avowed discipline – I believe a Mr John Arse put in an appearance at one point – we were off again with all our index fingers atop the beaker as it slid around the letters. The name George was forming up and, as usual, as the fourth letter revealed itself we were all noisily accusing each other of 'pushing it' and creating the kind of racket that might dissipate the chances of any drifting ghoul wanting to stick around. After the glass came to rest it was decided to ask a question that would flush out any charlatans, but we were momentarily stumped as to what that might be. Our ethereal chum waited patiently while we thrashed this out. Then I came up with the idea that I should remove a coin from my pocket and hold it in my hand without looking at the year engraved upon it. If the spirit guessed this date correctly then we knew we had a live one. I took a penny, one of the pre-decimal large ones, and without so much as glancing at it put it in my back pocket and sat down again.

'I thought you were going to hold it,' said Pete.

'Well, you'd all say I nicked a look at it if I did, so now nobody can, can they?' I replied. I wanted this thing watertight.

Tom remarked that the ghost would be forced to look at my bum now to find out what year was on the coin and after a good chuckle at this we asked the question formally.

The glass began to slide: 1 . . . 9 . . . 1 . . . 3. 1913.

Excitedly taking the penny from my pocket, I stared at the numbers beneath Britannia wielding her trident on the reverse: 1913. I showed this around and a strange sickly silence fell over us all. This was a bit weird. Placing our fingers back on the glass we started to ask each other what to request next. Our voices now were low and serious, all the effervescence knocked out by the inexplicable accuracy of the stunt. Before we could agree on a suitable enquiry, the glass began to move again: C . . . H . . . I . . . L . . . D . . . R . . . E . . . N.

'Children!' we all gasped as one, searching each other's eyes for the deeper meaning of this. Then it continued on.

S . . . T . . . O . . . P . . . N . . . O . . . W.

We paused and stared at each other, quite terrified. I broke the spell.

'I don't like it!' I said, my voice rising with fear. 'I don't like this bit!'

And we all jumped up and ran to the front door to leg it into the square outside.

I have absolutely no explanation for what happened there. All those who were present can confirm the events as recorded, and even if you rationalize the coin revelation as mere subconscious chance, none of us can think of a single reason why any of us would have concocted the mundane yet petrifying phrase that followed it. It really happened and there it is.

Possibly I should have brooded upon this bizarre incident more and allowed it to influence my world view from then on but it was soon made light of and only many years later did we all start to question what we experienced that afternoon. Thankfully, none of us have drawn a single spiritual conclusion from it and, quite sensibly, keep the story in a box labelled Derren Brown rather than a crystal ball named Uri Geller.

Anyway, the point of all these diversions into the fifth dimension is to tell you that on the day I was offered a job on BBC Radio 1 a pigeon pooped on my neck. This, coupled with the fire at my parents', the collision with the cellar beam and the later caravan tow-bar trauma lead me to believe that many of my career turning points have been presaged by portentous omens, although it wasn't until I set them all down in these pages that I recognized the inescapable pattern.

I may add that when we came to record the third series of the day-time game show *Win, Lose or Draw*, my schedule required that we record all twenty-eight programmes in four days. For the slower at maths among you, that is *seven TV shows a day*. And on the crucial evening I flew up to Edinburgh to start this lunatic undertaking the cab taking me to the airport broke down and I missed my plane. I grant you that I may be looking a little too hard here for mystical signs and that that the engine on a Peugeot 405 hardly qualifies as some kind of portal between worlds, but I insist this stuff all adds up when you look back over an eventful, if uneven, career.

The job at Radio 1 was never really a good fit and came at a two-pronged tipping point when the new boss at the station, a belea-guered Matthew Bannister once more, was attempting to haul the network out of its ageing complacency at the precise moment the British public began to feel that I was popping up a bit too much in their lives and might want to think about fucking off for a bit. In fact, the shows I did for Radio 1 on Saturday and Sunday lunchtimes were among the most peppy I've ever done, with an audience ready and willing for the more 'stunty' end of aural broadcasting that would include such feats as:

A Piano Played While Buried on Scarborough Beach
A Wardrobe Full of Empty Cans Pushed Off a Student Dorm Roof
A Builders' Skip Dropped on to a Microwave Oven
Two Men Racing Racing across a Supermarket Car Park in Shopping Trolleys Pulled by Teams of Dogs

Plus an inexplicably funny reccurring piece called the Universe of Turmoil, wherein my sometime co-host Danny Kelly would disappear from the studio with the day's newspapers only to re-emerge ten minutes later with a clutch of photographs and advertisements he had cut from them. On the foreheads of the people and animals in these pictures Danny would have written either the word 'turmoil' or the phrase 'we fear change' and I don't think anything in my life has ever reduced me to helpless hysteria quicker than when I would thumb through this pile of images trying to describe to the listeners what I was looking at. It became an extraordinarily popular spot, although neither we in the studio nor the listening millions could figure out just why it was so sublimely hilarious. Engineered or forced laughter in radio is easily detected and always irksome, so I think the genuine paroxysms I collapsed into as I hopelessly tried to convey the idiotic information that I could see a barn owl advertising British Gas with the word 'Turmoil' above its beak somehow infected the entire audience.

Less of a success was a visit from Dan Castellaneta, the voice of Homer Simpson. Though Sky TV had been showing the series for a couple of years, this was in the days when having a satellite dish was still far from compulsory. Dan arrived at Radio 1 with various promotional give-away items, including the first VHSs of the show and a bag full of character figures, but nobody seemed that keen to win any of them via the soft questions he posed about *The Simpsons* episodes, or indeed to have any questions for him concerning the programme. Booked for a half-hour spot, he actually stayed on for an hour performing in the guise of his many characters, each one today globally famous, and joining in with the other phone-in subjects that were getting far more attention than his presence. I had brought Sonny, then about seven, into the studio to meet with 'Homer' and afterwards we went for pizza with Dan personalizing all the left-over merchandize for my boy with various drawings and slogans. Those we still have, but lost to me are the dozen or so jingles he was good enough to record for the show as Krusty, Grandpa, Barney Gumbel, Mayor Quimby and Homer himself. Today I don't believe any of the Simpsons' cast are inclined, or indeed allowed, to be quite so free and easy with their gifts.

Though aware of the yowling mobs outside throwing rotten fruit at the windows, I was thoroughly enjoying my time at Britain's leading youth network, despite being in my thirties and inviting on movers and shakers like the actor/director Lionel Jeffries (sixty-seven) to talk about his work on the film *The Railway Children* (1970), also his friendship with Bernard Cribbins (sixty-five) and Peter Sellers (deceased). Despite scoops like this, the show didn't appear to be gaining any real traction among the kids. As far as most of the public and virtually all of the press were concerned, I was merely a radio interloper chosen to replace Dave Lee Travis just because I was the bloke on the Daz adverts. You can't bellyache about this too much and neither can you pathetically point to photographs of yourself in Bermuda shorts being hurried across stage at a New York Radio Festival or flash your broken TRIC Award as proof of broadcasting bona fides. You just have to do the work as best you can and accept that there may be legitimate reasons everyone thinks you're an absolute piece of cheese.

I had just the two spots in the weekly schedules, unlike dear old Emma Freud who was on every weekday lunchtime, yet my high profile elsewhere at the time saw to it that I became the poster boy for all that was new and revolting at the nation's pop-most network. I found myself cast as a hapless struggler, totally marooned once away from his box of soap powder and TV hangers on, whereas in reality I was in my natural habitat and as far as I could tell the shows themselves were bouncing along brightly. It was simply the wrong place and the wrong time. Despite shedding an impressive three million listeners from the previous incumbent's figures, I was holding on to something like nine million – my previous show at Radio 5 was lucky to get a third of that, so I couldn't see what all the fuss was about. However, one should never confuse popular with populist, and I think I might have done better at Radio 1 if I'd gone with the latter.

Though by my standards I was drumming up a sizeable audience for the peculiar, surprising and hopefully original programmes I continued to present, there will always be an even larger demographic that simply want the traditional, the generic, the norm, in the shape of big hit records and mild untaxing banter. This is completely understandable and so it was that many of DLT's faithful couldn't see what might be entertaining in hearing somebody doggedly walling up CDs they hated behind new tiles in their bathroom, or a small boy being ask to get inside a double bass upon which his father then played a solo. Yes, all that and Los Lobos too. I remember we received one furious email during a quite spectacular call where we were listening in to a woman's budgerigar walking up the fret board of her electric guitar. It said:

I DO NOT PAY MY LICENCE FEE TO HEAR BUDGIES PLAY MUSICAL INSTRUMENTS. YOU ARE INSULTING REAL MUSIC FANS. I AM WRITING TO THE PRIME MINISTER.

He probably did too, because some newspapers were organizing actual campaigns against what Matthew was doing at the station. Asked to meet with various journalists to mount some resistance to the swelling wave of negative, I encountered what remains for me the perfect example of the futility of such exercises. A woman from the *Sunday Mirror* asked how I felt about all the bad publicity my show was getting. Here is what I said:

Well, there's not a lot you can do about it and it may be there are other reasons why it's happening. If the programmes themselves were nervous and no good then I might take it to heart, but look; last year everyone was showering me with awards and calling me a genius, while this year, for doing basically the same show, I'm the leper of the airwaves. I think the only thing you can draw from that is, you know, there's no business like show business.'

And here's what she wrote:

Danny Baker looks down quietly at the drink he's been holding throughout our talk. When I ask him about the battering he's been taking from the critics recently he suddenly becomes angry and defiant. 'You know what? Let them say what they want. I don't care if I'm the leper of the airwaves. I still say there's no business like show business.'

Ladies and gentlemen, can you detect the shift in emphasis between those two extracts? From wry and philosophical to needy and tearful. But there it was. Matthew's revolution at Radio 1 was too much too soon and after about eighteen months of my not being DLT he took me to lunch and pulled the trigger. We both knew exactly what the meeting had been called for and so took the opportunity to get it out of the way immediately and spend the next few hours becoming nice and alight amid lashings of gallows humour. I may have reminded him more than once that he did ask me at one point to temporarily take over the Radio 1 breakfast show. A preposterous act of defiance that I think I'm right in recalling I answered by saying, 'Oh dear Lord, Matthew, no! Are you nuts? Why not just drop your trousers, show your arse to the audience and have done with it?'

I probably also recounted how on the day he had offered me the gig, a bird unloaded its guano down the back of my neck – a pretty handy metaphor by anyone's standards. Many years later the BBC made a TV documentary about those stormy years at Radio 1 as part of the hard-hitting series *Blood on the Carpet*, and one of the ousted old guard DJs, a droopy old string called Adrian Juste, whose gimmick was to edit himself into classic recordings of *Hancock*, *The Goon Show* and *Dad's Army*, gloomily recalled the few weeks when it was his misfortune to have to follow my Saturday programme.

'I remember hearing his show coming to a finish,' he sombrely intoned into camera, 'and I looked at my producer and just said,

"What the hell was that? Now we have got to go on and try to pick this station up off the floor."' And he sighed.

Dad, who saw this go out, was slightly more direct.

'See that twot talking about you on telly last night?' he barked the next day before even saying hello.

I said I had.

'You tell him if I see him, the only thing he'll be picking up off the floor will be his fucking hooter.'

I am happy to report that their paths never crossed.

We were recording a short sketch for the *After All . . .* talk show one afternoon when, glancing toward one of the TV monitors peppered around the set relaying the action, I saw the most extraordinary thing. It was a circular piece of sandwich meat just a little bigger than fifty-pence piece that, unbeknownst to me, someone must have placed in the centre of my hair. Was I now so unpopular both inside and outside television that open season had been declared to make me look even more ridiculous? Keeping my eyes on the screen, I felt upwards with one hand and tried to locate this bleached piece of baloney resting upon my crown. My plan was to quietly remove it, hoping that an unruffled, dignified way of dealing with the prank would disappoint and ultimately shame whoever had instigated the insult. However, upon placing the tips of my fingers on the strategically placed slice of sausage skin, I found it wouldn't budge. Not only that, but the harder I pressed, the more it hurt. After several seconds of this struggle it finally dawned on me that I was not in fact the victim of a cruel joke but witnessing the birth of a brand-new bald head. My bald head. I was not just going bald, I was technically bald already and it appeared follicles were abandoning the perimeter of my fledgling tonsure like the German army fleeing Mother Russia.

I have to say I was rather alarmed at the discovery and completed the sketch in an unblinking monotone. Your first thought on finding out you are now nurturing a flesh field at your North Pole is 'Has anybody else noticed this?' quickly followed by 'What can I do about it?' Understand that I was not by any means a vain type. May the record show I allowed myself to be dressed in some of the most terrifying and cumbersome 'fashions' of the period while in my TV pomp, none of which were sprung from my own wardrobe – a ropey enough affair in the first place. I remember as we approached the first programme of *After All . . .* I was asked what sort of style I had in mind for the series. My stock answer to this is 'Picture hat, off-the-shoulder blouse and glass shoes with a goldfish in the heel'. However I did say that because I had been scrubbed up and made TV presentable in so many other recent vehicles, wouldn't it be an idea if I did this talk show, usually so formal a forum, in a slightly less ragged version of my own street clothes, i.e., open-necked shirts and jeans. This suggestion was agreed and then later rescinded. I had no real problems with that, but sometimes as I looked at myself just before I went on, in a mauve jacket over a roll-neck jumper and a pair of casual trousers, I did wonder who the fuck that was looking back at me.

The worst stage-wear I ever got lumbered with was entirely my own fault. I was told to go and buy a couple of suits for the second run of the talk show and then give the receipts to BBC Wardrobe, who would reimburse me. I have never been one for claiming expenses and even way back at the *NME* would sit mystified as colleagues invented phantom business contacts to put down on their reimbursement forms as 'Drinks: £2.50'. I genuinely thought it was demeaning. This may strike people as odd, given the other rackets me and my old man got up to, but 'expenses' and similar petty entitlements have always seemed so mean and grasping – from a different culture altogether. I can happily get in a cab if one is provided, and make sure the driver gets plenty of waiting time too, but never once have I made my way somewhere under my own steam and then said at the other end, while waving a train ticket or taxi receipt, 'That'll be eight pounds seventy, please.' The very idea makes me cringe. Anyway, never having owned a wallet, I tend to lose receipts almost as soon as they are forked across to me and so it was on the occasion when I bought myself the heaviest suit since the Golden Age of Jousting. This was during a brief fashion window when gentlemen's suit jackets were worn at three-quarter length and so cut to finish just above the knees. I saw one of these ensembles in a Savile

Row shop window and decided that, though I wasn't particularly faddish, at last a style had arrived to chime with my own tastes. Long jackets, that was the thing, and I intended to hop on board the look while it was still hot – and hot is to be a key word in this disastrous sartorial misstep.

The problem may have lain in my impatience when in any kind of public changing room, coupled with only a passing interest in how I might look anyway. Hence my disastrous haste when grabbing the correct clothing for the New York awards ceremony. Even at the swimming baths as a kid I would get into my trunks as swiftly as possible and then roll all my belongings up into a ball to stuff into the locker so I could get on with the next bit of business – losing the locker key. In men's outfitters I am even more of a fluster. I seem to believe that if I don't get back out from behind the curtain in under twenty seconds the walls will start to move in like the garbage crusher in *Star Wars*. When trying on trousers – possibly my least favourite thing in the entire world – I go absolutely ape and inexplicably treat the exercise like it's a desperate competition where I'm already lagging behind with a ten-second handicap or that at any moment a member of staff will rap upon the cubicle door saying, 'Come on, Beau Brummel – what you doing, shooting up in there?'

Consequently I will only give the most cursory attention to whether a waistband is a little snug or if the trouser leg is over-running the heel of my shoe by several feet. In the dressing room at Savile Row I slapped the charcoal-grey three-piece on at my normal breakneck pace, looked at it in the mirror for barely a second and hauled it all off again, declaring the purchase made. So swift had been the process that my brain entirely failed to register that the thing had an overall weight like the pull of a black hole. Writing out a cheque for *nine hundred pounds* I walked out of the shop already composing my reply to Bryan Ferry's letter asking me where I had bought such a classic and modish outfit. It was only as I got down toward Piccadilly that I noticed that I kept changing the arm bearing the carrier bag's bulk as though it contained that month's coal ration for the Ukraine.

When I got it home Wendy said, 'Blimey, what you got in that bag, a couple of oxygen tanks? Isn't this gonna be a bit much to wear in a hot studio?' I of course told her that only nervous performers felt uncomfortable on camera and I would be no more ill at ease than if I were in a loose T-shirt and pyjama bottoms. I saw no reason to revise this opinion even when the burden of the jacket alone caused the coat hanger I had placed it on to crash to the bedroom floor.

'Do you need anything pressing?' said the woman from wardrobe on the night I planned to unveil the look. I told her I didn't and unzipped the suit bag to show her my choice.

'Ooh, dear, are you sure about that?' she puzzled. 'Isn't that going to get unbearable under the lights? It looks very heavy.'

I laughed again. What was it with these fashionistas and their obsession with the perfect temperature? I was going into a TV studio for a couple of hours, not jogging through the rain forest! Could nobody just appreciate how fine I was going to look in this cutting-edge combo? Perhaps these people wanted to pigeonhole me as the garishly-patterned-shirt-wearing youth they had grown up with on *Win, Lose or Draw* and the *Six O'Clock Show*. Hadn't they noticed I was a mature broadcaster now? I had my own BBC chat show and everything.

After she left, I began to get ready. To set off my new sober, dark-grey sensation I had decided to accompany it with a white collar-less shirt. This would have to be buttoned all the way up because I don't think these things really work when they are left to flap where they ought to encircle. Next I put on the trousers and, yes, as I held them up, they did, for the first time, strike me as a little more sub-stantial than some other trousers I have owned. If I hadn't been in such denial I might have conceded they tipped the scales at a weight close to the combined mass of the *Cutty Sark*'s sails and further-more, to button them up, I was forced to contort myself as though tearing in half the 1982 London phone directory. Why had I not registered any of this at the tailor's? Now for the waistcoat. Lifting this from the bag by its shoulders I couldn't believe I was actually going to climb inside what to all intents and purpose was a Victorian bulletproof vest. This too now appeared extraordinarily snug, with the middle button in particular under such tensile strength

I feared if it gave way during the show it would put somebody's eye out.

There came a knock at the dressing-room door. It was the sound department wondering if they could wire me up because it was getting very close to show time. I asked for a few more minutes. There is an old Norman Wisdom film, *On the Beat*, where he is denied a job as a policeman because he is not tall enough. In one bathetic scene he tries on his father's old police uniform and looks at himself in the mirror and, though swamped by the overflowing material, still attempts to look confident and commanding. As I heaved on the leaden, one-ton drape coat that completed my appearance I saw that I had inescapably become his hapless Pitkin character for real, and now I was going to have the moment recorded for all time on national television.

Momentarily my knees buckled at the realization of this indignity, aided and abetted by the gargantuan weight of the suit's mass bearing down on my frame. Eventually exiting the room with the exact gait of Jacob Marley hauling his burden of cash boxes through eternity, I made my way slowly to the studio. We were pre-recording a section of *After All . . .* that was to be inserted later. It was as I puffed my way through this not overly amusing skit, sweat cascading from my brow like those mocking Erith raindrops back at the dawn of my TV career, that I glimpsed the hairless halo confirming I was now going totally bald.

This jig, I inwardly reasoned, will very soon be up. And I have to say that as I sat there at the height of my ignominy, issuing steam like another kind of old geyser entirely, the prospect of the next phase of the voyage, whatever that might be, strangely excited me.

Mine is one of the last generations to not only use the expression 'Come in number fifty-nine, your time is up,' but to have actually experienced it. For anyone too tender in years to know the origin of the phrase, it stems from the era when most public parks had lakes in them where, for a shilling a throw, you could hire out a rowing boat to pass away the time on a hot summer's day. These rudimentary craft would be clearly numbered and rented by the half-hour. Thus when the thirty minutes had elapsed the park keeper on duty would bellow the necessary command through a battered old tin megaphone. The words later came to mean anyone or anything that had outstayed their welcome and, though hardly anybody uses it these days, I should like to employ it one last time to accurately reflect what happened to my star status as 1996 hove into view.

The precise moment my popularity boat was instructed to return to port forthwith is easy to pinpoint. I was in the front room of Scawen Road rubbing Twizzle's belly in the precise spot that used to make his back leg whizz round in circles. This, along with throwing an invisible ball that he would set off after at great speed before realizing he'd once again been tricked, were among our favourite games. The phone went. On the other end was a journalist from the *Daily Mirror* who wanted my reaction to the fact that I had been replaced as host of *Pets Win Prizes* by Dale Winton. This was news to me and I said as much, probably giving him the scoop he was after. After hanging up, I sat down on the settee. Then I lay down on it. Wendy came into the room and, noting my furrowed brow, asked if everything was OK.

'I don't know,' I replied after some thought. 'You remember you told me your family once moved house while your dad was in the army and didn't tell him the new address?' She confirmed the story. 'Well, I think the BBC are pulling the same gag on me.'

The thing that shocked me wasn't so much the loss of the job but the discovery I had become one of the woebegone tabloid Aunt Sallys who laid themselves open to such folly.

Now there may be some people who think that being removed as host of a show like *Pets Win Prizes* was tantamount to a last-minute reprieve from the hangman, but that's not how I saw it. *Pets Win Prizes*, the wonderful idea of a friend of mine from the *Six O'Clock Show*, Andy Meyer and his writing partner David McGrath, was a fantastic lunatic conceit that may be one of the few things to which I will attach the words 'ahead of its time'. Normally I shrink from this idiotic phrase with its suggestion that a current generation is somehow culturally superior to those that came before. I have heard everything from Oscar Wilde to the Marx Brothers to The Beatles described by this arrogance of chronology, ignoring that all of these artists were hugely successful in their own day and that a genius like W. C. Fields would be unlikely to find international fame in today's conservative world of mass marketing. Even somebody like Nick Drake, a complete commercial washout during the years he was recording, was very much *of* his time and not ahead of it and being *of* your time is a much harder trick than people imagine. I concede it may be argued that it is astoundingly presumptuous to elevate a vehicle like *Pets Win Prizes* to such august company. That is not for me to say, though I suspect one day History Will Vindicate Me. However, there is no doubt in my mind that the programme's much-castigated presence in the schedules would have found a more ready appreciation in the rapidly approaching irony-drenched, throwaway era that saw the decline of television. For sure, the BBC were very nervous about it at the time. They fretted that people would see it as a great clumping betrayal of its charter, that the very title shrieked of the cod and the cornball, and that to put chickens, sausage dogs and parrots in competition on prime-time TV might be interpreted as hopelessly low brow by the organization's vulture-like critics. These qualities, naturally, were what appealed to me most about the show and, having been shown the initial outline by its two creators, I personally took it to the controllers as what I wanted to do next. Leaning heavily on David Letterman's magnificent regular feature 'Stupid Pet Tricks' it struck me as an absolute hoot of an idea and on the pilot episode I couldn't have enjoyed myself more. I even came up with an instant catchphrase for the series. One round had featured three roosters that had fallen into a doze in their large cages that had been covered with a blackout cloth. As far as these cocks were concerned, night had fallen and all was quiet upon the farm. Then, to the accompaniment of Grieg's 'Morning', the covers were removed and, in front of a hushed and expectant studio audience, the birds began to rouse themselves. The deal was that the first one of the trio to go 'cock-a-doodle-doo' would be the winner. I may have been involved with more gripping slices of broadcasting in my time, but if I have I certainly can't recall one. Almost eight minutes went by with no result and every onlooker's nerves were stretched to breaking point. Occasionally one of the contestants would issue a low 'caw', but we decided not to allow these. It had to be the full crowing or else the entire exercise would be pointless. I have to tell you that when the middle of the three roosters suddenly flapped its wings and let go with its lusty alarm call, the release of tension in the studio was enormous. I have never heard applause like it. Elated and knowing a hit when I saw one, I raced across to my main camera and, gripping the lens by the corners of its cover, shouted directly into it above the cacophony, 'It's *Pets Win Prizes*! It's your licence fee at work!'

This became my go-to cry for the rest of the series, along with the equally true '*Pets Win Prizes*! Yes, it's come to this!' and 'This is exactly what Lord Reith had in mind when he legged it down the Patent Office!'

Sadly, when the shows started going out, such wilful exuberance was edited down to a compromised twee mush. Every mention of licence fees or the collapse of Reithian values was excised and wherever I had announced games with intentionally provocative declarations such as, 'Now we present a sensational round, possibly to the death, called "I Guarantee My Dog Will Sing"' I found they had cut that and inserted instead lame captions featuring 'cute' dog illustrations and the words, 'It's Pavarotti Pooches!' Well, I mean, what? Talk about making a fellow look like a sap. The tone was shifted completely, from one of swashbuckling defiance to pusillanimous collapse. For the love of God, it now looked like we were serious with all this hamster-based guff. Even so, the show was a ratings success, possibly, I suspect, to the embarrassment of BBC management.

About a week before they jettisoned me from the show I had been taken out to lunch to see if *Pets Win Prizes* could be made 'any better' for its second series. I voiced my views about how we needed to address the basic ludicrousness of the premise head on and not for a second try to appease all the pompous dopes who couldn't see anything at all wonderful in actual rat races. I was shown some sketches of some of the complicated sets they had built for this second season and also told that one of the spots on the show had tested badly with the audience and would not be returning this time around. This bit featured naturalist Terry Nutkins, who would pop up during items to bring us a few tips and facts about the pets involved and thus clunkily satisfy someone's dreary need to bring an educational angle to the merriment.

Of course, when the series did arrive back on BBC1, it wasn't Brer Nutkins who had been thrown overboard. Terry was all present and correct, telling us how we should keep an eye on the length of our guinea pig's teeth before handing over to Dale with this week's 'Crazy Kitten Capers' or some such rot. I stayed at home and brooded, wondering if the BBC would have been quite so swift to dump Professor Jacob Bronowski had *The Ascent of Man*'s producers cut out all his best gags. But dumped I had been, and plainly it was the talk of salons all over London where the smart set were doubtless creating stinging haikus celebrating my demise and ladies gossiped behind their fans, giggling, 'Have you heard about that portion of stinking fish, Baker? Not even fit to present programmes featuring pigs playing billiards these days, my dear. The nation seems to have come to its senses at last . . .'

So now what?

After The Goldrush

In ending the previous chapter with the frankly disingenuous phrase 'So now what?' I see I have given in to the temptation to set up a cliffhanger where, in reality, none existed. The only way I could justify such ominous ruminating was if we now entered my shadowy years of inactivity, substance abuse and failed business ventures culminating in my being rediscovered while selling matches and boot-laces from a tray outside one of London's busier Tube stations. However, that's where fiction trumps autobiography every time. The facts are that, having had five years of being a monkey up a stick, I once again found that as the whole potty phase wound down, fate was simply looking around for the next helping hand into which it could place the baton of my fortune.

It is perhaps indicative of my time as a teen idol that, apart from a gaggle of ten-minute programmes called *TV Heroes* that I made early on in the rise, and that remains my favourite project on which I have worked, I never wrote a single script for any of the shows I'd been part of. By and large these were not programmes that required too much structuring, so aside from routinely re-wording any links I was required to say – although more often than not I would just ad-lib my way through the nonsense – I played no part in the writing. When it came to writing for other people, however, it was a different matter. I had been writing scripts for established comedians and fellow presenters the entire time I was myself uttering some of the most notable bilge on British TV. This professional schizophrenia probably reached its zenith during the years I was providing waspish style and outrageous comment for both Angus Deayton and Jonathan Ross while, certainly in the public's eyes, being the

performer furthest away from the cutting edge those two so brilliantly represented. To be behind the scenes like this never bothered
me in the slightest. I have heard many times that writers of jokes
secretly resent the stars who get the laughs and that even the lowliest
foot soldier carries the field marshal's baton in his knapsack, waiting
for the chance to leap from behind the curtains. This is poppycock
of a rare hue. Your sole job as a scriptwriter is to make the turn
look as bulletproof as possible, verbally nimble and utterly secure,
and above all to give them status once they step out on to the stage.
They are the talent. A beautifully written line will crumble into rust
if it is not delivered by a gifted original, and I can't think of a single
thing that I have ever written that would have been improved if I
had said it myself. Besides, your own voice should not be present in
the work. Whoever I am writing for should sound exactly the way
the public expect them to, whether it's the actor Dennis Hopper or
big bad Jeremy Clarkson – to name but two disparate chumps for
whom I've penned. On top of all these considerations, though, is the
fact that I genuinely love writing for funny people and charge considerable amounts to indulge that pleasure. 'Win, win' is the current
phrase for this, I believe.

So when television stardom handed me my hat in 1996 I found I
was travelling back and forth to studios almost as much as I had in
the earlier part of the decade. The difference was that the shows I
was working on now people actually seemed to like. Within months
of my last BBC TV contract expiring I was to become involved in
one of the greatest extravaganzas and magnificent adventures of my
working life.

It all began with a phone call from an old friend called John
Revell. John had been one of the best producers at GLR and his
association with Chris Evans had flourished beyond the local station into the formation of Ginger TV, the production company
responsible for *Don't Forget Your Toothbrush*, the enormous success
of which, rightly or wrongly, continues to influence British TV to
this day. As a follow-up to *Toothbrush*, Chris was hoping to create a
brand-new kind of pop culture hub, a true slab of era-defining TV
incorporating wild live music, original comedy and stellar guests.

He also wanted it staged in 'the best bar in Britain', while exuding an endearing shabbiness that would root even the most famous headliners in a world far distant from their limousines and entourages. The show already had the title *TFI Friday* – the F, he explained, was for 'Four', the channel stumping up the eye-watering weekly budget for the project. Nobody believed him.

Over the phone, John explained that while the basic ideas were in place it just wasn't hanging together right. The comedy needed help and would I come along to the rehearsal rooms next week to have a look at what they'd got so far? 'It'll only take an hour or so,' he said. In fact, I would stay for the next four seismic and breathtaking years.

Meanwhile I was still opening the front door down in Deptford to delivery men or someone who'd come to fix the boiler and seeing them do a double take. Invariably they would then say, 'You Danny Baker? Blimey, I thought you'd live in a mansion somewhere! Don't see you on the telly much any more – did it all fall through?' And so help me I'd say I was mainly a writer now, often desperately adding, 'In fact I always was . . .' This cut so little ice with the workers that I may as well have said I was performing poetry down mines.

'Blimey, just shows ya,' they would say, setting down their tool bags. 'You have to grab the work while it's there, eh? You was on everything a couple of years back, weren't ya? Oh well, mate, I hope it picks up again for ya . . .'

At this I would usually check to make sure the arse wasn't literally hanging out of my trousers. One bizarre incident came when a man who had had to return to us after his initial repairs to our washing machine had proved incomplete, produced from his bag a large jar of horseradish. 'Do you remember yesterday when I was here I told you about my allotment?' he said.

I didn't, but being the sort who likes the day to go with some swing, I helpfully said, 'Oh yes! How's that going?' as though in the last twenty-four hours events down at his veg patch could have altered dramatically.

'No, you remember I said about me horseradish? How you can't whack real horseradish 'cos you'd only ever had the supermarket jars?'

The man seemed to be hallucinating or something. I'd never eaten horseradish in my life, and as for a conversational topic I'd place it a few notches below the varying coarseness of differing sandpapers. But naturally I nodded and may even have licked a lip as he shook the cream-coloured mulch about in its container.

'Well, here you go,' he said, unscrewing the lid. 'Have a smell of that.'

There may be people who, when offered a sniff of horseradish from a crouching repairman, would defer the sensation until after he had fixed the leak currently causing their kitchen to assume the aspect of the local lido, but I thought unless I satisfied the request he might do a half-arsed job, this time on purpose. So, leaning over the growing pond beneath my feet, I stuck my nose in the jar and inhaled deeply.

Now, have you ever taken in a full lungful of horseradish vapour? To call it powerful stuff does not begin to do it justice. It is devastating. It is cataclysmic. When the United Nations oversee the destruction of all chemical and gas-based weapons in unstable countries, that they leave them in possession of this stuff surely makes the whole process pointless. I have to tell you that you don't get too far into the sniff anyway because as soon as the fumes enter your nostrils they cause your head to snap backwards like Mike Tyson has just caught you on the point of your chin after a ten-yard run up. Pow! I jack-knifed to attention and then reeled backwards, falling over a mop and bucket full of effluent from the Hotpoint. Down I went and sat on the floor, a ring of stars and cartoon canaries flying around my head that later even Wendy says she saw. All I could hear was some ghastly demonic laughter. It was the washing machine man, now standing over me like the Jolly Green Giant.

'Sorry, mate,' he guffawed. 'That was a bad one, weren't it? I catch everyone with that – I was only fucking about! Everyone falls for it! Strong, innit?'

Mind totally scrambled by the blast, I gradually became aware that I had become victim of a hideous and degrading jest. And still he chuckled.

'Tell you what. If you ever get back on telly, you should use that. It's only horseradish, but it fucking kills ya, don't it? Your fuckin' face is a picture!'

I tried to laugh too but I'm told all that came out was a wisp of smoke. Walking away from the scene, my head throbbing from the olfactory coshing, I pondered the insult he'd added to the injury.

'If ever you get back on the telly . . .'

Hadn't I just told the man that I had recently finished the script for the *Smash Hits Pop Awards* presented by Pip Schofield? You can't get much closer to the media sun than that.

Horseradish pranks aside, his was an attitude that I was going to have to get used to. From now on, whenever anyone spotted me on the Tube, it wasn't because I had always used them, and still do, to get around the capital, it would be because I was now on Skid Row and had probably been forced to sell my Rolls at a knock-down price just to buy a pair of winter boots. I was the Daz Icarus who had flown too close to the celebrity sun and found its scorching heat to be way above the recommended forty degrees and now was all washed up himself.

This was really brought home to me a few months after the incident with the nerve gas, as Spud and I were sitting in Manze's pie-and-mash shop in Tower Bridge Road. Two things happened during that typically delicious sitting that made even my dad look at me from under his eyebrows. The first was when I was at the counter getting served; I noticed that of the two celebrity customer photographs the establishment boasted, only Roy Orbison's was still prominently displayed. Mine was now obscured on the shelf behind dozens of bottles of vinegar. I was later assured this was only temporary, and I believe it, but a more paranoid personality might have seen it as yet another straw in the wind. What happened as Spud and I wolfed down the liquored ambrosia though was unequivocal and perfectly mirrored the little mise-en-scène with which the first of these memoirs closed.

I had noticed a group of three younger men across the room who'd been casting glances in my direction. As they got up to leave, they stopped by our table. 'Excuse me interrupting while you're eating,' said one of them. 'But is your name Danny Baker?'

With a mouthful of pie-crust I confirmed that it was.

'I said it was,' carried on the bloke triumphantly. 'Do me a favour. He don't believe you used to be on telly. You did, didn't ya?'

Forcing down the now bitter crust I was forced to admit, that like Mr Bojangles, I had indeed once trod the boards. It would be no use producing my diary to show any string of current commitments. Either you are on TV. Or you are not. And now not only was I post-*Radio Times* but apparently some people didn't even recall the era of glittering prizes.

Still. As long as you've got your health, eh?

To be continued.

W&N

blog and newsletter

For literary discussion, author insight,
book news, exclusive content,
recipes and giveaways, visit the
Weidenfeld & Nicolson blog and
sign up for the newsletter at:

www.wnblog.co.uk

For breaking news, reviews and exclusive competitions
Follow us 🐦 @wnbooks
Find us f facebook.com/WNfiction